HEART CENTERED LIVING

Messages inspired by Christ consciousness

Pamela Kribbe

Jeshua.net
2012

First Edition

Cover photo by Anna de Leeuw, www.annadeleeuw.com

This book can be ordered at www.jeshua.net/book

Contents

Preface

This book is the result of years of workshops and public channelings. The messages were originally received in Dutch and have been translated into English largely by myself. However, I had the invaluable assistance of several people: Bart Lemahieu, Jeremy Stutsman, Lily Fu, Joep Boink, Maria Baes and Nicolette Suwoton. I am very grateful for their help in translating and editing the material.

I am grateful to Gerrit, my husband, for always being by my side when I channel in workshops or public meetings. He is my soul mate and although only my name is on the cover of this book, his implicit contribution to it has been essential.

Thank you to all the participants in our workshops, who feel so much like soul family to us. Because of your openness and trust, you inspired me to be open and trustful as well about bringing these channeled messages out in the open

Introduction

This book contains a collection of channeled messages on the transformation from ego to heart. We are entering a new era on Earth. More and more people feel the need for heart-centered living, rising above fear-based ways of living which do not honor who you really are. Who are you really? This book is based on the premise that you are an eternal soul temporarily dressed in a human body. You are here to experience what life is like as a human being. You are here also to express your soul's joy and wisdom on Earth, making it a more peaceful and loving place to be.

Heart-centered living leads you away from deeply ingrained ideas and habits which may have dictated a large part of your life for a long time. Living from the heart asks of you to be gentle and compassionate with yourself, and with others. However, it also challenges you to be completely honest with yourself and to let go of anything that doesn't align well with what your heart is telling you. Deciding to listen to the voice of your heart may mean that relationships change forever, and more importantly, it means that the relationship with yourself changes deeply. When you're no longer listening to what the voices of fear dictate to you, about who you should be and how you should behave, your soul awakens and will want to express itself in your everyday life. You feel like being "different", perhaps a stranger even within your own circle of friends and family.

This book means to offer suggestions, support and guidance for those who have chosen the way of heart-centered living. The messages in it mean to reassure you, encourage you and explain to you what is happening when you walk this path. How do you distinguish the voice of your heart from other voices within? How do you know your soul's purpose and how do you begin to express it in your life? When your heart opens, how do you deal with the overwhelming sensitivity which may occur? How do you balance male and female within? Why does the fear of truly expressing who you are run so deep? Are there soul mates out there who are like you and what does it feel like to bond with them?

All of these questions and more are the subject of the channelings in this book. Channeling is a way of receiving information from teachers who are not in the flesh anymore. In this book, the channelings have been inspired by the spirit and energy of Christ consciousness. What does that mean? In 2002, I had started my own practice as a spiritual coach and energy reader. After a while, I started to receive messages from a teacher who introduced himself as Jeshua ben Josef, which is the Aramaic name for Jesus. I have written more extensively about my first encounter with Jeshua in my first book The Jeshua Channelings. In the interview at the end of this book (chapter 28), you'll find more information on this as well. Here, I will only repeat Jeshua's own introduction of himself to me. I asked him who he was and this is how he answered.

I am the one who has been among you and who you have come to know as Jesus.
I am not the Jesus of your church tradition or the Jesus of your religious writings.
I am Jeshua-ben-Joseph; I have lived as a man of flesh and blood. I did reach Christ consciousness before you, but I was supported in this by powers which are beyond your imagination at present. My coming was a cosmic event - I made myself available for this.

It wasn't easy. I did not succeed in my endeavors to pass on to people the immensity of God's love. There was much misunderstanding. I came too early, but someone had to come. My coming was like throwing a stone in a large fishpond. All fish flee and the stone sinks into the deep. There are ripples noticeable long after though. One might say that the kind of consciousness I wished to convey, did its work underground after that. At the surface of the pool there were constant ruffles; well-meant but misguided interpretations rose to meet and fight each other in my name. The ones who were touched by my energy, moved by the impulse of Christ energy, could not really integrate it with their psychological and physical reality.

It has taken a long time before Christ consciousness could set foot on Earth. But now the time has come. And I have returned and speak through many, through all and to everyone who wants to hear me and who has come to understand me from the quietness of their hearts. I do not preach and I do not judge. My sincerest hope is to speak to you of the vast and unfailing presence of Love, accessible to you at any time.

I am part of a much larger consciousness, a greater entity, but I, Jeshua, am the incarnated part of that entity (or field of consciousness). I do not like the name Jesus much, for it has become so caught up with a distorted version of what I stand for. "Jesus" is owned by the church traditions and authorities. He has been molded to fit the interests of the church patriarchs for centuries, so much so that the prevailing image of Jesus is now so far removed from what I represent, that it would truly please me if you could just let it go and release me from that heritage.

I am Jeshua, man of flesh and blood.
I am your friend and brother.
I am familiar with being human in every way.
I am teacher and friend.
Do not fear me. Embrace me like you'd embrace one of your kin.
We are family.

As I grew more familiar with Jeshua's presence over the years, more messages came through and after six years, I also started to receive messages from other teachers, female ones especially. It started with Mary, mother of Jeshua, and later on I felt a strong inspiration to connect with mother Earth and channel her messages. In recent years, I have felt drawn to get in touch with Mary Magdalene, Jeshua's dearest female companion on Earth. One channeling from her is included at the end of this book.

This book has two parts. Part I holds fourteen messages from Jeshua. Part II, which is called "Rebirth of the feminine energy", holds messages from Mary, mother Earth and Mary Magdalene.

You will notice that all who pursue the path of heart centered living are often addressed as "lightworkers" in this book. In The Jeshua Channelings, a list of characteristics and a definition was given by Jeshua, which I will repeat here for the sake of clarity:

Lightworkers are souls who carry the strong inner desire to spread Light – knowledge, freedom and self-love – on Earth. They sense this as their mission. They are often attracted to spirituality and to therapeutic work of some kind.

Because of their deeply felt mission, lightworkers often feel different from other people. By experiencing different kinds of obstacles on their way, life provokes them to find their own unique path. Lightworkers are nearly always solitary individuals, not fitting into fixed societal structures.

The word "lightworker" may evoke misunderstanding, since it lifts out a particular group of souls from the rest. It may be taken to suggest that this particular group is somehow superior to the others, i.e. those "not working for the light." This whole line of thought is at odds with the very nature and intent of light work. Let us state briefly what is wrong with it.

First, claims of superiority are generally unenlightened. They block your growth toward a free and loving consciousness. Second, lightworkers are not "better" or "higher" than anyone else. They simply have a different history than the ones not belonging to this group. Because of this particular history, which we will discuss below, they have certain psychological characteristics which distinguish them as a group. Third, every soul becomes a lightworker at some stage of its unfolding, so the label "lightworker" is not reserved to a limited number of souls.

The reason we use the word "lightworker" despite possible misunderstandings is because it carries associations and stirs memories within you that help you remember. There is a practical convenience to it as well, since the term is frequently used in your current spiritual literature.

Characteristics of lightworkers

- *From early on in their life, they feel they are different. More often than not they feel isolated from others, lonely and misunderstood. They will often become individualists who will have to find their own unique ways in life.*

- *They have trouble feeling at home within traditional jobs and/or organization structures. Lightworkers are naturally anti-authoritarian which means that they naturally resist decisions or values based solely on power or hierarchy. This anti-authoritarian trait is present even if they seem timid and shy. It is connected to the very essence of their mission here on earth.*

- *Lightworkers feel drawn to helping people as a therapist or as a teacher. They may be psychologists, healers, teachers, nurses, etc. Even if their profession is not about helping people in a direct manner, the intent to contribute to the higher good of humanity is clearly present.*

- *Their vision of life is colored by a spiritual sense of how all things are related together. They consciously or subconsciously carry memories within them of non-earthly spheres of light. They may occasionally feel homesick for these spheres and feel like a stranger on earth.*

- *They deeply honor and respect life which often manifests as a fondness for animals and a concern for the environment. The destruction of parts of the animal and vegetable kingdoms on earth by human doing invokes deep feelings of loss and grief in them.*

- *They are kind-hearted, sensitive and empathic. They may have trouble dealing with aggressive behavior and they generally experience difficulties in standing up for themselves. They can be dreamy, naive or highly idealistic, as well as insufficiently grounded, i.e. down-to-earth. Because they easily pick up negative feelings and moods of people around them, it is important for them to spend time alone on a regular basis. This enables them to distinguish between their own feelings and those of others. They need solitary time to touch base with themselves and with mother earth.*

- *They have lived many lives on earth in which they were deeply involved with spirituality and/or religion. They were present in overwhelming numbers in the old religious orders of your past as monks, nuns, hermits, psychics, witches, shamans, priests, priestesses, etc. They were the ones providing a bridge between the visible and the invisible, between the daily context of earth life and the mysterious realms of the afterlife, realms of God and the spirits of good and evil. For fulfilling this role, they were often rejected and persecuted. Many of you were sentenced to the stake for the gifts you possessed. The traumas of persecution left deep traces within your soul's memory. This may presently manifest as a fear of being fully grounded, i.e. a fear to be really present, because you remember being brutally attacked for who you were.*

From: The Jeshua Channelings, p.37/38

Channeling – a bit of debunking

In conclusion, I would like to make some general remarks on the phenomenon of channeling. Perhaps, being Dutch (they are considered to be a very down-to-earth people) and still quite skeptical about some of the new age stuff I encounter, I would like to put some things about channeling into perspective.

The relationship between channeler and channeled entity

I think that channeling is a cooperation between a human being and a non-physical entity who acts as a teacher. The teacher offers inspiration and a larger perspective to the human being, and the human being translates the energy of the spiritual entity into the words and concepts he is acquainted with through his upbringing, education and culture. I do not believe that it is possible, or even desirable, that the human channel should completely set himself aside, in order to "purely channel" the non-physical entity's energy. I think it is inevitable that the channel's mind set, awareness and vocabulary greatly influence what comes through. Even if the channel goes into a deep trance state, they are the receiver, the vessel and therefore co-creator of the material. I think it is naïve to presume that the channeler can receive a message totally from without, taking no part in it. I believe the messages come from within, through their consciousness, *enlarged* by the spiritual teacher's consciousness, and that the quality of the channeling does not so much depend on the extent to which the channeler can eliminate themselves as on the level of consciousness that both the channeler and the channeled entity posses. Channeling is essentially a co-creation.

How to judge the quality of channeled information

Channeling can be beautiful and inspiring. But it can also lead to hollow phrases or fearful, moralistic tales of woe. At the worst, it leads to the worship of authorities who have nothing going for them except their name or rank in some invisible spiritual hierarchy. Looking up to elusive authorities outside of us - isn't that precisely what true spirituality warns us against?

The fact that information is channeled says absolutely nothing about the quality of it. In the philosophy of science, the branch of philosophy that investigates what makes scientific theories "scientific" or trustworthy, a useful distinction is made between the "context of discovery" and "the context of justification". What leads to the *discovery* of a scientific theory has no bearing on whether it can be *justified*. A scientist can make up any theory he wants, relying on personal dreams, associations, or reveries, but once he has formulated the theory, it will be judged by his peers on the basis of generally acknowledged criteria such as empirical confirmation, coherence, explanatory power, etc. So in the context of discovery, *anything goes*, whereas in the context of justification, the theory has to live up to certain standards of quality in order to be valued by the scientific community. I think the same goes for channeled material. Channeled messages should be judged by the same standards as spiritual texts from "mere humans": is the information clear, does it add new insights to your knowledge, does it inspire you to love yourself more, do you feel enlightened and uplifted by the message? I think if the answer is yes, the question of who channeled it and how it came about (the context of discovery) is relatively unimportant. The proof is in the pudding, not in the alleged rank or status of the one who prepared it.

My own experience as a channeler

When I channel Jeshua, I feel myself getting larger instead of smaller. I feel his energy helping me rise to the greatness of my own greater Self. I think he is in fact mediating between the small everyday me and the larger Me, helping me to embody it a little more. Every time he does this and I allow it, I am expanding my consciousness a little more, and it affects my own growth and empowerment. One time, I did a channeling in which I so strongly felt the presence of my own higher of greater self (who I call Aurelia), that I doubted whether I was still channeling Jeshua. I asked him that evening before I went to sleep, and then he said something very endearing to me: "Remember always, *I am there for you, you are not there for me*". This made it very clear to me. We are all meant to fully embody and manifest our greater Selves here on Earth. Teachers come along to help us on our path, and if it's a true teacher, he or she will help you as long as you need it, and then get out of the way.

Jeshua is still with me, although I feel I am not "chatting" as much with him as I used to in the beginning. Often nowadays when I ask him a personal question, he asks me: what do you truly feel about it? And when I focus on that, the answer is there, from my own inner knowing and intuition. So, Jeshua encourages us all to take up our own power, and to see channeling as a means and not as an end. Perhaps one day I will be able to channel my own higher or Christ self, and not rely on Jeshua anymore. I am sure he would be the first to applaud me!

Jeshua on channeling

I will conclude with a "channeling on channeling", a few words from Jeshua on his relationship with me as channeler.

Channeling is a way of getting closer to yourself with the help of another – non-physical – being. This being temporarily plays the role of a teacher. The energy of the teacher helps you get to a deeper level of yourself. The teacher's energy lifts you out of the fears that keep your own light veiled.

A teacher shows you your own light. The teacher is more aware of your light than you are. As soon as this light, your inner knowing, is accessible to yourself, the teacher becomes superfluous. You are then able to channel your own light. The teacher does not have to act as a bridge any more between you and your higher self.

I am reminding you for a while of your own light. I mirror your greatness to you in the shape of Jeshua ben Joseph. *In me you see yourself, your Christ self, but you do not realize this fully yet. I am like a frame of reference to you, my energy serves as a beacon. I help you get more deeply acquainted with your own Christ self. It slowly will move to the foreground, and I will move to the background. This is all right. It is as it should be. Don't forget, in this relationship, I am there for you, you are not there for me. I am not the aim, but the means. The rebirth of Christ is the awakening of your Christ self, not mine.*

I act according to what serves your greater Self. My aim is that you make me superfluous. When you channel me, do not try to make yourself small or invisible. I wish that you make yourself bigger, feel your true strength flow out of you and shine upon the world.

A teacher points at the road but it is you who walk it. After a while, you find yourself walking alone, having left the teacher behind. This is a grand and sacred moment. The teacher will stay with you, will live on in your heart as an inner presence, but the separate figure will disappear.

We stay connected, but as you grow, you will less and less see me, or want to call upon me, as a separate being. I will slowly become part of your own energy. And at some point, you will not know me as separate from you anymore. This will show that you have truly heard and seen me.

PART I

MESSAGES FROM JESHUA

1 - Surrendering to your soul's passion

I speak to you from the heart of Christ consciousness. I am Jeshua, but I am not solely that one particular personality who lived on Earth two thousand years ago. Here, I represent more than that. I represent the Christ energy that lives and vibrates in all of your hearts. The one who speaks here now thus also represents your own energy and vibration; it is your own heart-felt longing that is turned into words in this room we are sitting in.

Being together like this, is not simply about delivering a lecture….it is a gathering and celebration of the New Era. The awakening of a new consciousness seems to be far off at times. There seems to be so much disharmony and conflict in your world and, indeed, within yourselves as well. Yet the awakening has begun. A new dimension of consciousness is being birthed on Earth right now, and after a long stage of preparation, it will gradually gain a foothold and spread a wave of enlightenment across Earth. You all take part in this wave of newly awakening consciousness, engulfing the Earth right now. In many senses, you *are* that wave of energy.

Whether you trust to surrender to your heart's calling is a big issue within this process of spiritual awakening, both at the individual level and at the collective level. At the political level, world leaders often find themselves confronted with this issue. It still is very difficult to be in charge politically and make decisions from the heart. Politics does not seem to be ready for this yet. Nonetheless, surrendering to the wisdom of the heart is the only way out of the great conflicts on Earth right now, the only chance for a peaceful resolution of these conflicts.

The universal sense of connectedness and unity that is possible between people of very different races, religions or cultures, is the foundation for world peace. The recognition of each other as human beings, despite the external dissimilarities, is growing among the world population, and it is stimulated by your modern information technology, which greatly diminishes distances in time and space. At the same time, the growth towards mutual understanding is threatened by old, fear-based notions of "us" and "them". Thinking in terms of good and bad, right and wrong, "us" and "them", perpetuates age old hostilities and fuels a great deal of emotional turmoil. These divisive notions are still used by politicians to sustain their power.

However, what ultimately determines reality at the political level is you, the individual. Politics mirror the consciousness of the majority of individuals together. It is by the awareness of many independent individuals together that a new level of consciousness comes alive. Rather than dwell on the political level, I would now like to speak of the individual level, at which you are all working to integrate the energy of the heart into your lives and at which you are dealing with the issue of surrender and control.

Meanwhile I ask you to simply feel the energy of surrender, as it is gathered here today and flowing out of your hearts. You all strongly crave for the sense of liberation and trust that is inherent in surrender, letting go. But often, you do not know yet how to integrate this energy into your day to day lives.

What is the source of control in life? By control I mean: wanting to exert power over life, forcing it to flow according to your desires, which you perceive as right and just. Why do you mean to exert control over your life, and continually live in tension and anxiety because of it? The source of control is fear. Fear is deeply ingrained in the structure of your life: your upbringing, education and society. Control mechanisms are present everywhere and are taught to you as good habits. Apparently, you are a sensible, rational person if you want to have control over your life and organize it accordingly.

Surrender and unpredictability instill a sense of fear in you. Surrender you associate with giving up, not knowing what to do, being overwhelmed by emotional turmoil or crisis. This, however, is a very limited conception of surrender. It is a conception born from fear, from ego based consciousness. There is a much more positive notion of surrender, one that points at a lifestyle, a way of being, in which you live your life in trust, without the need to control, force or manipulate it.

The ego craves control because it is scared. The ego identifies with images that do not come from the soul but are fed to you from the outside world. The ego is constantly running around to preserve its self-image, be it successful businessman, caring housewife, or able therapist. It wants to keep up this image to have control over other people's thoughts about you. However, there are always moments in which the ego fails and loses. This may be the case when you get overworked, sick or your relationship breaks down. The ego considers such crises, which at some point force you to let go and surrender, to be deadly blows.

The ego thus associates surrender with crisis. The ego lives in a continual alternation of control and crisis. Often, in moments of true crisis in your life, you are invited to look at the hidden treasure inside of it. There is always a positive element hiding within the crisis, which beckons you to get closer to the heart of you. In that way, life is always moving you closer to yourself, your inner knowing and wisdom, even if you live by the ego's dictates. For there will always be situations in your life that challenge you to surrender sooner or later. Life is always offering you opportunities to choose surrender as a lifestyle.

You know this. You all know these moments of surrender after a crisis, precious moments of clarity and awareness, in which you realize you are carried by the flow of an invisible, divine breath. You realize this divine flow of life wants the best for you, and that you can rely on it even if it does not necessarily bring you what you expected. What you all long for is to live according to this higher consciousness more permanently; to incorporate this way of being into your everyday life, without having to be pushed into it by deep crisis and despair. You all long for surrender as a lifestyle.

You are all worn-out warriors. You have come a long way. Sometimes you feel very old and tired within, but it is better to say that you are very tired of the old...... You are searching for a way of being that is effortless – inspiring and yet light and flowing. The key is that you do not empty yourself out in your relationships, work or other goals, until you crash and crisis forces you to surrender. Take one step further, or rather take one step back, and focus on a lifestyle that is always marked by letting go, trust and surrender. Surrendering means: not struggling, not resisting but going along with the flow of life, trusting that life will offer you precisely what you need. Trust that your needs are known and will be met. Accept what is in your life right now and be present with it. About this way of living I wish to speak, as your longing for it is deep and sincere. It is a spiritual longing that comes from your soul, the divine flow within you.

Blockages on the way to surrender: three false gods

On the one hand, you desire to put down your masks and live openly according to the original blueprint of your soul. You long for sincerity, honesty, love and connectedness. On the other hand, letting down those masks is a very difficult thing for you. You have been raised with beliefs and structures that have become rooted in your psyches and that keep you from connecting to your own soul. In particular, I would like to address three idols or "false gods" that you often turn towards for guidance but which in fact take you off-center, out of the balance needed to live in surrender to who you really are.

The first idol: God as an authority above you

The first false god is God himself, that is to say God conceived as the lord and master of creation. That type of God is a human construction, an image of God that has deeply influenced your culture.

Many of you think that you have let go of this traditional image of God. You say you do not believe anymore in a judging and punishing God, who stands high above you and keeps a record of your successes and failures like a school master. You say you believe in a God of Love, who forgives you at all times and who cherishes and encourages you. However, in the rigid and loveless way you often treat yourselves, this old God is still very much alive! Do you not often say to yourself that you have failed, that you are not right, that you should have progressed further, whether in the area of relationships, work, or the spiritual. You torture yourself with ideas like: I do not live up to God's expectations, I am disappointing my spiritual guides or higher Self, I have failed my mission, I am not contributing anything meaningful to the world.

Many of you believe, secretly so to speak, that there is a higher order that you are supposed to obey or answer to. Whether it is a "soul mission" or a "life path" that has been laid out for you, a spiritual hierarchy that has an "assignment" for you, or a spiritual guide telling you what to do or where to go......in all those cases you believe in the existence of a higher authority, a spiritual level above you, that you had better listen to. But as soon as you believe in an authority outside of you, who is able to offer guidelines about what you should do in your life, we are back with the traditional God. According to this image, there is a level of truth, at which things are fixed and determined, and all you can do is live according to it or not. This is a false image.

Certainly, when you are born, there are intentions in your soul for the lifetime to come. One might call these your higher purpose for this lifetime, but it has not been ordained by anything outside of you. It is you yourself who has chosen it and it was born from your own desires and wishes. The things in your life that are "predetermined"- in the sense of very likely to happen, nothing is ever fixed completely - have been created and chosen by you. You can connect to your life purpose or higher inspiration anytime by listening to your feelings, to the voice of your heart, your deepest longings. I would advise you not to listen too much to high-strung spiritual doctrines about how you should live. Listen especially to the so-called lower part of you: powerful emotions that manifest in your everyday life. Through these emotions, the soul is trying to reach out to you and tell you something.

If you would like to know what your soul wants to tell you right now, look at the emotions that recur in your life often and absorb you the most. Look at them in a kind but honest way. Do not accuse anyone else of your emotions, do not pay attention to causes outside of you; see them as the result of your choices. For instance, if you are angry and annoyed often, where does that come from? Is there something you are lacking? What does the anger tell you? What is the message hidden within? Is it a sense of not being recognized or valued by others? Are you afraid to show them who you are, afraid to stand for your truth? Do you hide your true feelings often and is it difficult for you to clearly state your boundaries? Often, through the anger, a genuine message is crying out to you: a longing to be who you are, to show your original soul energy to the world. If you recognise your soul's longing through the anger, you are seeing your angelic self shining through your inner child.

The angel inside of you is the "higher self" who wants to connect with physical reality, incarnate and shine its light upon Earth reality. It is the knowing part. Your inner child is the passion of life itself: it is desire, emotion and creativity. It is the experiencing part. The child part in you is your "lower self". The inner child is a source of joy and creativity if it lives in harmony with the angel within. But if it breaks away from the angel's caress and goes

17

adrift, it is the source of emotions running wild. Anger will turn into hatred and vengeance. Fear will pervert into defense, neurosis and frustration. Sadness will deteriorate into depression and bitterness. The original emotions are pointers…messages from the experiencing part of you. It is the child that, through these emotions, reaches out its hands to the angel inside of you. The emotions express the pure, un-knowing experience. They are an expression of misunderstanding. It is in the connection to the angel that emotions can be picked up as pointers and understood. As such, the emotions become instruments for transformation and exploration: the "lower self" enriches and fulfils the higher self as it provides the knowing part with felt content. The angel in you comes to life and experiences deep joy if she is allowed to enlighten the child. And if the higher self shines through in this way, your emotional body quiets down and gains balance. The fruit of the flowing together of angel and child is an intuitive, inner knowing that can imbue your life with light and effortlessness.

The higher and lower principles in you, the angel and the child, are an organic, meaningful whole. The notions "higher" and "lower" therefore are not really right. It is about a joyful playing together of "knowing" and "experiencing". It is this interplay that leads to true, incarnated (as opposed to theoretical) wisdom.

To find guidance about your life in the now moment, you can best address your inner child. By giving it the attention it needs, you shower it with your higher consciousness, the touch of the angel. To illustrate this, let's return to the example above in which I spoke of anger and irritation. Once you have connected with this emotion and envisage it as a child, you can invite the child to come to you. You can ask it what it is upset about and what it needs from you to heal. Let the child answer you and allow it to express itself very clearly. Imagine it talking to you in a lively way, with a distinct expression on its face and clear body language. Perhaps it is giving you specific answers, such as "I want you to quit your job!" or "I want to take dancing lessons", or they may be more general, like "I need to play and relax more" or "I can't be nice all the time, you know!" Take the answer seriously and live according to it as much as possible. Maybe you cannot instantly do the things your inner child desires. But you can start small and step by step start to realize your longings.

If you embrace the angry, frightened or sad child inside of you with love and acceptance, it is touched by the angel inside of you and the result is that your soul speaks to you. Start with the emotions, find the true longing behind those emotions, and find a way to realize them step by step.

In the image I am drawing of the angel and the child within, there is no place for an authoritarian God figure. The "higher" and the "lower" complement each other in an open, dynamically evolving relationship. The angel does not dictate anything to the child, nor does the child have authority over the angel. It is in their interplay that you discover what is right for you in this moment.

You will find your life's goals through this intimate connection between angel and child. In this connection, you discover what really moves you. No authority outside of you can replace this connection, or make the connection for you. A teacher can only point to that sacred area within, where you can allow the child inside to be cherished and inspired by the angel in you. In this area, you find out who you are and what your passion is. General guidelines about how to live a spiritual life are nearly always inadequate, or at least not universal in nature. Truth is formless. Every creature has its own form, its own way of living the Truth. That is the miracle of your unique soul essence. Real spiritual teachers do not teach specific do's and don'ts, such as "do not eat meat" or "meditate two hours a day". A real teacher knows that it is all about you finding your own truth, in deep communion with yourself. Teachers may indicate what has been helpful to them on their way, but they will not turn this into a rule or dogma.

If you take a look at the way God has been portrayed in most of your religious traditions, this is exactly what happened there. Most of them are traditions of fear and power abuse. The need for clear cut rules and dogma and the tendency toward hierarchic organizations always show that fear and power are at play. The same thing however also happens in new age spirituality. Take for instance the many predictions and speculative theories currently circulating. If you go along with this without consulting your own basic feelings about it, you may get insecure and start to wonder "am I doing things right?", "what if I don't become enlightened in 2012?" or "is the state of my chakras pure enough to enter 5th dimension?" These types of questions are certainly not helpful to your inner growth. I ask you: turn towards yourself. Do not focus on the movement of the planets and stars, the climate changes, or the judgment of an "ascended master" to determine your level of self realization. You are the center of your universe, the standard and touch stone of your world. There is no God outside of you who knows better or who determines things for you. Not only does the God you formerly projected outside of you, reside in you, this God is not all-knowing either. The divine principle in you and all of creation is a playful force, growing and evolving in open and unpredictable ways.

In this image, the "lower" has an indubitable reason for existence: it is the fuel for growth and fulfillment. Light and dark have their own role to play and it is in the acceptance of both, that you find enlightenment. Reaching out for the light in a one sided way, ignoring or fighting the dark, which some spiritual groups aspire, creates imbalance and a subtle resistance to (and contempt for) life on Earth.

Doing things wrong, making mistakes, is alright and it may even bring you greater growth than trying to avoid mistakes. In the "bad things" the seed of light is dormant. Only by experiencing the bad from within, can you experience the good as beautiful, pure and true. You cannot learn "from without". You, God inside of you, has plunged into the deep (into material reality) to become knowing through experience, not to apply knowledge to experience. In that sense, not many things are non-spiritual. All experience is sacred and meaningful. Do not let yourself be guided by outside rules, dictating what is healthy, right and spiritual for you to do. The touchstone is your own heart: if it feels right for you, then it is okay. Let go of anything else.

The second idol: the standards and ideals of society

Another false god which estranges you from your original soul energy is "society": the standards and values which control your social world and are passed on to you through your upbringing, education and job environment. Many of society's ideals are rooted in fear, in the need to control and structure life so that it becomes a neatly arranged playground. Many rules of behavior are not so much inspired by what people truly feel and experience, but on what it looks like from the outside.

Trying to live up to such external standards of conduct can put a great pressure on you. Think of the fear of "not fitting in", not having accomplished enough, not being beautiful enough, having no relationship, etcetera. By comparing yourself to unreal images of success and happiness, your creative energy gets stuck and you do not feel at home in this world anymore.

Because of all these do's and don'ts, which have become like a second skin, you hardly dare to explore your original creativity. You are afraid to step outside the beaten track. But it is exactly this original soul energy, the energy which wants to flow uniquely from you, that is so welcome on Earth! It is this part of you that is meant to bring about the transformation of consciousness on Earth right now.

Connecting to your creative impulses and expressing them in your own unique way often demands that you deviate from society's aims and ideals. It may be the case that your natural rhythm of exploring yourself and then expressing who you are on the material level, does not fit in with society's schedule of how and when to achieve certain things in life. You may first go through a long process of getting to know yourself deeply, not achieving or producing anything on the outer level. While this may seem ineffective or unsuccessful to people, you may be working very hard on the inner level, discovering a lot of valuable things about yourself. Take your time to discover who you are, where your natural energy leads you, and to integrate it into your emotional and physical being. Do not pay attention to external success. Focus on what feels good and right to you, what makes you feel relaxed and inspired. If you find that way of living, and experience peace and quiet within, you will most easily get in touch with your original soul energy.

There is much fear in people about what society dictates and expects from them. The strange thing is that "society" as such does not even exist. What we have is a lot of people together, each with their own sincere longings and their deep-seated fears. Everyone longs to be free in the deepest sense of the word: to simply be who they are without fear of being judged by "the others". Think again therefore, whenever you are paying a lot of attention to what others think of you. You are in fact becoming the other's worst enemy too, since by abiding to their rules and fearing their judgment, you keep false ideals alive and suffocate the both of you even stronger. You become "society" to someone else.

Especially you, who are the pioneers of the New Era, can be an example to people who are caught in fear. You are that example when you truly stand by yourself, listen closely to your feelings, live accordingly and let go of outside judgments. These judgments are born from fear, not love, and they are often based on old rules and codes that no one remembers the true origin of. These old standards, which bear no connection to the human heart anymore, wait to be transformed from within, by people who dare to open up new vistas. Society waits for you; it waits for inspired ideals and standards that help people connect to their hearts and their true desires. You contribute to the collective transformation of consciousness by being an example of love instead of a follower of fear.

Dare to invite in the playful, childlike part of you. Get in touch with your inner child often: it knows very well what it wants. Often you can hardly sense what your heart truly longs for and you feel like you have lost your passion. This is because you do not let the inner child play, fantasize and dream anymore. When you measure yourself to external codes (what is appropriate for my age, gender, social background) you limit yourself and you do not allow the child, the dreamer and visionary, to take you outside of those limits and connect you to your "inner code".

You were all born with an inspiration, a desire to manifest something on Earth, both for yourself and for others ("society"). You have not come here to live in an ivory tower. You are part of collective consciousness on Earth and you have come here to be a leader and inspirer of change. That will make you happy and fulfilled. By connecting to your inner child, and once again feeling the magic of that original passion, illusory limits and boundaries will be lifted and you will find your way in life in a much easier and lighter way. The more you set yourself free from the false gods that keep you small and fearful, the more you live from a sense of freedom and surrender to the heart, and the more the universe will support you and provide you with the means necessary to bring your passion to fruition.

The third idol: pitying others and going along with their suffering

There is one other false god which I would like to mention and which perhaps preoccupies you the most in everyday life. It is pitying your fellows, sharing the burden with your dear ones by suffering along with them. Now, you may ask: how can that be an idol? Am I not supposed to connect with others, especially my loved ones, and help them if I can? What I am talking about is a tendency of yours to connect so deeply with people around you, that you are drawn into their pain, their problems and negative emotions and lose touch with your own core and inner peace. This kind of pity and co-suffering is not your duty, it is not helpful to the other person and does not speak to the truth of who you are.

Much of what you call "high sensitivity" is being so open to other people's energy that it wipes away your own. Your empathy (i.e. the ability to feel other people's moods and emotions) is in that case insufficiently balanced by the insight that the negative energies in that person belong to them and not to you. You are not realizing clearly enough that this negativity plays a viable role in the other person's life and that you may enlighten them through your compassion and understanding, but that it does not serve anyone's purpose if you suffer along with them.

Of course you would love to see your dear ones lead happy and fulfilling lives (whether it be spouse, child, parent or friend). You wish they would feel better and that their problems would be solved. Always remember though that the problems they have are their own creations. Relationship problems, money issues, health problems, psychological disorders....they all mirror deep-seated inner conflicts within the soul. Somewhere deep down people want to experience these problems, in order to get clear about something. It may seem that they are victims, especially when they are running around in circles over and over again. But often that means they still want to experience some aspect of that problem more thoroughly and that they are not open yet to your help. If you try to help them anyway, you will easily become pushy and controlling and you will exhaust your own energy sources. You then give up on surrender as a lifestyle.

By giving too much or inappropriately, you waste energy and you chain yourself emotionally to the one you are helping. This makes you dependent on the other person for your sense of well-being. Your emotional energies get mixed up and this is one of the major causes for loss of strength, vitality and self-awareness. Few things can break down your energy so easily as a persistent sense of duty, guilt and responsibility for someone else.

In such a "helping relationship" power issues often arise, even if no one intended this. By giving too much or inappropriately, the helper in fact tries to cover up an inner emptiness that goes unnoticed if one is preoccupied with someone else. Helping someone else may make you feel stronger and more self-assured. The one who gets all this attention from you experiences this as nice and comfortable, and they soon notice they can influence you with their moods and emotions. They know that if things get worse for them, they get more attention from you (because you want them to get well so badly). The "sufferer" therefore senses that they have power over you and that it pays off to remain in the victim role. In such a relationship, a strong energy exchange is taking place, and it will drain the both of you, because it is not in alignment with what your souls really want. There is no spiritual truth in the way you are reducing each other to very limiting roles. The helper will eventually get frustrated because the sufferer will not progress enough: it is not in their interest to change, for they have invested in the victim role. And the sufferer gets even more stuck in their victim role; they dig themselves deeper into it, which may completely paralyze them. Both will get angry and blame one another.

You easily sympathize with and feel sorry for the people around you. Especially lightworker souls, who have a deep impulse to spread light and awareness on Earth, are very sensitive to the suffering of others. It is hard for you to see suffering on a global scale, for instance in regions in the world devastated by poverty or war, or the destruction and pollution of the environment. But when it comes to suffering that is close to you, in your personal environment, you are affected most profoundly. And it is especially here that you are challenged to take back your power.

It is important to realize that you are not helping someone by making yourself smaller. You often think that if you absorb and swallow part of the other person's emotions, you connect deeper to them and therefore help them. It is like you are sharing the burden. But by taking in the other one's troubles, you only double the burden. The shadow deepens. By going along with the other person's suffering, your power gets fragmentized and shattered by the negativity in them. You will think you are not entitled to be happy, peaceful and satisfied yourself, while they are suffering. This is a grave mistake. In actuality, the opposite is true.

To be truly helpful to someone means that you put your energy at the service of the solution of the problem, not of the problem itself. To do so you need to make yourself bigger rather than smaller. The more self-consciousness and independence you radiate, the more you represent the "energy of the solution" and the more you can mean for someone else without exhausting yourself. If you are going to suffer with them, you are really only affirming the problem.

If you stay centered and calm, not resonating with the heavy emotions of the other, you open up another angle, another way of looking at the problem. Precisely by not resonating with the energy of the problem, you shed new light on it.

True spiritual guidance never involves solving someone else's problem. Rather, it means to be a beacon of light and awareness to them, which mirrors their problems back to them in a way that enables them to take another look at it. It enables them to see meaning and value in the problem; it returns to them a sense of free will and responsibility. Something inside of you touches their heart and inspires them: it is the energy of love. It is the energy of acceptance. In this way, you offer the "energy of the solution" to them, not by doing anything for them, but by being it. That is light work: being your natural self, having peace with yourself and radiating that peace to others. It is not about carrying other people's burdens or finding solutions to their problems. It is about carrying the energy of the solution in your own being and openly sharing it with others. That is the core of your mission on Earth, the core of what it means to bring light.

Being true to yourself, taking good care of yourself and listening to what your intuition tells you is a prerequisite to anchor the frequency of love to Earth. This is what your soul wants for you. Anytime you let others run away with your energy, or give too much of yourself out of fear or a need to control, a part of your light gets shattered and you will need to recuperate and emotionally heal yourself to regain your natural balance and vitality. Notice how this happens in your everyday life. If you are worrying about other people, about how they perceive you or how you should help them, and your thoughts are going in circles, and the same emotions repeat themselves, you are stuck in the rut of fear and control. Often, you tend to give away your energy because you think you are making things better, helping people out or solving a problem. But pay attention: does your contribution really serve the solution of the problem or does it affirm and thereby perpetuate the problem. Ask yourself whether you aren't really serving an idol, instead of your own inner light.

Trying to control things often seems right and sensible, but often it is just fear that forces you to. You frequently feel tired and exhausted from all your exertions in different areas of your life, but often you stick to it and feel that you are obliged to put even more energy into it. You think you owe it to

25

someone, to some organization, to society or even to God. But anytime you feel emotionally exhausted, pushing it too far, it is really time to let go and find some quiet space for yourself. It is time to let go of the world and turn within. Cutting the cords for a while and reconnecting to your inner child is of great importance to remain centered and balanced. By connecting to the child, you also awaken the angelic you, the keeper of the child. You connect to your "lower self" and "higher self" and by feeling them inside, and listening to them carefully, you start to sense how they can play together joyfully in your present. It becomes clear what things you need to do or pursue to become centered and peaceful again.

Finding and following your passion

Everyone is born with a passion. Imagine that passion to be a beautiful red rose. Imagine that, just before you are born, you are standing at the edge of heaven, holding this exquisite red rose in your hand. Though you may hesitate to take the leap into the Earth realm, even wondering gloomily whether you are really up to it, you sense a fire deep within, a passion, which presents itself to you as the red rose. Now imagine that you take the leap, you incarnate, and now you carry the rose within, in your belly and heart. Let the energy of the rose come to you now. Allow your original passion, your inspiration to present itself to you in this moment. Take a look at the rose, what does it look like now? Take the first image that springs to your mind. Does the rose look a bit sad and worn out, or does it radiate vibrantly? Do you see a rose bud or a blooming flower? Does it need anything from you in this moment? Perhaps more water or sunlight, or some more love and attention, or does it want to be removed to another spot, to more nurturing surroundings? Imagine that you give it exactly what it needs, and feel how this affects you on the inner level.

Red is the color of the Earth and of the base or root chakra. Red is the color of passion. You are often afraid of your own passion. You are afraid to let this original flow express itself openly in your lives, because it goes against what society or tradition considers proper, right and sane. However, in each one of you there is an original passion and inspiration that is the very source of your existence here and now. You cannot really be fulfilled and inspired, until you allow that energy to run through your life and guide it. The essence of surrender as a lifestyle is that you surrender to yourself, to your soul's passion, the inspiration that cradled your current lifetime.

There are a few ways in which you can recognize whether you are connected to your soul's passion.

1. Feeling inspiration – wherever it flows, that's where you need to be

Surrender as a lifestyle means that you let yourself be guided by what truly inspires you. Surrender is not a passive energy. By surrendering to what really motivates and inspires you, you open the gate to a lively and active flow of energy within. To discover that flow for yourself, you need to find out with what kind of activities your energy naturally flows. What things make you feel happy and peaceful? In what kind of occupation or pursuit do you feel that things move effortlessly and gracefully? What is the essence of these things or activities? Feel the essence of it – and know that there may be a variety of ways for this essence to take shape and form.

2. Being true to your own nature - what you do naturally, is what you are good at

To recognize your passion you need to realize that it is always something that is very natural to you. It is something, an activity or occupation or expression form, that you are drawn to, feel interested in and enjoy pursuing. It is something close and natural to you, almost self evident from your perspective. To bring your natural gift to fruition, you may have to learn some skills or pursue some formal education, but it will be relatively easy and joyful for you to do so. Your passion is something that your abilities and talents are attuned to; it involves activities that you are good at from the start.

3. Maintaining clear boundaries and daring to say "no" – take yourself seriously

You are in the flow of surrender to yourself if you take yourself seriously enough to say no to things or people that inhibit or cut off that flow. You can only follow your passion if you dare to say no to what does not fit or feel right to you. Surrendering to yourself, to your unique inspiration, entails being precocious and stubborn sometimes, standing apart and trusting the messages of your heart even if people say you are silly and foolish. It is about loyalty to yourself. Dare to be grand, dare to make a difference! There is really no alternative, you know. The alternative is that your natural flow of inspiration gets stuck and dries up and you start to feel frustrated, empty, angry and unfulfilled. If you do not choose for yourself, you choose against yourself. The energy of the rose, your passion, withdraws and this creates psychological problems such as loneliness, estrangement and eventually depression. Therefore, dare to say no, dare to take up space with clear boundaries. Do not fear to be "egotistical" according to the standards of false gods.

4. Patience and rhythm – do it step by step

If you are connected to the energy of your soul, your inspiration, it will clear a path for you in your everyday life. Opportunities (in the form or people or situations you encounter) will come to you in a pace and rhythm that suits you. If you want to be attuned to that flow of manifestation, stay in the present and take it step by step. Try to not run ahead of all the things that need to happen to realise your dreams and passion. Life takes care of you, you need not take care of life. Simply feel your passion and entrust it to the hands of the God within you. Let the angel inside keep and watch over the dreams and longings of your inner child. Surrender and trust!

Thank you so much for being here today. It is a great pleasure to be with you and remember that the I who is saying this also very much represents your own energy. It is your own energy that beckons and invites you: dare to live, dare to be who you are!

2 - The Atlantis heritage

I am Jeshua. I stand before you and send you my energy and love. I would like to be of support to you in these challenging times. This time of transition on Earth brings many old issues to the surface. Old energies emerge from times long gone by, times in which you were incarnate and had lives in which you experienced much. All these old layers now resurface.

I would like to speak of these old times today, to bring you to a deeper understanding of yourselves, of who you are here-and-now. You are old, ancient beings, who carry within a great deal of experience. Long journeys through time and space you have made, and not just on planet Earth. Please let me take you back to the beginning. There was never a beginning, but for the sake of this story, I speak of a beginning in time, because there was a starting point to the large cycle of lifetimes in which you are now caught up.

I am taking you to the time of your birth as an individual soul, as a separate "I". The "I-ness" that is so familiar to you now, was an altogether new phenomenon in the universe. Being separate and individual, enables you to gather a multitude of experiences, and yes, illusions as well. But that does not make it less valuable. It is precisely in being an "I", in being separate from the whole, and experiencing the illusions that go with it, that you can discover what is not. You can discover an illusion and experience it from the inside out. At first, this was not possible. At first, there was the One and nothing outside of it, like an undifferentiated ocean of love and oneness. Now try and experience fear and ignorance from in there!

In being vulnerable and prone to illusion, you gather an enormous amount of experience, which enables you to really understand what oneness means, what love means at the level of experience. You will understand what love is, not as an abstract concept, but as a living, creative force that moves you and fills your heart and spirit with a deep sense of joy and satisfaction. This is the end goal of your journey, the Homecoming you are longing for: to be God-as-you, to experience oneness as an "I". You do not want to give up your "I-ness". It is through the connection of your "I" with the whole, that you experience the deepest joy and that you add your own unique energy stamp to the whole of creation. God-as-you adds something new and precious to creation.

I ask you to go back to the time that this "being an I" took shape for the first time. Back then you were, or were created as, angels. Can you feel the tenderness and innocence of that original energy, that distant beginning in which you were first "molded", got to know form. All of a sudden you were *you*, distinct and separate from the others around you, and you experienced the miracle of being an individual. You were still so close to the source of divine light, that you were filled with love and overflowed with joy and creativity. There was an incredible desire in you to experience, to know, to feel and to create. Please go within for a moment, and see whether you can sense the truth of it: that you are an angel in the deepest part of you....

I now take a big leap in time, as I can only give a broad outline of this extensive history. I take you to the beginning of planet Earth. You were present there, you are older than the existence of Earth as a physical planet. Your birth as a pristine I-consciousness, lies much further back than the origin of Earth.

Now imagine that you were contributing to the development of life on Earth. Slowly, life evolved on Earth, through the presence of material elements which offered a broad range of possibilities for consciousnesses to incarnate in material forms or bodies: minerals, plants, and later on, animals. And you were deeply involved in this process of creation. How?

You were the angels and devas who supported and nurtured the vegetable kingdom, who knew the "web of life" on Earth intimately and cared for it deeply. You have also provided animal life forms with love, care and etheric nourishment.

Memories you carry within of "paradise" or the Garden of Eden, of a perfectly balanced nature in which you participated as caregiver and keeper of life, stem from this ancient age. You were not incarnate yet then, but hovering between the ethereal and the physical realms. You were an angel on the verge of being born into matter.

Remember the innocence of that age, remember what it was like to be this angel-deva-consciousness and how dearly you loved the Earth and all manifestations of life on it. Feel the childlike aspect of your consciousness back then. You were like children playing in paradise, always in the mood for adventures, kidding around, laughing, experiencing the joy of freely expressing yourself in a safe environment. Despite your playfulness, you were in great awe of the guiding laws of life and you would not think of treating life forms with anything less than deep fondness and respect.

So, you have been in some sense the parents of life on Earth. This explains why you can be thoroughly shocked by the disturbances of nature by modern technologies, and the general abuse of the forces of nature. Why does it affect you so? It is because you have cherished and nurtured these very energies from the beginning. From your essence you are connected to it, to Earth and its many life forms, as a parent is to her child and a creator to his creation. And back then, when you were angels nurturing Earth life, you knew not why you were doing it. You acted as children who felt drawn by the calling of yet another adventure, the thrill of the new, and you let yourself be guided simply by what felt joyful and exciting to you. You planted your energy wherever it felt welcome.

Thus, you helped create paradise on Earth: the splendor of life, the abundance of the plant and animal kingdoms, the diversity of life forms and the unconstrained development of it all.

Please hold on to this image for a moment.......remember who you are.

Even if it seems too grandiose, when I tell you this, just allow yourself to fantasize that you were part of this, that you were present as an angel in that Garden of Life, playful, innocent, nurturing and cherishing life.

Out of paradise - the first Fall into Experience

Many developments occurred on Earth over millions of years, which are hard to describe in a nutshell. But, at a certain point in time, your blissful adventure in the Garden of Eden was disturbed by an outside influence, which might be termed "bad" or "dark".

From other dimensions in the universe, beings started to meddle with Earth. Their purpose was to exert power and influence over life on Earth. This happening, the interference of powerful dark energies which emerged out of nothing from your point of view, deeply shocked your angel-selves. You were not prepared. This was your first encounter with "evil" and it shook your world to its foundations. For the first time, you experienced what it was like to not feel safe anymore. You got to know "human emotions": fear, shock, anger, disappointment, grief, outrage: what is this?, what is happening here?!

Sense how the shadows fell upon you in that first encounter with darkness, the dark side of duality. Slowly, the craving for power, which had shocked and horrified you, started to take possession of you yourself. This was because you felt indignation and outrage towards the attackers, and you wanted to defend and protect the Earth against this strange invasion.

I speak of an extraterrestrial influence, a certain race so to speak, the origin of which does not matter much for our tale. What matters is that you partly absorbed the energy of these beings, and thus made a fall. I do not speak of a biblical Fall, as this phrase is associated with sin and guilt, but a fall into experience, into darkness, which was in a sense "predestined" because you were part of the world of duality. By being an "I", by experiencing separateness from the whole, the seeds for duality were born inside of you. It is part of the logic of creation that you will explore all extremes of duality, once you are in it.

You gradually became warriors yourselves, as you desired the power to protect your "territory". A new stage ensued in your history, in which you got caught up in various galactic wars and struggles. Please take a moment to feel this happening, the fall from the playful energy of the angel-child to the harsh and angry energy of the galactic warrior. We are speaking of long periods of time. It may seem grand and unfathomable that you have gone through all this, yet I ask you to allow your imagination to travel with me for a while.

You got caught up in a fierce and grand battle. Part of the science fiction literature familiar to you, describes all this and is actually inspired by real events in a distant past. It is not mere fiction. Much has actually happened and you were deeply involved in it. You lost yourselves in the struggle for power and during this stage of your history you thoroughly experienced the energy of the ego.

I have talked of this before in the Lightworker series (published in the first book *The Jeshua Channelings*), and I now want to take another huge leap and tell you what the next important stage was.

After a long, long time, you got tired of fighting. You had had enough. You were getting sad and battle-weary, and a kind of homesickness crept into your hearts. You had long been obsessed with the wars and conflicts you were involved in. The illusion of power can exert an hypnotic influence over an untested, naïve mind. You were naïve and untested when you experienced your first fall into darkness.

But then, at a certain point, an awakening occurred within you. A vague memory of the old days in Paradise stirred in your minds and hearts, reminding you of the joy and innocence you once knew. You wished you could go back there and did not desire to fight anymore. One might say that the energies of the ego had been exhausted in you, by the full experience of it. You had known all sides of the battle, the whole range of emotions having to do with winning and losing, controlling and surrendering, being slayer and slain. You had become disillusioned with power and had discovered that power does not give you what it promises to: love, happiness, fulfillment. You awoke from your hypnotic slumber and yearned for something new.

When you reached out to rise above the energy of struggle, and connect to the energy of the heart, you were again naïve and "untested". You were like children who popped your head over the wall of an altogether new country, in which not struggle or power were the leading forces but love and connection. You followed the calling of your soul and climbed over the wall. And you started to meet each other again and to recognize each other as soul mates, members of the same family. Once you had played together as angels in the Garden of Eden.

The members of the lightworker family, who are part of a same birth wave of souls, looked up on each other again and felt drawn by a common calling, a shared mission. You knew you had to do something to make the major step towards heart consciousness, the return to Paradise, actually happen for you. You felt you had dealings with Earth once again, but this time as a human being, incarnated in a human body, to experience from within what had happened on Earth due to the galactic wars, and your abuse of power.

In your struggle for power, the Earth had always been the focal point of attention. Many galactic parties battled for dominion on Earth and this negatively affected the Earth, all life upon her and the collective soul of evolving humanity. The reason why Earth was such an important target for all these warring parties is not so easily explained. Briefly put, Earth is the starting point of something new: it is a place that brings many different dimensions and realities together and therefore constitutes a crossroads toward the future. Many, many energies meet and mix together on Earth – within the plant, animal, and especially the human kingdom. This is very special. When these energies can peacefully coexist together, it will bring about a huge explosion of light throughout the cosmos. That is why Earth is playing a key role and why she had been in the centre of a great Battle.

You were once part of this battle, as offenders, trying to manipulate life and consciousness on Earth in quite an aggressive manner. This caused harm to the developing human being. Humanity was then in its infant stage, the "stage of innocence". Humanity was "inhabited" by souls who were from a different birth wave than you. We have called them "Earth souls" in the Lightworker Series (See *The Jeshua Channelings*). It was a group of souls younger than you were, who had manifested on Earth from early on and had to deal with outside, extraterrestrial manipulations which narrowed down the capabilities of the human being. The extraterrestrial forces projected energies of fear and inferiority into the open and young consciousness of man. This enabled them to gain control over them.

I return now to your decision to incarnate on Earth as a human being. You had two motives. First, you sensed you were ready for an inner change and transformation. You wanted to let go of the ego's battling attitude and grow towards another way of being. You did not know what exactly this meant; you could not grasp it fully yet, but you sensed that incarnating on Earth would offer you precisely the challenges and possibilities you needed.

Secondly, you knew you had to make up for things that happened on Earth, partly because of your doing. You somehow sensed that, originally, you had a deep bond with Earth based on love and mutual respect, and it had gotten corrupted when you let yourself be enmeshed in war and battle for this very Earth. The two extremes of you, of angel-child and hardened warrior, needed to be brought together and transformed, and what place could be more suitable for this than Earth? You felt deeply connected to this planet and you also sensed a karmic obligation to improve conditions on Earth. You wished to change and lift the state of consciousness on Earth. So you became lightworkers.

You incarnated on Earth at the time of Atlantis.

Atlantis - the second Fall into Experience

Atlantis was a civilization that lies much further back in time than the familiar historical eras. Atlantis gradually came into being about 100,000 years ago and it ended about 10,000 years ago. The first beginnings even predate 100,000 years. Atlantis gradually evolved when extraterrestrial races started to "invade" Earth by actually incarnating in human bodies. These souls in general had a high level of mental development. At that time, societies and communities on Earth were largely made up of Earth souls, and they were "primitive societies" as you call them.

There were, even before Atlantis, many extraterrestrial influences on Earth, from galactic realms that sent thought forms to Earth in different ways. Thought forms are energies that connect themselves to humans at the ethereal or auric level, and thus influence the thoughts and emotions of people. This happens continuously as you absorb ideas and beliefs from your upbringing and society. These surround you as an infectious web. But it can also happen from the "astral levels" surrounding you. The thought forms projected unto you by the galactic warriors were in general controlling and manipulative, but there have always been influences of light and gentleness as well. It is the human himself who decides what he allows in and what not. At a certain moment, the galactic parties wished to have a more profound influence on Earth and there was an opportunity for them to actually inhabit human bodies, in short to incarnate on Earth. Spirit or Life opened up this possibility for them because it fit into their inner path of development. You were one of these parties. In your spiritual literature, folks that stem from these galactic realms are often referred to as "star people" or "star seeds".

Atlantis was the result of a coming together, a mixture of the native Earth societies and the influx of souls that came "from the outside". You, the wave of the lightworker souls, incarnated on Earth because you wished to bring about change and progress and because you wanted to grow yourselves, from an ego-based consciousness to a heart-based consciousness.

When you arrived, it felt very awkward and uncomfortable at first, to be inside of physical human bodies. Living in such dense physical matter gave you a sense of oppression and imprisonment, as you were used to much more fluid and volatile bodies that possessed more psychic power. In higher (less material or dense) frequencies or dimensions, your psyche has a much greater direct influence on the material environment. By simply thinking of, or wanting something, you can create or attract it immediately to you on these planes. Your mind was used to creating much faster than was possible on Earth. You might say that the reaction time on Earth is much slower. So when you are here for the first time, you have the sensation that you are somehow locked into a solid and unyielding body. You become insecure, since what you desire and aspire does not materialize so easily anymore and your hold over your life and circumstances seems to be quite limited.

So you were confused when you got here. At the same time, you had highly trained mental abilities that were developed during your previous galactic lifetimes. To send out thought forms and project them unto other living beings requires that you have attained considerable psychic power. Your mind was like a set of sharp knives, which had to prove their value in an altogether different environment. Your trained mental capacities were an old attainment, and because of the sense of alienation and oppression you experienced on Earth, you instinctively tried to find your way here by using this old attainment. You thus started to exert your mental powers on Earth. Originally, your intention had been to connect with Earth reality from the heart. Before you incarnated, you knew that, despite your formidable analytical and psychic powers, the grounds of your heart lay fallow and were in need of seeds, little seedlings of light. This, however, you forgot when you plunged into Earth reality and your consciousness became veiled.

On Earth, you had to deal with the Earth souls, who lived there as human beings, and you did not understand them well. You thought they were instinctive and barbaric beings. You did not understand their direct, spontaneous way of expressing emotions. They were primitive in your eyes; they were attuned to their emotions and instincts more than to their minds. You had abilities and gifts that were different from the natural dispositions of the people on Earth.

Even though you were frequently born and raised as their children (when you were born to Earth soul parents) there gradually developed a social divide between you and them. Because of your superior mental skills, you developed technologies that were formerly unknown. This all happened slowly and naturally. We speak of thousands, even ten thousand years of time.

Without going into the details of this process, I want to ask you to feel the essence of what was happening there. Can you imagine you were part of that? Can you imagine what it must have felt like to end up somewhere you do not truly feel at home and to know: there's something I planned to do here, but what was it...? Let me see, I have certain abilities and powers at my command......this distinguishes me from many others in my environment......I will make use of these talents to assert myself. Do you recognize this kind of pride and ambition within you? Can you remember it was yours? This is a typical Atlantean energy.

Gradually, a new culture came into being on Earth, a civilisation that brought forth an unprecedented technological development which affected all parts of society. I would like to say a little more about the kind of technology that evolved in Atlantis. What you as star people still remembered brightly, despite the veil of forgetfulness, was that you can influence material reality by using the power of your mind, specifically the third eye. The third eye is the energy centre (chakra) of intuition and psychic awareness, and it is located behind your two physical eyes.

The power of the third eye was still very familiar to you in those first incarnations, like a second nature to your soul. You knew "how it worked". You knew that matter (physical reality) has a form of consciousness, *is* consciousness in a certain state of being. Through this essential insight into the oneness of consciousness and matter, you could affect and form matter, by making inner contact with the consciousness in the piece of matter. In this way, you could literally move matter, manipulate it from the mind. You knew a secret that was forgotten in more recent times.

Presently, you see matter (physical reality) as separated from consciousness (the mind). Influenced by modern science, you have forgotten that all beings are ensouled: all that is has some form of consciousness that you can connect with and cooperate with in a creative way. This knowledge was self evident to you in those ancient times. But, during Atlantis, when your heart centers had not been awakened fully, your third eye was predominantly controlled by the centre of the will or ego (the solar plexus or third chakra). You stood on the doorway of a new inner reality, the reality of heart-based consciousness, but due to the shock of being submerged in the dense reality of Earth, your tender and fresh inspirations were temporarily lost. You allowed yourselves to be led astray by the excessive use of the will mixed with the power of the third eye. You did aspire to make things better on a larger scale ("light work") but you did it in a self-centered way, with an authoritarian attitude toward the Earth souls and nature.

In the hey-day of Atlantis, there were many possibilities and the technology was highly advanced, in some areas even more so than your present technology, because the power of telepathy and psychic manipulation was much better used and understood. Instantaneous telepathic communication could take place between different persons at great distance from each other. It was possible to leave your body consciously and travel around. Communication with extraterrestrial civilizations was pursued and effected.

Much became possible during Atlantis, but much went wrong as well. There generally was a divide between the political-spiritual elite and the "common people", which were predominantly made up of Earth souls. They were looked upon as inferior beings, means to an end, and they were actually used for genetic experiments that were part of the Atlantean ambition to manipulate life on the biological level, so that more superior life forms could be created.

A positive aspect of the Atlantean society, by the way, was the equality of men and women during that age. The power struggle of man and woman, in which women were horribly oppressed during the last stage, was not a part of Atlantis. The feminine energy was fully respected, especially because it is directly related to the power of the third eye (intuition, clairvoyance, spiritual power).

I now wish to take you to the downfall of Atlantis. Energies were at work there that you are still trying to come to terms with. You were deeply involved in what went wrong at that stage.

In Atlantis, you lived from the centers of the will and the third eye. Your heart energy did not open up significantly. At a certain point, you fell in love with the possibilities of your own technology and the ambition of creating more superior life forms. You applied genetic engineering and experimented on several life forms, and you were unable to understand, to feel, that you were disrespectful to Life in this. The ones you experimented upon could not count on your empathy and compassion.

The energy present at this stage of perversion in the Atlantean civilisation specifically returned in the 20th century as the Nazi regime in Germany. Cruel experimenting and a general attitude of clinical coldness towards "inferior life forms" was a substantial part of that regime. The lack of compassion and empathy displayed towards the victims, the lack of emotion and the mechanical way of dealing with them, was similar to the Atlantean attitude. This now fills you with a deep sense of horror. You have seen and felt the other side of it, the victim side, in lifetimes that came after Atlantis.

But during Atlantis, you were the offender. That's where a particular karma ensued. Atlantis is the key to your "offender lifetimes", your dark side. I'm telling you this, not to make you feel ashamed or guilty, not at all. We are all part of this history, taking on various roles and disguises, and this is what it is like to be in duality. It is to experience and play all thinkable roles, from very light to very dark. If you allow yourself to know your dark side, if you can accept that you played the role of perpetrator as well, you will be more balanced, free and joyful. That is why I tell you this.

At one point, the technological developments that you - and other soul groups - pursued, had such a great impact upon nature, that the ecological systems on Earth were disrupted. The downfall of Atlantis did not take place all at once. There were many warning signs - nature's beckoning - but when they were not heeded, enormous natural disasters occurred through which the Atlantean civilization was flooded and destructed.

How did it affect you on the inner level? It was a shocking experience, a traumatic experience; it was another Fall, a second Fall of Experience into the realm of duality.

During your incarnations on Earth, you had eventually lost the connection to the heart energy that you had reached out to. Stronger than ever, you realized after the downfall of Atlantis that truth was not to be found in the controlling of life, even if the purpose seemed noble. You then really began to open up to the still voice of the heart, which tells you that there is a wisdom working through Life itself, that needs no managing or controlling. In the flow of life itself, in the flow of the heart and the feelings, there is a wisdom that you can attune to, or align with, by listening and surrendering. It is not a wisdom created from the head or by the will, it is a wisdom that comes from allowing in a higher perspective, the voice of love.

This mystical knowing, which is accompanied by a sense of humbleness and surrender, you slowly started to feel from within. But even then, the time was not yet ripe for a joyful awakening of the heart energies. A shadow had fallen upon you during Atlantis, the shadow of having affected other beings negatively. The effects of this would have to be deeply felt and experienced by you before the awakening could take place.

Again I take another huge step in this old history, and I take you to the moment you return to Earth after Atlantis had vanished, washed away by ocean waves. Once again you incarnated in human bodies, the memory of Atlantis buried deep within your soul memory, tied with a sense of shame and self-doubt. The downfall of Atlantis had stunned and perplexed you, but it had also opened up your hearts a little wider.

What immense developments taking place on such a grand scale of time!

Rejection as a lightworker- the third Fall into Experience

The next important cycle started with the coming of the Christ energy on Earth, most visibly represented by me. Many of you were present then or around that time. A few centuries before my birth, you started to incarnate again in great numbers. A voice from your heart enticed you, summoned you. You sensed that "you had to be there", that it was time for you to take another step on your spiritual journey, which had become so intertwined with Earth.

The coming of the Christ energy, my coming to Earth, was partly prepared by you. I could not have come without a layer of energy present on Earth that would receive me, "catch me" so to speak. Your energy provided the channel through which I could anchor the Christ energy on Earth. It was a joint effort, truly. Your hearts had opened up to me, to what I represented. At that time, you were the part of humanity most open to receive the love and wisdom from the heart.

A certain humbleness had arisen within you, in the best sense of the word: a surrender to not-knowing, not wanting to control or manage things, and a genuine openness to something new, something that stands apart from power and control, something different. And because of this trust and openness in your hearts, you could receive me.

I was like a light beam falling on Earth, reminding the ones who were ready of their angelic nature, their divine core. You were moved by me, by what I expressed and radiated to you from my inner core, and the Christ energy has thenceforth affected you deeply, in that lifetime around Christ and in the lifetimes after it, up to now. In all of those lives, you have tried to bring the Christ energy down to Earth, spread it through teaching and healing in different forms. You were inspired and passionate lightworkers, working hard to bring more justice, fairness and love to this planet.

In that era, the era of the awakening Christ energy, you were the ones who were opposed to religions that were too tightly organized, to authoritarian ways of subduing people. You fought for freedom, emancipation of the female energy, heart-based values in an age that was still barely aware of it. In the past two thousand years, you were freedom fighters and you were rejected and persecuted for it. You were punished and tortured for who you were, and frequently ended up on the stake or the scaffold. You carry a lot of emotional trauma from this episode of history.

In the struggles and the resistance you met, the Atlantean (and galactic) karma was working. The roles were now reversed. You became victims and went through the depths of loneliness, fear and despair. You became intimately acquainted with the deep emotion pain of rejection. This was your third Fall, a third Fall into Experience, and the one that brought you to the heart of your mission: understanding the oneness underlying both light and dark, learning what love truly means. This third Fall has led you to the present, to who you are now.

Today, at the edge of a new cycle, in these transformative times, you are truly open to the meaning of the Christ energy. In your heart, a wisdom is sprouting that embraces and transcends opposites and recognizes the one divine flow in all different manifestations. Your love is not a mere abstract knowing, but a real, pure and sincere flow from the heart, that reaches out to others, and to Earth. You now recognize yourself in the countenance of the other, whether they are light or dark, rich or poor, lightworker or Earth soul, man, animal or plant. The love embedded in the Christ consciousness bridges the gap between opposites and gives you a palpable sense of the interconnectedness of all that is.

As an angel, you once guarded paradise on Earth. You cut yourself off from this state of innocence when you engaged in the dance of power with energies that wanted to steal paradise from you. Through this, you abandoned the spiritual realm and incarnated deeper into the material reality of form and illusion. From angel you became warrior. When you incarnated on Earth and sought to experience what it was like to be human, you were again tempted by the desire to control things and this led to the downfall of Atlantis and of you as a warrior. You came back to Earth to experience the downside of the power play, to feel what it is like to fall prey to aggression and violence. The aftermath of this latter part of the cycle is still clearly present in your way of experiencing things and you are all working hard to overcome the trauma of rejection inside of you. With that, you are coming full circle, to the point where it began. You come back to your true nature as an angel, but now a fully incarnate angel, with a real and alive knowledge of the extremes of light and dark, love and fear. You are a wise and compassionate angel, a human angel…

I have great respect for you, for the incredible journey you have made. I stand before you now as your equal. I am here as a teacher and guide, but also as a brother and a friend. I would like to offer you my love and friendship, not in an abstract manner, but as a tangible energy of companionship and understanding. I know who you are. Now recognize yourself in my countenance.

You are at the end of great cycles of time, in which you have gone through many experiences. Today I wanted to speak of Atlantis, as the recognition of the energies that you embodied there can help you get into a state of peace and wholeness with yourself. The Atlantean energy is the energy of great mental power, combined with a distinctive pride and arrogance. Dare to recognize this "dark energy" within, dare to accept that you have experienced and lived it once. Feel that you have been offender and perpetrator as well as victim. Allowing this fact into your consciousness opens the gateway to the greatest wisdom you can embrace in your life: the wisdom of non-judgmentalness. By being aware of your dark side you will let go of judging others and yourself for being right or wrong. All grounds for judgment will fall away. Judgment makes way for understanding and compassion. Then you really start to understand what love is, what light work means. The word "light work'" in fact suggests falsely that there is some kind of struggle going on between the light and the dark, and that the lightworker is the one beating the dark. But true light work is none of that. Real light work entails that you are able to recognize the light of love and consciousness in all that is, even if it is hiding behind masks of hatred and aggression.

You are still often tempted to pass judgments on the reality of Earth, for instance on the way politics work or the way people are treating the environment. It is easy to say that it's all wrong and to feel yourself a stranger on this planet Earth, alienated and homeless. Try to make contact with the offender energy within you in such moments. Allow yourself to access the Atlantean energy, which is still there in your soul memory, and feel that you have been that too, and even that it was okay. All of your "falls into experience" eventually bring you full circle and open up your heart to the essence of God's creation: love, creativity, innocence. You, who have experienced the extremes of darkness and light, have all along your journey been none other than an innocent child from paradise, setting out with a spirit of frankness, bold curiosity and zest for life. On this journey, you could only learn from experience. The "falls into experience" could not have been avoided, as they were the means to reach out for something new and more fulfilling. The essence of your journey is that you reach wisdom through experience. Therefore, please recognize and honor the courage of this angel-child that you were. See its vitality, courage and perseverance in venturing into the unknown, and then feel your own innocence, even in your darkest side.

I ask you to respect yourself, including the dark side of you. Just feel the power and self-consciousness of the Atlantean energy for a moment. There is a positive side to it as well. You were gifted in many ways. Invite that energy in, here and now. Allow the sense of self-esteem and self-command to return to you, and forgive yourself for the atrocities that took place in the past. Yes, you have inflicted pain on others, you were the aggressor there......but feel also how you have come to regret this deeply, and how much you have opened up now to genuine respect for all that lives. When you forgive yourself, you open up to the joy of letting go of judgment. That is the consequence, you see: if you recognize the dark part of you and are able to forgive yourself for it, you need not judge either yourself or others any more. This is such a delight for your soul......

So often you still put yourself on the rack of your judgments. You tell yourself there is so much you have to accomplish yet. Today, I ask you to look back and see what you have accomplished already. Be aware of the profundity of your journey throughout these great cycles of time. And do not look up to me as a master anymore. I have fulfilled that role, two thousand years ago, but that time is over. You are the Christs of this new era, you will bring peace in a world of duality and polarity, by radiating the peace that lies within your own hearts. Feel how you are ready for this role and let me simply offer you some support and encouragement as your friend and brother. We are one.

3 - It's about you!

I am Jeshua. I am filled with joy as I come near to you today and share my energy. I share my energy with you, but you are sharing as well. Your light shines upon the world, even though you do not always realize this. You are making the difference on Earth, here and now, in this age in which so much is changing.

Consciousness is evolving on Earth and it stirs the dark to come out of its hiding place. It brings to the surface much that is old and rotten, for all to see. This is why this age appears so contradictory in its manifestations. Consciousness grows, but it may become darker before the Light gains a foothold and truly shines in your world.

You are the ones that drive the old to the surface, you force it into openness by your consciousness, by your light. This is what you feel called to, this is who you are. You are lightworkers. You are souls with a deeply sensed mission; you are moved by a calling that gripped me as well during my life on Earth. Many of you were followers of me back then, or better put, followers of the teaching and energy that I disseminated.

I am your heart, I am your soul. I am not just that one human being who once lived on Earth and who is now returning to you. I come here before you as the expression of the Christ energy: your oversoul, the energy that binds you, that is your source and origin. It is a field of energy that is now moving closer and closer to Earth, touching the hearts of many people and affecting their emotions.

This wave of light brings much confusion to people who are not ready for change. They feel insecure, they experience a lack of meaning in their lives, and they do not know how to deal with these confused emotions. And you are the ones on Earth who are here to radiate light to these people. You are the pioneers, you are the teachers of this New Age. Now you may ask yourselves: am I ready to do that? How should I go about? How do I radiate or express my light? The answer is simpler than you think: you are already doing it. You are doing what you came to do.

One of the reasons why you have so many doubts about yourself is that you fear to face up to your own grandness. In your everyday life, you still harbor a lot of negative thoughts and emotions about yourself which make you wonder: "Can I really be anchored and rooted in this place called Earth, am I really at home here? Do I truly fulfill my mission here?" And I am telling you: especially when you are challenged by fear, despair or gloominess, you are able to fulfill your mission. Because right there is where your light is needed the most. No one is better equipped to heal the pain inside of you than you are. In lighting up your own inner darkness, with love and compassion, you are setting up an example of light work that radiates outward to others and encourages them to light up themselves.

You are old and come from afar. You are nearing the completion of a cycle of lifetimes. And now, at the end of this cycle, your energy has become gentle, full of compassion and wisdom. But you have also become discouraged, and you get depressed now and then, when you look at the state of mother Earth, this beautiful creation of plant, animal, and human kingdoms, which could be so full of life and vitality. Also, when you observe your relationships to others, you often feel that something is lacking. You miss a certain openness, love, gaiety, connectedness. You are homesick for a reality in which you can share this with others. This pains you. You have pain about the world. You have pain about the people near to you. You have pain about yourself. You sense homesickness and a deep love within that you find hard to express and embody here on Earth.

But I say to you that you are on the threshold of a New Era. Have faith, I am here with you to support and encourage you. However you are the ones who cross the barrier, you are the ones who carry on my work. You are the Christs of the New Era. Especially when you feel down and tired, losing all confidence, please open up to this new possibility, the light that is dawning, and surrender to it. Do not try to fight or struggle with your fears and gloominess. They are there – let me take care of it. Feel my energy here and now, I am with you.

I am you, we are one. Allow the light and comfort of the Christ energy to be with you and feel how we are all connected by this powerful carrier of light. You are the Christ of the New Era.

Now I would like to ask you to direct your attention to the hurt part of you, the inner child which has felt beaten and humiliated throughout many lifetimes on Earth. You have gone through a lot, both in this lifetime and in past ones. It is this dear child within you, physically located in your belly, that needs care and attention. Especially, it needs patience and trust from you. This child, this emotional part of you, does not heal at once. It has been wounded deeply, and from this hurt it creates negative emotions in your life, such as loneliness, fear, feeling abandoned or rejected. These emotions point at your deepest wound. It is not even death that you fear most. It is the sense of total disconnection from God that constitutes the deepest agony. Feeling separated from the loving presence of Spirit, cut off from the natural light and connectedness of Creation, has created the heaviest burden inside of you. I am asking you to see that pain inside of you and to reach out your hands to the hurt child inside.

Just imagine that you are an angel, a representative of the realms of light, and feel how your angel energy envelops your body with a soft and warm cloak. It is a golden energy that cherishes you and you can feel how it circles around you, from head to toe. Notice how hands of gold reach out to your belly, to the small and innocent child within. Tell the child it is welcome and precious beyond words.

Say "hello" to that old pain of yours and allow it to be there. "You can be a part of my life, I am not letting you down". This is the compassion that you long for, this is what makes you whole, let it be. Standing by your own wounded self, not letting the child within suffer all by itself, is the energy that makes you a Christ. In your everyday life, any time you resist your own pain, wishing you could get rid of your fear and anger all at once, cursing yourself for it, you are letting the child inside you down. By resisting your pain, and judging the behavior coming from it, you alienate the child from you. You say "I do not want to be sad or angry or afraid anymore, I just want to be happy, why can't I get over it, I hate myself." But the child within is crying and calling out for you, and it will not be healed by your resistance or condemnation.

Take the time to heal yourself. When you feel resistance, stop right there and sit down. Do not turn away, let the resistance go, for the child's sake. Be present with your wounded child, allow the golden energy of your angel self to embrace it. Do not be afraid to be so grand! Take as much time and space as your need to heal yourself. Do not belittle your needs and the depth of your pain. Take it seriously. This healing process is the very reason you chose this lifetime on Earth. The inner transformation you are going through is precisely what you aimed to accomplish, what you are called to do, and what Earth is waiting for.

Have compassion with your pain. Face the desolation deep within and tell that part of you "I am there for you, I AM the angel who brings light, I will bring you to the promised land. Have no fear, for I stand beside you, I stand behind you, I am before you and I am inside you. I do not come from above, I do not come from below, I come from your soul. I am the essence of You."

You are becoming angels in the flesh. You are angels incarnated in physical matter. You have much to give and share with people, but do not let that distract you. You are the number one in your life, and you always need to be connected to that inner child part of you. As soon as you notice that your emotions become unruly, that you feel uneasy, tense, anxious or annoyed, face up to it immediately. This is more important than any other thing you need to do in your life. Even other people are second place. Your life is about you. You can only channel your angel light into your human existence, if you are also willing to reach out to the darkest part of you.

Take time and space for self healing. Do anything that helps or comforts you, whether it is spiritual counseling, reading books, taking a walk or preparing yourself a fine meal. Nurture yourself both on the spiritual and on the human level. Stay focused and take your time. This is how self healing occurs. This is how you embody your angel light and do what you came to do in this lifetime. It is about you!

We salute you. We are here in great numbers, much greater than you think! There are angels and guides surrounding each one of you. They want to help you find your way in life. There is a lot of support for you from the cosmos, much respect and encouragement. You are the ones who are doing it here on Earth, this we cannot do for you. But we will do anything we can to send you joy and consolation. This is truly an age of transformation. Please call upon us, we are there for you. We are crossing that threshold together and it looks like it is going to be a great (new) time!

4 - The birth of Christ consciousness in you

I wish you a warm welcome. I am delighted to share this moment in time and space with you. Actually it's not really an "I" that speaks to you. It's more a communal energy that does the talking. We together form this field of energy. The rebirth of the Christ energy is currently taking place on Earth on an unprecedented scale. I, Jeshua was a precursor, a founder of a new current, a new consciousness. The "I" that speaks here is more than he, for I am also you. Your hearts are united with mine. Together we form a field of new consciousness, a field of Christ energy reborn. It fills me with joy that we have come together here to celebrate this.

Feel the recognition that brought us together. We are guided by a common desire, a belief, an ancient feeling that survived the ages. During many lifetimes you have cherished the Christ energy in your hearts and waited until the time that it could flow out upon the Earth. Now that time has come. You live in an age of transformation on a worldwide scale. It's no coincidence that you were born precisely in these times, for you wanted to be present when the Christ energy would globally thrive, you wanted to assist.

The evolution of both the Earth and your soul occurs like cycles in time. Growth processes follow a certain rhythm, from birth to completion. At this moment you are in the phase of completion of an old cycle and you reach out to a new cycle of which you already feel the beginning.

The Earth is likewise completing an old cycle. For long she has put up with the disrespectful manner in which humanity lived upon her. Now it is enough. It is not that the Earth passes judgment on how people treat her. She has compassion and understanding and she wants to support humanity on its way to inner growth and freedom. Nevertheless, she now reaches out to a new consciousness and rises above the ego dominated forces that had her enthralled. The Earth moves to a higher frequency and you as humans have the choice to go along with this transformation or to resist it.

In many of you there is sadness present for the destruction caused on Earth; the deforestation, the disappearance of plant and animal species and the air pollution. Yet Earth is going through a process of growth and self-realization. She disposes of incredible forces and will clear a path to the new, even if it seems she is dragged down in a downward spiral of destruction and pollution. Humanity isn't as powerful as they think. The great force of Earth is that she knows how to adjust herself to a higher order, to the energy of wisdom and love which moves the cosmos. Therefore she will be preserved and find a new form of existence so that all beings living upon her will coexist together in harmony.

Humanity stands before a choice. Will people tune in on this higher order, which speaks through the voice of intuition, the call of the heart? Will they collaborate with this change or –at the expense of everything– hold on to the old, of that what seems safe and secure, but what isn't anymore. You lightworkers are souls who, from birth, experience a deep inner urge to change and renew. You make up the leading edge within humanity, the first ones to germinate a new consciousness. In that your cycle is in sync with that of the Earth and so both cycles support and reinforce each other.

You are on Earth in these times to assist, as best as you can, in the smooth transition to a heart centered consciousness. You do this by being an example of what it's like to live from the heart.

Your society overemphasizes thinking and the driving force behind thinking is, only too often, fear. Fear generates the need for control and mental thoughts seem to satisfy this need. However, with your mind you will never be able to grasp what life is. Your mind is incompetent when it comes to the true questions of life. In fact, there's an old masculine energy dominant in your society that withholds you from trusting your feeling, your heart. One of the features of the transformation in which you find yourselves is the revival of the feminine energy. The feminine energy, which expresses itself through the feelings, emotions and intuitions, asks of you to make contact with what you deeply desire in your heart. Listen to it, listen to what your deepest desires tell you in this moment. There's no time for delay. Live up to it. Everything is accelerating in these times, together with the soul of Earth.

Before you were born you knew that these times would give you enormous opportunity for inner growth and development. As always, your reincarnation was a leap into the deep, into uncertainty, but there was a knowing that when the time was right there would be the possibility to return home, which really means to be at home with yourself. You are bringing to conclusion a long cycle of lives, to realize who you truly are: an angel in your deepest essence, but now an incarnated angel of flesh and blood.

What is ascension?

In these times there is much talk about "ascension". Ascension –literally: to rise– means to raise one's frequency by inner growth and awareness. The expansion of consciousness shows itself, amongst other things, by an increased sensitivity, the capability and willingness to empathize with others and to focus less on the material, on success and appearance. But ascension is in essence not a movement from the low to the high, but a movement from the periphery to the centre, that is, from the outside to the inside.

Imagine yourself to be a radiant star, a shining sun. In the core of that sun you are one with God, you are unconditional love and creative power. You're not bound to time and space, you are not bound to any form. You don't need a body to feel or to be who you truly are. At a certain point, from this core the desire to experience originates. A desire arises for dynamics and movement. The God within you, the formless and unbound essence, seeks out material reality to experience emotion and the duality of love and fear. In God existed the desire to experience and therefore you created yourself. You are Creator and creation in one.

Every life you have, every incarnation in form, represents one ray of the big star that you are. When you reach the outer point of such a ray, and you are as far as possible from the sun, you have become deeply rooted into form. It's then that you possibly lose touch with the divine source, out of which you derived. You forget who you are and you identify yourself with beliefs and behavior patterns that don't reflect your true solar essence.

What happens when you ascend, when you raise your vibration is that you move back along the ray. You come closer to your core and identify less and less with your identity at the end of the ray: your body and personality in this earthly lifetime. You start to feel who you truly are. You regain contact with your soul, that part of you that is not bound to the body and to the forms of time and space. You get more in touch with your divine origin, with the joy and creativity that are intrinsic to it. The more you move to the centre while remaining present in your body, the more you will embody your essential self on Earth. So ascension means that you embody a greater part of your "higher self" or soul here on Earth. So one might just as well say that a "descension" is taking place of your soul to Earth. As your consciousness is opening up, a larger part of your soul is able to manifest on Earth. True ascension is not really about rising up, away from Earth. It is about heart-centered living on this planet, it's about being present here from your divine core.

In all of you reading this, there's a strong desire to reconnect with your greater self and to let this energy flow out to relationships with others and to the area of work and creativity. Why do you feel this so strongly in this lifetime? It has to do with where you're at now, at the end of a cycle.

In your many lifetimes on Earth and elsewhere in the cosmos you've gained a lot of experience. Like explained before (see chapter 2 on the heritage of Atlantis), you lived many lives in which you played many different roles: the role of cherished angel, the role of mighty warrior, the role of hurt victim. You have explored the extremes of human experience and with that also the furthest alienation possible from your divine core. There comes a time in the cycle of lives in which you feel so totally estranged from who you truly are that you feel you cannot become separated from God any further. Darkness appears to be on all sides. Such a moment of deep crisis and utter desolation often leads to a turning point in the development of the soul. This point of utmost disillusion also holds the possibility of a breakthrough, a sudden awakening and urge to return to Source. In such a moment you are invited to let go and surrender all of your expectations. Your human ego is tired and exhausted of the struggle. You don't know what to do anymore. It's precisely then that the grander reality of your soul can touch you. When you give up the struggle and reach out to something that is beyond what you know, you allow your soul to connect with you and inspire you with her light. Your ascension begins.

Many of you have reached this turning point, and are faced with the choice to resist or surrender to your heart's calling. The opportunity to surrender instead of struggle will occur several times in your lifetime. When you choose surrender, you let go of what feels safe to you and open up to something new. You trust that your soul will guide you towards what is right and joyful for you to experience in this lifetime. You are not alone in walking this path.

There is a group of souls (often called lightworkers) going through this turnabout and returning Home. Together you are making a difference on Earth. Your inner transformation from ego-based to heart-centered living influences the collective consciousness of humanity.

As soon as you start the process of ascension, you'll start to develop rapidly. You'll notice that a lot that concerned you before will fade into the background. Rigid structures in your life concerning relations and work situations will dissolve. Your thoughts and feelings will undergo a major transformation.

The most important difference with the old, ego based consciousness is that you start to live from a heart based consciousness. To live from your heart means trusting your intuition, trusting your inner voice, and not the endless flow of information that's forced upon you from the outside world. To live from your heart means that you've become so silent within that you're finally able to hear your inner voice. It means you are conscious of the emotional patterns that get in your way. You've learned to identify them and with that they won't control your life anymore. As soon as you feel emotions like fear, anger or sadness, you keep your consciousness awake and you won't be swept over by these energies. Ascension means that you, more and more often, converge with your own core, which is timeless, silent and pure.

While growing towards this state of consciousness, you will encounter a lot of old pain within: rage, fear, sadness, frustration and disappointment. These emotions want to be acknowledged and lived through. By welcoming them and surrounding them with consciousness when they arise, you release them. Be patient with yourself in this process of emotional purification. Old pains may surface that will only gradually resolve by your attention and acceptance. Even if the road seems long and you sometimes lose hope, you will certainly reach momentary states of inner peace and freedom. These are moments of aligning with your soul. Your heart opens like a flower and you understand the meaning of self-love. There may still be some negative believes influencing your emotional life, but you will resolve them as you go. You now have the understanding what it is like to be connected with your true self, your divine core.

The incarnation pain of lightworkers

An emotional blockage that many lightworkers have to deal with is their resistance to being on Earth. Many of you entered this lifetime with resistance; you entered with an emotional mixture of fear, old pain, anger and distrust. These resulted from experiences in earlier lives. Many of you began your current lifetime with incarnation pain.

The pain you carry within is partly to be explained by your incarnations here during the last two thousand years. In the centuries after my arrival on Earth, you felt inspired by the Christ energy that I tried to seed and you endeavored to bring in a new consciousness on Earth. In your own soul history, you had already dealt with the biggest extremes of ego-based consciousness. The energies of power and control did not seduce you so much anymore. You came to Earth with a mission of peace, although in many cases you weren't understood by your peers. Your energy was too progressive and radical for the age you were in. You were pioneers who were often mistaken for rebels. You felt attracted to the non-organized, mystical side of religion; there you felt the Christ energy still flowing. You were labeled a heretic or a witch and sometimes you were tortured, killed or burned at the stake for that reason. This history of persecution left deep traces in your emotional body. Before you were born into this lifetime, you remembered this pain. Deep inside, there's a level of distrust that is hard to eradicate.

On all of you rest certain burdens from the past, traumas and scars on your soul. Because of these burdens you are afraid in the present time to truly manifest yourselves from the heart. This makes you vulnerable and brings back memories of being rejected precisely for those qualities of the heart. You were once a spiritual warrior and you can still feel this old fire flare up inside at times. On the other hand you are fearful to truly express this energy. You know and feel within what once were the consequences. You hesitate and hold back. As a result, your spiritual energy remains unexpressed and backfires upon you and. It causes uneasiness, self doubt and even depression. For what is your reason to be here on Earth, if your true inspiration cannot flow and be expressed in the world? This is the dilemma which many lightworkers find themselves in.

When your soul began this lifetime, you were, in one respect, enthusiastic about the unprecedented possibilities for inner growth that these times offer.

On the other hand you felt the resistance to return again to Earth. You can still feel this ambiguity in yourself here and now. Within you reside high ideals, the hope for solidarity between all humans and a renewed balance between humanity and Earth. Your heart can flame up in passion for these ideals. You may feel outraged about the destructive aspects of humanity and passionate to bring change to the situation. At the same time there's a dark, little voice that whispers: "Don't do it. Don't show yourself. You will get hurt. Be careful now and don't take that risk again." Within this voice lie anger, disappointment and bitterness. Even deeper lies the fear to be rejected again, the fear of not being welcome on Earth.

I am here to tell you that you are welcome here and now on Earth. Your time has come. It is safe now to be who you are. The cycle has completed. You have played all the roles there are to play in the game of victim and offender. You have explored the extremes of duality. Now is the time to manifest yourself joyfully from the sense of oneness that has been born into your heart. Your soul has come here in peace and if you speak and act from the heart, you will be received in peace. You are invited now to show your wisdom and depth of experience to the world. This is not about persuading people to adopt a certain world view or converting them to another life style. It is about radiating the reality of heart-centered living and sharing it with all who are willing to receive, who –in biblical terms– "have ears to hear". They will come to you, they will cross your path naturally when you dare to shine out the light from your heart. And this shining has nothing to do with struggling; it doesn't require labor or effort on your part.

Being a lightworker in these times means to be in balance with yourself and to share the peace and simplicity that comes with it. The energy you have to offer to the world will flow from you effortlessly and without the resistance you experienced in earlier lifetimes. As soon as you trust the inner voice of your intuition you'll notice that the right opportunities and possibilities will cross your path in a natural way. In this age, you are to experience light work as something joyful again, as something that is fully appreciated and welcome on Earth. These times are for healing the old wounds of rejection for being different. Trust again what you know and feel inside and come forward with your knowledge and wisdom. Do it for your own sake, because it is your nature to shine out light, and because you want to heal yourself and wash away your own history of pain.

The meek shall inherit the Earth

I would like to remind you of some words from the Bible: "The meek shall inherit the Earth". What does this phrase mean and who are the meek? The meek are those who have put aside their ego, who converge with the inspiration of their grander self, their divine source. The meek are those who have felt through the extremes of light and darkness during many lifetimes on Earth. The meek are those who have become humble and do not judge on the deeds of others. The meek carry around a knowingness of the one consciousness that supports and connects all life. The meek are you.

The meek shall inherit the Earth. The legacy of the New Earth is yours. Precisely by the struggles you have been through, you have explored all that duality has to offer to the utmost limit. Now is the time to break the hold it has on you and to recognize the oneness that underlies everything. You need not battle with duality; you let go of it by becoming deeply and silently aware of who you truly are. As you become aware of the flow of oneness that permeates all that is, incusing you, you sense safety and peace and thereby release the fear and doubt that are part of duality. As you align more and more with the oneness behind duality, your soul's energy will flow more easily into the world. You then become a lightworker, and you will feel drawn to types of work or to relationships that nourish your soul.

Many of you ask: "What is my purpose in life? What do I have to do to complete my mission on Earth?" My answer is: "*You* are the purpose, *you* are the mission." The Christ consciousness that is being born in your soul is the purpose and meaning of the grand cycle of lifetimes you experienced. It is time you take yourself seriously. Accept the fears and doubts still present inside you but don't be led astray by these emotions. You are the carriers of Christ consciousness today. Receive your mission with joy and dignity. Receive what is yours and let your light shine out upon the world. Blessed are the meek, for they shall inherit the Earth.

5 - Rebalancing the male and female energy within

Let us celebrate the coming of a New Era. It is present already and it is growing and evolving because of your inner transformation. You are the forerunners, the pioneers who help birth a new consciousness on Earth today. In the present stage of your inner transformation, there is still much confusion inside of you. You have one foot in a new reality, a new way of conceiving and experiencing things. But the other leg is "in suspension", in a vacuum so to speak. It cannot get back to the old and familiar ways, but at the same time you are frightened to make the whole switch and go forward with both feet on new ground. This new paradigm of consciousness is unknown territory and it does not seem to resonate yet with the outside world, the traditional values and habits which you learned at school or at home.

A large part of society still seems to embrace old and worn out belief systems, fed by fear or the need to control. But a lot is changing and much that was self evident before is tumbling down and falling apart. In western societies, many people experience a lack of meaning in their lives. People have also started to pay much more attention to the inner aspect of what happens around them. They are interested in psychology and spirituality. They are less focused on mere external success and material wealth. Especially in affluent societies, people discover that success and material wealth do not necessarily create true happiness and real contentment. Success is different from fulfillment. You will feel truly fulfilled in your life when you are able to connect with and express your own soul energy. That is what creativity essentially is: discovering what your soul energy is about and expressing it on Earth through your own unique gifts and abilities. This is what makes you truly happy inside, warm and radiant. And at that point you will touch others and they get to see who you really are: an angel of light. You have then become an angel who consciously brings light to the Earth realm that is so often overshadowed by illusions which prevent you from seeing the inner light in every living being.

You all have chosen to be here to give shape to your soul energy on Earth. Especially in this stage of history, you are not solely here for yourself. Your inner development is such that you have much to share with others. Presently, much is happening on a global and planetary level. Huge shifts of energy are taking place and can affect you in your daily life. Whenever people are changing their consciousness and start to think differently, when they ask new questions and doubt the existing order, they are inviting a new energy into their lives. A new dynamic will enter that more often than not drastically alter your lifestyle and circumstances. Now, part of you wants this and is constantly trying to achieve it. But other parts of you resist the new and do not want to go along so easily. These are the most fearful and distrustful parts of you. The inner tension and conflict that results, causes a split in your consciousness, and in the consciousness of millions of people who are in the same process. This can cause the atmosphere around the Earth to be heavy with resistance and tension at times. It is resistance towards change and movement, and it is part of being a human being. Even if you live a very conscious life, you can be affected by this heaviness, because at some point it resonates with fears and doubts that you have not let go of.

How do you deal with this inner conflict and how do you let go of old fears and belief systems? How do you connect to your own soul energy and find a way of expressing it in the world? Today I would like to approach this question by talking a little about the balance between the male and the female energies within you.

Every soul has access to both the male and the female energy. Essentially, the male energy has to do with the aspect of manifesting yourself outwardly, in the material world. Male energy is related to focus, discernment and the power to act. It enables you to take up space, to be an "I" with clear boundaries. The female energy is naturally inclined to turn inwards, to the inner dimension of things. It is related to feeling, inspiration and transcending the boundaries of "you" to connect with others. The female energy is flowing and receptive and when combined with the male energy, it leads to the highest form of creativity. Balance between the two enables you to realize your highest potential.

The feminine energy is in a sense the energy of the unmanifested, the realm of the potential. It is also the source of true inspiration – heartfelt desires that spring from your soul. Your feminine energy is the bridge to your soul. Your soul is formless. Just feel this. At this moment you experience yourself as having a body that enables you to be part of this reality. You have eyes, hands and you are either male or female. But you can feel that although this way of being is now a part of you, it is not all that you are. You are that which ensouls the body, the form. You bring it to life from within. But you, in your essence, are formless, you are pure consciousness, one and undivided. Feel the freedom and bliss of it! Feel how you, as consciousness, are totally independent of your body and that you have freely chosen it to be part of this reality for a while.

You have temporarily merged with your body for a reason. You are here because you want to be here. The flowing, unbound energy of the female wanted to enter into a dance with the male energy of manifestation and form. The male energy enables the soul to enter and experience this specific physical reality. It helps the soul to express itself creatively in this particular realm of Earth. The masculine and feminine energies are the building blocks of creation and if both play together in peace and joy, they bring forth beauty and fulfillment.

However, in many of you the masculine and the feminine have become artificially separated and they are not working well together. Roughly speaking, you can either have too much male energy or too much female energy. If there is a surplus of male energy, the female energy gets suppressed and there is too much focus on manifestation in the outside world and being recognized and valued by others. You are cut off from your soul energy, the living flow of feelings and emotions which constantly tries to tell you what you need and truly want. If you are identified too much with the male energy, you are caught up in the expectations and demands from the outside world. Essentially, you are driven by insecurity and you try to handle that insecurity by forcing yourself to comply with standards not your own. You do not feel truly safe and nurtured by your female energy and seek to establish an external sense of safety by being competitive and controlling. All of this makes you very dependent on how others think, feel and act. Disconnected from your unique inner guidance, you get a tense and anxious ego that constantly needs recognition and wants to be in control all the time. It lives by a false image of power that suffocates the soul.

People who are overbalanced towards the male are afraid to surrender to the formless, flowing nature of the feminine energy. In your society, that as a whole has a surplus of male energy, this fear is apparent from the fact that people are neurotically busy all the time. They hardly take time for themselves, spent freely without a purpose. Everything seems to have to be ordered and planned, with an almost compulsive efficiency. Also, when you long for something and you truly feel you would like a particular change to happen in your life, you want to act upon it immediately. You often do not take enough time to let an idea or purpose grow and evolve and gradually be birthed in your reality. It is like an organic process. The inner dynamics which are set in motion once you set your intention to do or have something, are governed by an natural rhythm that you cannot force or control. Because of a dominant or disconnected male energy you are inclined to think and worry far too much. Your thoughts jump up and down like crazy. This leads to a general restlessness, a sense of emptiness and lack of inspiration in your life. You are not really trusting your feminine energy. She seems to want to head in a very different direction than you. Your emotions tell you, for instance, to let go of things, take time for yourself, and communicate more openly to others. At a certain point, you will not be able to ignore this call of your soul anymore. If you try to live solely from the male energy, you are heading for a crisis in some form, whether it is illness or some other discomfort. This crisis will essentially be an opportunity to find a new balance between the male and the female in your life.

What happens when the female energy stands too much on her own and does not sufficiently connect to the male? As opposed to a tense and controlling ego, this will lead to a weak and wobbly ego. Being overbalanced towards the female means that things are easily "too much" for you. You are reacting to other people's energies in a highly sensitive way. It is hard to say no and set clear boundaries around yourself because the male energy of taking up your own space does not seem available to you. It is hard to even know what you want as you get easily drawn into other people's moods and desires. Having a surplus of feminine energy means that you are empathic and that it is easy for you to understand what other people feel. You are also capable of going deep into your own emotions and moods, but you feel unable to really express yourself emotionally and creatively in the world. You have insufficient access to the male energies of self-consciousness, standing up for yourself and feeling centered and focused. The female energy, which is naturally flowing and receptive, needs to be anchored to a well defined "I". This is what the male energy can give to her, if the female part is willing to trust him and let go of her fear to be a separate "I" with its own needs and clear boundaries.

This is feared by the female energy in many people, especially women, because women are taught that it is a good thing to be sensitive, sweet and compliant (whereas men are taught that it is right to be tough and competitive). But if they do not develop that male ability to be centered into one's own being, their creative energy will be squandered and fragmentized. Their soul energy will not get adequately expressed and this creates sadness in the soul, causing melancholy and depression.

This era asks for a rebalancing of the male and the female energies. It is important to realize that the female is in a sense basic or primary. I do not mean this in the sense of "better" or "higher". The feminine and the masculine relate to each other as represented in the yin-yang symbol: both are equal and complementary. But the feminine energy within you is the bridge to your soul, your formless essence. By connecting to your female aspect, you open yourself up to your deepest inspiration and you get in touch with your purpose of being here.

Just imagine that you are now connecting to your female energy. Imagine that she is seated in your heart. Feel a soft, warm energy in your heart that is very familiar to you, very close to who you are. You feel that energy in your heart and now imagine that she creates an opening at the back of your heart. From there she connects with light, the light of Source, the light of your soul. Take a moment to feel this. Perhaps you are seeing angel-like figures or guides, it does not matter what you see. You just need to feel the presence of loving, cosmic support, the presence of Home. This is how you channel your soul energy. Just sense the lightness and lucidity of that energy. It enters your heart and now you may notice how close we actually are to you. We "from the other side" are part of a reality that runs right through yours. You are actually a part of that other reality right now. Your greater or higher self is there now while it merges with you on Earth.

Now imagine that you are calling upon the male energy inside of you. You ask this energy to help you ground and connect your heart energy fully to the reality of Earth. Feel the power of the male energy gently and easily flow into your arms and legs. It creates clarity in your being, self confidence and focus. You feel how it anchors your heart energy to your body and to Earth. The masculine energy gives you the qualities of courage, discernment and stability. Realize that your male aspect loves to connect with the female aspect in this way. It wants to serve the female energy, to enable the soul energy to embody itself in time, space and matter. Protected and enveloped by the male energy, the feminine energy feels safe and joyful. Feel how heaven and Earth connect inside of you.

We go a little further on our inner journey. Imagine you are now walking through a beautiful forest. The sky is deep blue. It is autumn and the trees are starting to lose their leaves. Yet the sun is still warm on your skin. You enjoy walking there and after a while you notice a nice spot to sit down for a moment. Perhaps there's a bench or a soft spot beneath a tree. You sit down and become quiet. You breathe consciously and let go of any tensions you feel in your body. You feel how the Earth carries you. You become still and peaceful within. Then you hear the sound of gay children's voices in the air. It moves you and makes you smile. You notice two children are walking towards you. They are a boy and a girl. And they walk towards you in a determined way, for they want to give something to you.

They are now standing next to you and their faces look happy and carefree. Then the girl steps forward and gives you something. It may be a thing but it doesn't have to be. She may also simply radiate something by her presence or with her eyes, reminding you. What is she reminding you of? What quality is she vibrating as she looks you in the eye? What she gives to you energetically is more important than what she physically hands to you. Absorb her energy and thank her. Then ask her to sit down next to you on your left side. You now focus on the boy, who also wants to give you something. You look at him and you receive his gift. It may be a symbol, an object or a feeling, or maybe he simply touches you and you know. You feel his message and take it in. You thank him and invite him to sit down at your right side.

Feel how these children are a part of you. They are always by your side to remind you of who you are. Their original qualities belong to you. Now take their hands, holding them in your lap, and let everything inside of you that feels old and worn out, dissipate. Fear, worry, gloom, just imagine how the Earth opens up and takes it from you. It becomes neutral in her womb. Allow the new and fresh energies of the children to enter your energy field and bring back to you your zest for life and your childlike sense of magic and trust. When you return to the present in a moment, you do not have to let go of these children. They are a part of you and they keep alive your original inspiration. Any time you feel tense, uncomfortable or dissatisfied, you can connect to these children. They can let you know how to rebalance yourself.

When you go to that forest again, or any other spot you like, you may see just the girl or just the boy wanting to address you this time. Trust whatever your imagination comes up with. Just keep it light and playful. This is not supposed to be a serious exercise. It is just play. It is a means of connecting to the powerful core energies of the female and male within.

You are all working to create a new balance between these two energies, which have become so alienated and misunderstood in your society. Anytime you reconnect the two and recreate that balance within, you radiate this out to others and help bring about a lighter and more loving consciousness on Earth. We thank you for this. We love you deeply.

6 - Releasing struggle from your life

We are gathered here to bring to you a message of love and hope, as we see how much difficulty you are experiencing at this time. I who am speaking am Jeshua but today I am closely aligned with the female aspect of the Christ energy.

In these times of transition, there is a huge influx of female energy in the realm of Earth. This wave of energy helps bring about a new birth, a rebirthing of you as well as of Earth. We would like to say a little more about the current developments, which often create resistance, disharmony and insecurity within you.

You are all enveloped in a deep inner transformation. This has been your conscious choice. There was a longing in your heart, even before you were born, to clean out the past and make way for a new energetic reality to be born on Earth. You knew beforehand that this lifetime was going to offer you major opportunities for growth and healing. You sensed, before you started this lifetime, that Earth was going to come to the end of a long cycle of power abuse and destruction.

You have been part of this cycle, in many past lifetimes on Earth, and now you, as well as Earth, have reached a point of departure, an opportunity to round off the cycle and move on. This is why you wanted to be born in this age and time, because this opportunity could only be seized while living on Earth. The cycle could only be brought to a close by incarnating once more and integrating the energies of this whole cycle into this lifetime. Do you wonder why it is heavy sometimes?!

Before you can even get to this mission in a minimally conscious way, you first have to be born into a human body, into a personality that is partly shaped by external influences such as your parents, your community and your society. During your childhood, you generally forget who you are, as you are influenced and practically hypnotized by the convictions and anxieties of those who bring you up. Generally, you are surrounded by energies that are old and stifling, stemming from a tradition of fear and unconsciousness. Your original soul energy gets narrowed down and often it goes into hiding for some time.

Now, it has been your intention for this lifetime to rise above these restrictions and free yourself from it, and not just for yourself, but also to be the living bridge to a new level of consciousness on Earth. You are here for yourself, but as you are growing and evolving, you are helping to lift the consciousness of humanity. You are supporting the movement of Earth as a spiritual being and you are contributing to developments which affect your whole solar system and beyond.

But to be a part of this transformation and make a contribution to it, you first had to incarnate into an earthly personality, with all the burdens of tradition thrown into your lap for you to deal with. You are brave warriors indeed. We love you. And you have now reached a point at which you truly and deeply wish to let go of the old. You cannot stand the energy of the past anymore. You are in the midst of the labor pain. You are being born again in this very body you have lived in for decades, but as a new You. You are actually in the process of reincarnating again while in this body, but now as the higher you, the expansive you that consciously wanted to be here to seize this opportunity to finish the cycle.

It is now your desire to let your deepest inner knowing, your true self, be born on Earth and manifest itself with joy and creativity. This radical and yet "predetermined" desire has brought you to the place that you are now and we know it is difficult. You are turning yourself inside out, leaving no stone unturned and to others you may seem to be walking to the beat of an intangible drummer.

A huge battle is taking place within you between the old and the new. You are carrying the old to its grave, but before you can do so you have to look it into the eye and make peace with it. Otherwise it will not rest in peace. So you have to face and accept the darkness in you and in the world, before you can rise above it and be free. There is no such thing as darkness really, but as you feel tied down by heavy emotions of grief, fear and anger, you seem to be dealing with the demons of darkness. However, you are mostly dealing with your resistance to look these demons into the eye, to face up to them and accept them as viable presences. They are a part of you, the part that got hurt, frustrated and misguided. They are calling out to you to be recognized and understood by you! You are their guide, not their enemy! As you resist them, they knock on your door even harder. Only as they are embraced by your loving compassion, can they find peace and be laid to rest.

As you are going through this immense purgatory process of facing your inner demons and making room for the new, your body gets affected by the movements of your consciousness. It may react in strange ways, giving you discomfort and pain, but generally, it is all passing. It is part of the purgatory process. Emotionally, you go through highs and lows and you are faced with deep fear and doubts as everything familiar seems to slip through your hands at some point. You have to let go of it all. There's no balancing the old and the new. This is a genuinely new beginning. The only compass you can go by is your own soul. Especially lightworkers, who are the pioneers, will find little or no support and recognition from your environment. You have to rely on yourself. You know deep down where you are heading. You planned this before your birth. Your innate knowledge and instincts in this area will bring you home.

As a human on Earth you have been hypnotized by the collective belief system and traumatized energy surrounding Earth. The collective human notion of life fosters the idea that life is about struggle and suffering. "You have to fight to survive, you cannot trust your fellow human, you need to be vigilant all the time." All these beliefs and emotional structures now rise to the surface, especially now that you want to let go of them. As you want to trust and surrender, your habits of distrust and control raise their head and protest. As you want to open up and express your innermost inspiration, fear of rejection seems to block you and make you mute. A lot of inner conflict is going on, causing turmoil in your minds and hearts. The old thought patterns do not die so easily, as they are embedded in your way of being. This is a gradual process and you are moving forward. The key to remember is that you cannot overcome the old by struggling or fighting.

Letting go of struggle

You have gone through many lifetimes on Earth in which struggle was your middle name. Many times you have tried to kindle the light of consciousness on Earth and many of you were inspired by the Christ energy in whatever form it took. You were deeply moved by its inherent vision of a better world, based on equality, peace and harmony. At the same time, you were deeply involved in struggle: you often felt you were different, and had to find your own way in life. You had to struggle to understand yourself, and then to express yourself in a world that, again, seemed to walk to the beat of a different drummer. You were "aliens" so to speak, ahead of the times, and in many lifetimes you were persecuted and violently rejected for your different way of looking at things. Therefore, spirituality and struggle seem to go hand in hand for you.

What is asked of you now is to release that struggle. This is a different time. This is your time. You are here now not to struggle or defend yourselves or convince anyone. You are here to release yourself and surrender to the birth of You, your grander Self who has been waiting for this to happen.

Many of you now feel a lot of struggle and resistance in your life, like things are not flowing easily. What you need to do is go even deeper into yourself and relax into that boundless Inner Being who is not of this world. Your soul energy is available to you and it can help you remember why you are here now. Remember how clearly you knew, before you jumped into this lifetime, that this would be a profound and meaningful lifetime, including the frustrations and difficulties. Remember that you came here not to struggle but to release all struggle and come Home. Home is in the here and now, where your consciousness dwells. Wherever you are, lies the possibility to release and let go of struggle. You can accept where you are right now, and let expectations go. This is who you are now. Stand behind yourself and comfort yourself with the knowing that you are very close to what you came to do here.

To get there, you only need to give up your resistance, the idea that you have to get somewhere through struggling. You are so tied up with the notion of growing through pain that you actually think you are doing good work when you are suffering and trying and working hard on your spiritual growth. However, especially when you are confronted with heavy and dense energies from the past, the solution is to find a point of stillness within. It is not to "do anything" but to retreat into a point of neutrality, neutral awareness, "just being". From that point, you will look at yourself and not try to change yourself. You just let yourself be.

One of the things that is still clinging to you from your last cycle of lifetimes on Earth is a strong, male oriented energy of "doing". Often you have been "warriors of the light" who wanted to change things for the better with great zest and passion. You were a bit overbearing there too. It is now asked of this male, action oriented energy to quiet down and enter into a new balance with the female side. The feminine aspect in this context is the carrier of lightness, ease and joy. It tells you to go with the flow of your feelings, to not focus so much on results as on what feels right to you now.

Allowing in the female energy will raise the question of how the flow of giving and the flow of receiving are related to each other in your life. Can you do what feels right to you and not mind other people's expectations or your own internalized demands to yourself? Can you really take care of yourself and give yourself all that you truly long for in your life? This is not the typical lightworker's question to ask. You have been focused enormously on the outside world, wanting to change it, improve it, etcetera. "What is my mission on Earth?" and "how can I contribute to a better world?" – these are your favorite questions. And often you approach these issues with a warrior attitude that has become second nature. The idea that you are here also to nurture yourself, to enjoy and go with the flow of life, is hard to swallow for most of you! If you recognize this, it actually means that there is an imbalance between giving and receiving in your life. You are giving too much.

If you are giving a lot, working for the good of others and feeling very responsible for their needs, you are often struggling and you are "doing" a lot. You have trouble receiving and you are losing sight of your own humanness. You will likely end up frustrated and empty. To balance the male and the female energy, you need to get to that flow of living in which you feel inspired and joyful by what you do without feeling pressured to do so. Pressure signals that you are not free, that you are attached to results.

Whenever there's pressure, withdraw and go into stillness.

When a lot is moving on the inner level, it can be hard to find the right way of expressing or manifesting yourself in the world. Instead of trying, struggling and pushing at such a time, it is easier, lighter, wiser to stay calm and not do much at all. Just feel what is going on inside of you. This new birth you are going through asks a lot from you on all levels, emotionally, mentally and physically, so perhaps this is not the time to abundantly express yourself in the outside world. Surrender is the key here, and that's what the feminine energy is all about. Go with the flow and trust.

Think of the physical birthing process of a child. Primal forces of nature are guiding this process. You cannot control these forces, you cannot decide when you are going to get a contraction, but what you can do is either resist it or go along with it. Going along with it means allowing the pain of the contraction to go through you and trusting that it will subside in a while and you can catch your breath again. What you can do is align yourself with the inner flow of your feelings and therefore make the whole process more easy and gentle. So, instead of judging yourself from an external viewpoint, measuring yourself up to all kinds of expectations and demands, feel what is really going on inside of you. Feel the truth of it and see how your external reality adequately reflects this.

I now would like to invite you to travel with me for a while. I would like to take you to a future reality which may help you feel more relaxed and trustful in the Now. Just travel with me in your imagination. We are going to visit the New Earth.

Visiting the New Earth

The New Earth is an energetic reality that is gaining more foothold gradually, thanks to your inner work. Now let us enter that world and draw in its energy. Just imagine yourself walking through a lovely forest with beautiful old trees and a soft breeze on your skin. You sense how the burdens of the past, the burdens of your current present, have dropped from your shoulders. You are a different you. You have already been born into the New Era. You feel light, with a clear inner knowing, and you realize it has all been meaningful. You have learned from everything you went through and your soul has become deep and wise because of it. You feel light and comfortable and your heart is open in joyful anticipation. You enjoy nature and as you feel the Earth beneath your feet, you sense peace and calmness. Something has changed on the planet. People have now learned to live in harmony with nature.

Now you are approaching a settlement, a small community, in an open area that blends in naturally with the forest. This is where you live. You feel your heart open up as you realize who live there with you. These are your friends and soul mates. Your kinship is old, you have met in many lifetimes and they are like brothers and sister to you. It is always a blessing to be with them. You do not have to pretend or hide yourself in their presence, you can simply be who you are. You understand each other easily and you speak with each other almost telepathically, using very few words.

You have your own house there too. Take a look at it. Somewhere in that place there is a spot just for you and you go there now and take in some of the details of your house. Is it big or small, what materials is it made of, and especially....how does the house feel to you? Earth has offered you the materials to build it. Feel how the colors, materials and the view nurture you. This house is an energetic extension of you. Whenever you feel the need to withdraw yourself, you sit in this house. It allows you to enter into a deep connection with your own Being, while you are safely held by Earth.

Now we are going to take a closer look at the group of people you are involved with. In the middle of this settlement there is a square, where people meet and join for mutual activities. This place holds the "energy of together" and there is something going on there right now. Let's go see what it is about. You approach the square with a sense of curiosity and people welcome you with an open and loving smile. There is a grand circle of people holding hands, and two people immediately make room for you so that you can participate as well. You sense a deeply vibrant energy running through this group that you are part of. You sense the unity, the fellowship and the joy that you have made it together. You are now the inhabitants of the New Earth and there is much to do for you. You are engaged in various activities, in the area of building, growing food, communication, healing, whatever your area of expertise is. But all activities are pursued against the background of an all pervading harmony. No struggle, but peace. You let yourself be guided by your intuition, in the moment. There is plenty of room for play and relaxation as well.

Here you are, together, and you can feel how each one of you has gone through that birthing process that we described today. An old identity has made way for a new presence. You have been born into the light of the New Earth.

And now you hear a call coming towards you. As you stand there, joined with your brothers and sisters, you hear a call from the old Earth crying out at you. It is your call, from the present, as we sit here today. As you are gathered here, feeling tired and worn out sometimes by the intensity of the birthing process, you can ask your future self and your soul family "over there" for love and support. You in the future can feel this summoning and you are able to send love and wisdom to the old you. Close your eyes and do this for a moment. Be that future self and send love to your present self. And you may sense that the group energy in that future reality knows exactly what you all need right now, for they have been you and have gone through that dark night of the soul.

Now change the perspective and come back to the present. Be on the receiving side. Accept the love and consolation coming from your soul family, and rejoice in the fact that you have indeed "made it". Feel the respect they are paying you, for you are the ones who persevered and kept faith in yourselves as you gave birth to the New Earth. Ask your future self whether she or he has a message for you. What is important for you to know right now? Let the answer come to you, easily, lightly. There need be no words, or images, just feel the energy. Visualize how your future self takes your hands and looks you into deep the eye, transmitting hope and trust to you. Sense how you can truly let go, go with the flow of the labor contractions and take your time to integrate and ground the new energies.

We believe in you! Take it a day at a time and dare to be truly sweet and gentle for yourself. As soon as you turn hard on yourself, by being impatient and critical about yourself, you slip back into the old energy of struggle. You can release it now, the time is ripe for gentleness and kindness toward yourself. Be the face of compassion for yourself, and your radiance will bless others as well. Be the angel that you are and all else will fall into place.

7 - Death and beyond

Beloved angels of light, I am with you. It is from the heart of the Christ energy that I, Jeshua, reach out and extend my greeting to you.

Beloved angel, know that you are cherished. You are loved unconditionally while you reside in this body of flesh and blood, a mortal body. Even while living within the boundaries of this temporary home, you are still unconditionally part of God, the Home for which you long so much. You have never truly left Home, yet you do not recognize the eternal flame which remains alight forever within your being. Get in touch with that light in this moment, cherish yourself, know who you are. A light burns within you, so beautiful and pure. How come you ever doubted this?

Today we speak about dying. Much fear exists concerning death. Fear of annihilation, fear of oblivion, fear of being swallowed up by the big black hole associated with death. As so often the case in the earthly dimension, you tend to turn things topsy-turvy and present them exactly opposite to the way they actually are. In reality, death is liberation, a homecoming, a remembrance of who you really are.

When death comes, you effortlessly return to your natural state of being. Your consciousness blends with the flame of light which is your true identity. Earthly burdens are lifted from your shoulders. Residing within a physical body imposes limitations on you. It is true that you chose to dive into this state of limitation because of the possibility for experience it had to offer. Nevertheless it's a sensation of bliss to be restored to your natural angelic state. The angel inside you loves to fly and be free, to freely investigate the myriad of worlds which constitute the universe. There is so much to explore and to experience. Once you are born into an earthly body, you more or less lose touch with this angelic freedom and sense of being without limits.

Please join me now, as we go back to the moment just before the dive into your present incarnation. On an inner level you permitted yourself to commence this earthly life. It was a conscious choice. Perhaps you have forgotten about this, and you occasionally feel doubtful about whether you really want to be here. Yet there has been a moment in which you said "yes". This was a courageous choice. It is an act of great bravery to temporarily trade your angelic freedom and sense of non-limitation for the adventure of becoming human, of becoming mortal. That adventure holds a promise that makes it all worthwhile. Feel the "yes!" that once rose from your soul. Remember also being drawn to Earth. Feel how you connected to Earth reality, and feel the moment you descended into the embryo within your mother's womb. You may notice there is heaviness surrounding planet Earth, a certain greyness or thickness.

There is much suffering on Earth. Pain, loss, fear, negative thoughts are part of Earth's collective atmosphere. And that is what you, as a freshly incarnating soul, passed through. Your light found itself a way through this darkness and in doing so an unavoidable veil of ignorance fell over your original angelic awareness. Feel the sadness of that event, and behind it, your courage and bravery. You were determined: "I am going to do it. Once more, I am going to root myself into this Earth reality, in order to find my own light, in order to recognize it, to rediscover it, and to pass it on to this world which is so in need of it."

Yes, it has been a leap into ignorance. Temporarily forgetting who you are, not remembering your unbound state of being is part of being human. You forget that you are safe and free, no matter where you are. Being human, you set out to reclaim that natural sense of freedom and safety. In your quest, you can become ensnared by powers that seem to offer you what you are looking for, but in fact are making you dependent on something outside of you. You may lean upon judgments coming from outside yourself, telling you how to behave in order to be loved. These false images of Home, these substitutes, tend to sadden and depress you. Indeed, the journey down from heaven to Earth has been a tough one. Death, however, transports you back to the plane of eternal love and safety. It is in dying that you surrender to who you have always been. If you die consciously, if you can accept death and surrender to it, dying becomes a joyous event.

What happens when you die? Before you die, you pass through a stage of parting and letting go. It is a phase wherein you say farewell to earthly life, to your loved ones. This can be difficult, yet at the same time it offers you the possibility to reflect deeply upon who you are, and what you have learned and accomplished on Earth during your lifetime. In the grief you may sense in letting go of your loved ones, it becomes ever so clear what connects you to them. It is a bond of love which is immortal. This bond is so powerful that it effortlessly passes across the boundary that is death. Love is an inexhaustible source, forever giving rise to new life. Do not fear to lose your loved ones, for it is in the moment of saying goodbye that the bonds of unconditional love are reinforced and given new life. For it is certain: when you part in love, you will meet again. You will find one another again, effortlessly, because the shortest way to another always remains the way of the heart.

If you have loved ones who passed over, you can be sure that they are near to you at the level of the heart. Feel their presence, for they are here among us, extending their greeting to you. They feel privileged and free. They are free from the doubt which plagues so many on Earth and they yearn to share with you the love and kindness which is available to you at all times.

Those who remain behind often associate the phase prior to their loved one's dying with feelings of sadness and loss. It is natural to grieve the departure of a loved one; it is natural to miss and yearn for the loved one's physical presence. However, we encourage you to try and feel that with their departure a gate toward a new dimension is opened, a dimension where communication is of a nature so pure, clear and direct that it rises above the methods for communication commonly used on Earth. You can have direct communication with a loved one after they die, from your heart to their heart. This way, misconceptions which used to stand between you can easily be cleared, once you honestly and openly communicate with the other. Your message will be received, always.

Once you yourself have died, you will view people who are living on Earth from a different perspective. You will be more tolerant, mild and you will find yourself with an increased sense of wisdom. You will not be completely balanced all at once, because there are emotions and feelings that you take with you and which need to be dealt with. You will not be perfect or omniscient once you let go of physical life. And that's not so bad really, for there is still so much to experience and discover on this side! Yet, in most of you there is a new perspective. The dimension of eternity is tangible and this respectfully mitigates your view of what occupied you and the people directly around you during your stay on Earth.

Once you have gone through the mourning stage, the stage of saying farewell, you will feel start to feel death drawing closer. The focus of your consciousness now changes. Letting go of the outside world, the people, your body, it will now turn within and move deeper inside of you. Your awareness of the outside world diminishes and this allows you to prepare for the inner journey you are about to embark on. If you consciously accept death, you will experience a "getting ready", a readiness to truly let go. For your loved ones, this is the moment to let you go, for you need all your strength to turn within and prepare yourself.

Dying need not be a painful process. What actually takes place is of a grand and majestic nature. Dying is a holy event wherein the soul connects with itself in a most intimate manner. During the final stage, the dying person senses the earthly dimension in a detached way: the body, the scents, colours, and other physical sensations. Another dimension is entering their awareness, with a radiance so promising and inviting, that it is not so hard anymore to surrender and leave all things earthly behind. Even the presence of your loved ones will not stop you from going now. The energy of Home - God, heaven or whatever you want to call it - is so overwhelmingly kind, warm and reassuring that it become easy to let go and return your tired and worn-out body to Earth.

Once you let go in peace, your soul will rise up from your body gently and fluidly. You will feel supported by universal forces of wisdom and love. If you die without resistance, your immediate surroundings will be filled with warm and loving energy. You will experience an unspeakable sense of relief. You are free, and everything becomes clear. You remember the omnipresence of Love, not as an abstract idea but as a palpable reality. While on Earth, you called this kind of love "God", and you kept a biased, human image of what this God "wanted from you". You were convinced that there were certain demands made by this God, demands to which you usually did not comply. But here in this dimension, you recall what God's will truly is: to ensoul you, to inspire you, to experience creation through you and to finally recognize Itself in your countenance. God wanted to become human through you. The goal of the universe's evolution is YOU: God become human!

God is the source of creation, and you are its fulfillment. You, who have given the light of God human form, are never judged for being human. Instead you are honored. The idea of a vengeful God is yet another perversion, a reversal of truth instigated by fear. God recognizes Itself in you, regardless of what you do or don't do. When you are back on this side, you become aware of this again, and a truckload of self-judgment and feelings of inferiority will slide off your shoulders. You will feel the original joy of living again, safe in God's hand.

Soon after your arrival here, you will perceive light beings around you. There will be guides to assist you and people you knew who passed over before you. Sometimes it will surprise you who you will run into over there: people who you met only briefly, but who touched your heart deeply, may be there alongside lifelong friends and relatives. Anyone with whom you had a loving connection will come to greet you at some point. Once again, it becomes so clear to you that saying farewell is but an illusion, that the heart-connection is eternal. You will experience a sense of thankfulness and of awe, as you enter this plane of unconditional love and wisdom.

After you arrive on this side, there is a phase of adjustment, in which you get used to your new environment and slowly release your attachment to Earth life. You will need to acclimatize. There will be guides to support you who are specialized in this. You will still have a body yet it will feel more fluid than the physical body you were used to. Most likely it will take on the appearance of your most recent physical body. Although there is freedom to take on any appearance that you desire, most people appreciate some continuity for a while. You are also free to create your own living conditions, for instance a beautiful house with a lovely garden, in a natural environment you were fond of while on Earth. It is quite all right to live out your earthly fantasies on this plane, which I refer to as the astral plane. This is a dimension or realm of being which allows for much creative freedom, although it still resembles and is closely connected to the dimension of physical Earth.

Some people have had difficulty accepting death on Earth and their transition to the other side may have been less peaceful. They usually need more time to adapt to their new life circumstances. Sometimes it takes a while before they truly realize that they have passed on. Some people have suffered a long-term illness, and find it hard to shake the idea of being ill. They cannot fully believe they are healthy again, and it often takes the patient and gentle support of a spiritual guide to help them release their old body. The old body can stick to the soul, purely as a concept, as a thought-form. The same goes for emotional habits and patterns of behavior. They can repeat themselves on the astral plane until the soul discovers its freedom, its power to let go and open up to something new.

Another possibility is that a soul remains attached to the Earth realm, to loved ones in particular, because they died suddenly or very young. This can happen in the case of accidents, disasters, or when the person was in the prime of life. These are situations in which a particular soul did not feel ready or prepared to make the departure. Dying in those cases is more or less traumatic. There is loving support on this side for these traumatized souls, as there always is. Sooner or later the soul will reach a state of acceptance and understanding of the situation. There is always a viable reason for what seems to be a premature departure from the Earth plane. Dying is never a coincidence.

As your stay on the other side extends, your spirit expands into wider and deeper levels of awareness. More and more will you let go of the ways of thinking and feeling you were used to on Earth. Essentially, you gradually go back to the core of who you are, your soul, the divine spark within. The more you enter – or return - to that state of consciousness, the more you detach yourself from your earthly personality and the dimension of Earth. You will sense a flow of being which reaches beyond that aspect of you. You will get in touch with other lifetimes you spent on Earth, incarnations wherein you embodied other aspects of your soul. You become aware of the boundless space that is your soul and the many experiences you have gathered on your journey through the universe.

When people on Earth connect to you now, they will sense a person who has gained in wisdom and spiritual love. In fact, as you are moving closer the core of your soul, you are leaving the astral plane and entering what I call the essential plane, the realm of Essence. Most people stay on the astral plane for quite a while after they have died. They look back on their life on Earth and reflect on all the experiences they have gone through. In the astral realm, you can experience both joy and depression, both positive and negative emotions. Your surroundings mirror your inner psychological reality. The emotions you have to come to terms with, take on the form of colours, landscapes and encounters. You often visit the astral realm in your dreams, so you are familiar with this field of awareness. In your esoteric literature, when they speak of many layers or spheres in the afterlife, ranging from dark to light, it is the astral plane that is referred to.

On the astral plane, you get a chance to sort out the emotional luggage you've brought along from your recent life on Earth. In this you are assisted by several loving guides. At some point, you will let go of all your attachments and emotional pain, and you're ready to move beyond the astral plane altogether. That's when you pass on to the plane of essence. When this happens, it is like a second death. You leave behind anything that does not truly belong to you and allow yourself to merge with the greater You, your divine core. The moment you pass on to the essential plane, you will be aware of the immense power that moves you. You will experience your oneness with God.

The plane of essence, the plane of the eternal You, is the seat of the divine consciousness from which all creation originates. I ask you to take a moment to connect to this plane, here and now. It is not far away. It permeates everything, both the astral plane and the Earth plane; it permeates the entire cosmos. The presence you sense here is the presence of God, pure and untainted. It may be sensed as a deep silence, completely peaceful yet brimming with life and creativity. From this source springs all of creation and to this source it shall return.

When you reach the essential plane in afterlife, you will be able to make conscious choices regarding your future destination. On this plane you may arrange, with the help of teachers and guides, another incarnation on Earth, or plan a different journey, dependent on your goals. You can clearly hear the voice of your soul on the essential plane. It is from this plane that you once said "yes" to the life in which you now find yourself.

Take a moment to remember what it felt like to be on this plane. The more you become aware of this dimension during your life on Earth, the easier it will be to die peacefully and, after your death, to move beyond the astral plane into the plane of essence.

Death is nothing more than a transition, one of the many transitions you go through in life. Birth is a transition. Life on Earth knows so many moments of transition, of passing through and letting go. Just think of it. The body you now reside in has at one time been very small, a vulnerable little baby. And yet your soul, the divine essence inside you, was already working through you when you were that vulnerable little baby. When you reached maturity, many of you got swallowed up by the demands which life on Earth made on you, and you were confronted by fears and doubts. The awareness of your divine core, your soul, got pushed to the background. However, there arrived moments in your life when the dimension of divine awareness opened up again. This often happened at moments during which you had to let go, when you had to say farewell.

Maybe it was saying farewell to a loved one, perhaps letting go of a job; any conceivable scenario. Such events are transitions which resemble dying, not in a literal sense but on a psychological level. You are being asked to let go on a deep level, and it is exactly during those moments of letting go that you can start to feel the reality of your eternal Self, the divine light that burns inside you. This reality remains with you unconditionally, even when everything around you falls away. And so it is when it comes to physically dying. If at that moment you are courageous enough to let go, the plane of the eternal will embrace you and you will experience a very strong awareness of who you really are.

Dying in conscious surrender is a sacred event, filled with life and beauty. The majesty of what is enfolding will be tangible for those present. The more the ones who are present have experienced "dying while being alive", the more they will be filled with awe and reverence about the transition they are witnessing.

With regard to all the transitions available in creation, ranging from physical birth and death to moments of intense emotional detachment during your life, the pivotal question ever remains not whether you will survive, but whether you are able to retain the connection with your own divine core. Can you stay in touch with the plane of Essence, your origins, Creation's heartbeat? Connecting with the essential plane often during your life is the best way of preparing yourself for death, and for what lies beyond. By becoming aware now - prior to physical death – that the very core of who you are does not depend on the current physical body you reside in, nor on the identity which you assume in the world, you set yourself free to smoothly make the transition once the moment arrives.

Connecting with the essential plane is a choice you make. Dying in itself won't get you any closer to it. After dying, you will very much be the same person as you are now, albeit endowed with different possibilities and given a wider perspective. Yet the crucial question ever remains: do you remember yourself? Are you able to consciously connect with that dimension of timelessness which flows through you and which truly inspires you?

You are imperishable, dear angels of light. Take faith in this. Let yourself be comforted and supported by this knowledge when your hour of death arrives; and now also, while you struggle with the issues of your life.

In order to die peacefully, you are asked to detach yourself on the inner level from anything that ties you to earthly existence. Practice this detachment continually while you are living, and you will be prepared to die. You may ask: "Isn't it tragic to detach yourself from life, while you are standing in the middle of it?" The answer is: "No. Instead, it is testament to a truly powerful spirit."

What does detachment mean? It means that you pay attention to essence, that you do not get caught up in non-essential matters. It means you do not create unnecessary emotional drama; it means you experience joy in the simple things of life. To practice detachment and stay tuned to the plane of essence entails being aware of a hidden dimension, which lies directly underneath and behind the observable. It means to renounce quick judgment in terms of good and bad, and to trust the cosmic intelligence which by far exceeds the human mind.

Many of you are trapped in a thinking fever. You feverishly ponder life; how to solve problems, how to accomplish all the things you think you need to do. You are very fixed on organizing life through your will and your mind. Detachment means you take this thinking aspect of yourself less seriously. Is this a tragic thing to do? No. Instead, it brings light and space to your life.

It is by your excessive urge for control that life becomes a struggle, tiring and heavy. Detachment brings peace of mind, sense of humor and thoughtfulness. Being aware of the finiteness of life inspires the natural desire to cherish life. Then your divine core can effortlessly flow through you, from the essential plane to your earthly reality. Once that happens, you will have conquered death before you have died.

8 - Connecting with your guides

It fills me with great joy and happiness to be with you. All of you are old friends of mine. You are beings of light who have come to Earth to express the energy of your soul on this planet. However, while planting your torch of light here on Earth, you have been confronted with darkness. You became entrapped in it and had to deal with anxieties and dark feelings which caused you to doubt your mission on Earth, even doubt the presence of light in yourself.

I invite you to travel back in time in your imagination and go to the moment before you began this incarnation. See yourself as an angel of light, sitting on the brink of heaven. Watch how you are looking down on Earth intently and taking in its energetic qualities. Picture Earth as a globe around which exist a number of different spheres. You are an all-knowing angel of light who is watching Earth from the spiritual realm.

You see the physical qualities of Earth. On the most substantial, material level, you observe the human body, made of bones, flesh and blood. That's where you are going to live in. That will be your home for the duration of a lifetime. Around and throughout the body there are energies which are more transient: the emotions, feelings and thoughts. These are less tangible and yet very real, because you are dwelling in them day by day. It is like a field of energy that surrounds you continuously.

You can distinguish various levels within this field of emotions, thoughts and feelings. The level that is most close to home, to the angel in you, is that of the heart. In its very essence your heart is the dwelling place of your inner light. It holds the light that you are and that has undertaken the journey into the dense matter of Earth. Your emotions, often residing in the area of the belly, are much more influenced by the illusions and the ignorance that is part of living in the Earth realm. Yet, emotions are there for a reason. They enable you to experience life in a human body. As a result of experiencing the emotions that are part of human life, you become able to understand spiritual truth from the perspective of a fully embodied being.

There is a difference between the spiritual knowingness that you have as an angel high above and the spiritual knowingness that you have as a human being. The latter is more profound. You can compare it with the idea of a beautiful sculpture in your head, and having the actual sculpture cut in stone before you. The latter is more impressive. Having the sculpture cut out in stone involves a deeply creative process on the part of the sculptor. That is the reason why all of you chose to incarnate. Why would you do that, sitting on the brink of heaven looking down, being the perfect angel that you are? Why did you jump into the realm of density? You came here to understand the spiritual truths of life from an experiential level. By taking your light you to the dense realm of Earth, you expand creation. You are an artist, and a daring one.

Emotions are important on this journey. To understand their value, think of moments in your life in which you feel perfectly happy and satisfied; moments in which you are fully present, body and mind, and experience joy or fulfilment. This could happen while being immersed in a creative activity, expressing your inner light in a way that is uniquely yours. Or you may have a moment of joy and happiness with someone close to you, your spouse, a child or a friend. The mixture of emotions taking place inside you cannot be experienced in this way in the heavenly realms. It is only within the physical reality of this Earth, with all of its imperfection and tragedy, that moments of pure joy, which always reflect spiritual truth, can be sensed so passionately. The fact that you have emotions enables you to expand creation on the level of feeling; it adds beauty and joy to all that is.

That's why you shouldn't condemn your emotions. It is true that they can cause you pain and confusion. It's best to see them as frightened children who are at the same time your guides. As pointed out in earlier channelings, even the darkest emotions may reveal something important and valuable to you. Emotions are messengers; they carry truth within which can be uncovered by your willingness to receive them with love and kindness. It is like you are their mother: you ease them and yet, you are open to their messages.

Connecting with your spiritual guides

In this channeling, I wish to speak about how you can receive guidance from the spiritual realm. During your life on Earth you mistakenly see yourself as a limited human being in need of higher guidance from some superior being. This point of view starts you off at the wrong foot when you try to get in touch with your guides. It's important to let that thought go, and I'd like to explain why.

Roughly speaking, spirit beings can dwell in two types of realms or planes of existence. As a human, you can connect to both realms. The first one is the astral realm, close to Earth. This is the place where many disembodied) spirits dwell after they die, if they are not able to set themselves free from their past life on Earth. These beings are not embodied anymore at the physical level, but they do have (ethereal) bodies and very human emotions. Often, they feel confused and in need of love and recognition. They are not "evil", but they certainly aren't to be looked up to as spiritual teachers or guides.

In connecting with them, you may feel some of the fearful emotions they live through. Spiritual guides never speak the language of fear; nor do they command or push you in any way. Their energy feels light, gentle and inviting. They do not dwell in the astral plane, close to Earth. They are part of the spiritual realm, as I call it, or the realm of Oneness. The energy there is much more detached from Earth and the emotions generated by living in duality. The realm of Oneness is where you come from; it is your home. You are connected with it through your heart. The connection is always there, whether you are aware of it or not. It may be obscured by your fear, self doubt or lack of hope. But the connection is always there. You are and will forever remain an angelic being from the realm of Oneness who chose to descend on Earth.

From your heart, there is a direct, "horizontal" link to the spiritual realm of your guides. There is no hierarchy between them and you. The guides who accompany you in your earthly life are not "higher up the ladder" than you. You are equals n the realm of Oneness. The only difference is that at this time they are not embodied as a human being. So they are not bothered by the foggy and heavy energy of the Earth realm that you are coping with now. Your guides are your friends and companions. Do not view them as your teacher or guru. They are like brothers and sisters who remind you of home.

Feeling the energy of home reminds you of who you are: an angelic being trying to embody the reality Oneness in a realm that has forgotten about it.

What do guides do? They inspire you to trust the wisdom of your own heart. They never try to push you or force you into anything. The energy of a true guide feels joyful, light and clear. Guides from the realm of Oneness have a delightful sense of humour; they like to share a joke with you. Because of the plane of existence they operate from, they offer a wider perspective which can help you look at situations more light-heartedly. Also, guides are very patient. Their perspective on time is very different from yours. They help you realize that it is your inner development that counts, not what society expects from you at some point in time. They can accept it fully if you repeatedly choose a painful experience over a joyful one. They are wise and know that finding your true path will happen only after you make some pretty grand detours first. They never tire of encouraging and inspiring you along the way.

Your guides dwell in a realm of timelessness and unconditional love. In being with you, they do not have a specific blueprint in mind; there are no deadlines, no timetables for you to keep. They are present with an ongoing deep and caring love. Actually, the challenge for you in connecting with your guides is to be able to receive this kind of love. The art of receiving messages from your guides is the art of opening yourself to unconditional love.

Trusting your first impressions

As you try to open up to guidance, you often receive glimpses of light and reassurance from them. But then your inner critic gets in the way, and your thinking starts to interfere. You tell yourself: "I am making it all up". So you push aside your first impressions. And you ask yourself if there's a certain technique you should learn to get in touch with your guides. You don't trust your first impressions, but they are often true and valuable. In wanting to connect with your guides, dare to be open like a child. Do not censure yourself, dare to think big and receive big.

The moment your mind interferes with the process, infused as it is with energies of fear and distrust, the energy becomes heavier and you lose touch with the ease and lightness which belongs to the realm of Oneness. It cannot be comprehended by your usual frame of reference. Just try to consistently hold on to your first impression, the glimpses that you get in opening up to your guide. To open up to the realm of Oneness doesn't require any techniques; it asks of you to let go of fear and remember your true origin.

You often feel that your own thinking is driving you mad. However, what is really driving you mad is the energy of fear and distrust that is running through your thinking. Thinking can be useful, if it follows the flow of the heart, supporting it instead of obstructing it. The faculty of thought and language can help you put your intuitions and inner awareness into words, so you can communicate them to other humans. The kind of thinking that you are used to is not natural. You are by and large taught to use thinking as a way of controlling your life, your emotions and your environment. Do not judge your mind as such. It can be a useful tool. Ask your thinking to help you put into words what you are sensing when you open up to Oneness. Put the mind to good use instead of fighting it.

Connecting with your guides is like returning home for a little while, dipping into the realm of Oneness and remembering. When you do that you realize that truly, you are your own guide. All the wisdom you seek is there in your own heart. It is okay to let your guides help you remember it. They represent the true you for you in moments of darkness. But as soon as you emerge in the light, connecting with the realm of Oneness, you realize that of course, you know it all yourself. The guides are a stand-in for your true Self so to speak and once you cast of the veil of illusion, you recognise them as dearly loved family members.

If you want to know whether the connection you feel with your guides is real, look at what it does to you emotionally. True contact is marked by emotions of joy, warmth and relief. Tears may run down your cheeks, as you realize what home feels like, and how you've missed it. These are tears of joy, because you are reconnecting to home in that very instant and once you know the energy of our true self, it will be easier the next time to come back to it.

In this moment, I invite you to remember yourself as the spiritual being that you are. You do not need anyone outside you to tell you what to do. Nonetheless, I am willing to represent the face of your own true wisdom for you. Look at me now, with your inner eye. See me as you want to. Allow your imagination to conjure up an image of me. Any image will do. Man, woman or child. A blue sky, a huge tree, a bird or a shining stone. I will go with any form. My energy does not depend on any material shape or body. Neither does yours. So allow yourself to play with images in your head. It's okay. You cannot go wrong. Then, as you see me, open up to my essence. If I have eyes, look into them. Feel me. Can you receive me? I want to tell you of love, ever present for you. I want to tell you of kindness and forgiveness. If it's easier for you to have me, Jeshua, tell you that you are innocent and lovely, then see me as someone outside of you. But remember, we share the same divine core, we are One.

9 - Being a teacher in the new era

Dear friends,

I am Jeshua. I was the bearer of Christ consciousness two thousand years ago, and now you are the ones carrying that torch. It is a torch of light that brings change in this world, a world that is in need of change at this very moment. You live in an age of crisis. There is a financial crisis, an economic crisis going on right now, and there is also crisis of the planet, an environmental crisis going on. You live in the midst of this crisis, which is also an opportunity for change. For fundamental changes to happen, the existing structures often need to break down in a dramatic way.

You who feel drawn to my messages are the ones who are to lead the way for others. Yes, you have been born in this time on purpose; you wanted to make a difference, to *be* the change that humanity needs. You are the teachers of the new era. It is to you that I bring a message of hope an encouragement. I wish to encourage you to take up the role of the teacher that you are. Many lifetimes, you have spent on Earth preparing for this time, for now the planet and humanity are ready for a transformation toward a heart-based consciousness that recognizes the oneness of all that lives and breathes on Earth. You have been the carrier of this sense of oneness for centuries; you have been lightworkers on Earth before, and now the times are with you. Look beneath the surface of what appears to be negative and bad news. Look behind it all. This is a great opportunity for change.

Humanity is asked to go deep within and to address the negative emotions and fear that rise to the surface in times of crisis. Now more than ever humanity needs healing, and is prepared to receive healing. You are the ones who are leading the way. You are the teachers of the new era, and I ask you not to be shy about yourselves. Because of all the experiences you had on Earth before, you have become shy and withdrawn about who you are, about the light that you carry within. There is passion in your heart and your soul. You long to be the shining light that you are, but you are also hiding from your own power, because you carry old memories of being rejected for this and even being persecuted and killed for it. I can see your fears and insecurity but you are grand and powerful if you believe in yourself. You have come a long way. Many times you visited Earth and gained experience. You are a mature and old soul now and you wish to share the wisdom of your heart. I want you to look inside yourself and feel the passion that you were born with, the passion to make a difference. I ask you not to hide anymore.

How do you teach? What is this teaching that I speak of? It is not about conveying theories and knowledge from books to others; it is not about preaching or telling people what to do. It is about a vibration that you bring into the world, a vibration of compassion and inner peace. And so when you address your own darkest parts, your emotions of fear, anger and distrust, your vibration rises, and you bring a new light into this world. It will be visible in your eyes, in the way you speak or listen to others. Do not hide it; be as open as you can because you are beautiful and true. It is when you bring this vibration into the world that people are drawn to you. Not because you know the truth or because you know what is going to happen to them, but because there is a space of compassion and understanding around you. They feel safe and accepted in your presence. That is what teaching in the new era is about: offering understanding and deep compassion to people, accepting their dark as well as their light aspects, making them aware of their inner light, their strength and their creative abilities.

Being a teacher in the new era is different from what you may have expected. It is about finding peace deep within and not being led astray by the negativity that is around you. It means to let go of the world, to not be dependent on it, and yet to be open to everyone, and to offer the world the vibration of peace and deep understanding that you carry in your heart.

How your teaching will look like, what form it will take is different for every individual. Each one of you has natural skills or talents and a passion to do one specific thing rather than another. Your energy, your light can take many forms and to me the specific form is of less importance. What I'd like you to be aware of today is that you are a teacher and that you have come a long way. I encourage you especially in these times not to hide it any more, to share your wisdom with others and bring your passion alive. That is what it means to bring new energy into this world.

Dealing with high sensitivity

You all have become very sensitive. Your hearts have been opened. In many ways, in this era the feminine energy is being re-birthed through you, as you are the first to open up to heart-based consciousness, recognizing the oneness of all life. You have opened up your heart and as a side effect, you take in the negative feelings and emotions of those around you, as well as the feelings that are simply present in the atmosphere around Earth. This sensitivity can sometimes be a burden. You sometimes absorb so much negativity, that you feel down and depressed, and you do not even know where it is coming from.

Opening your heart, developing your feminine side, being receptive and open to energies around you is part of the development you are going through. But it is very important for you to also embrace your male energy, not in the traditional sense, but in a new and higher way. In the past, an aggressive male energy has dominated your history. This energy aimed at gaining power and manipulating reality. Generally, you now have a bad association with male energy; you think it is by nature oppressive, aggressive, and egotistical. You need a new definition of male energy.

A mature variety of male energy is essential now to support and balance your feminine sensitive side. The male energy in its mature variety is about focus, setting boundaries around yourself and being very determined about what you allow into your energy field. If you have a well-developed male energy, this will prevent you from being absorbed by negativity around you. It will help you set boundaries around you. The mature and sophisticated male energy is like a knight standing at the gate of your energy field, distinguishing what nurtures and inspires you and what doesn't. You need the male energy within to protect your very sensitive female side. So I ask you to rethink the male energy, and to find within yourself a new definition, a new feeling about this. Perhaps the image of a knight or a peaceful warrior can serve you; you call on him to help you distinguish what is right for you or to withdraw from situations that aren't serving you anymore.

Being a lightworker and a teacher means, on the one hand, to be in the world and be open and willing to spread your vibration when people ask for it. But on the other hand, it also means that you know when to withdraw and to take good care of yourself, especially when the energy around feels very heavy and strained.

Honor yourself and create space for yourself every day to come back to yourself, to feel who you are. Creating a space for yourself can be taken literally, finding a physical space in your house, or out in nature, where you can feel at ease, where you can completely be with yourself. In such a relaxing space, you can enter the space inside, and that is what really matters. Inside of you, there is a space that is really a state of consciousness. It is the beingness of you, the very core of who you are and it cannot be expressed in words. You can feel this consciousness more easily in stillness, when you are by yourself, not bombarded by external noises, situations, things that distract you. To find this stillness within every day is important to remain aware of who you are, a teacher and carrier of light. So, in order to find the right balance between being by yourself and being in the world, use the male energy inside to guard you.

Redefining the male energy

It is time now for lightworkers to balance the male and female energies within. In a sense, you have become afraid of your own power. There have been times, very ancient times, in which you yourself used your power in a way that you later on regretted. These were the ages before Christ; they go back to Atlantis and before. You still have memories of those ages and at some point you decided you never wanted to misuse your power again. But in your remorse and sense of guilt you tended to go to the other extreme of not using any force at all. You so much wanted to safeguard yourself from your own power that you now often feel unable to stand up for yourself in a very basic way. You are sensitive about other people's needs and you find it hard to be clear about who you are and what you do or do not want. This is regrettable because eventually, you will become exhausted and depressed by the suffering around you and your inability to solve it. The real problem is that you refuse to take up your power: not power in the sense of ruling over others, but in the sense of connecting to your natural passion, your natural instincts, your knowingness. Again, I tell you that you need to find a positive definition of the male energy, and embrace it from the inside, so that your sensitivity and empathy are balanced out by clarity, discernment and self esteem.

The female energy connects you to your soul. Your female energy allows your soul to speak to you through your intuitions and feelings. However, to bring the inner knowingness of your feminine side out into the world, to manifest your soul's passion in the world, you need the qualities of the male energy. The mature male energy helps you to protect your feminine energy, take your distance when needed and remain centered and calm amidst energies that do not resonate with you. To be the teacher and the pioneer that you truly want to be, you need to embrace both the male and female aspects of yourself.

Take courage in all of this. Things are changing and you are not alone. Many people around the world go through the same process as you are. There are many fellow lightworkers alive now, and if you connect with them from the heart, you can feel they are your brothers and sisters. Distance in time and space do not matter, nor do nationality or race. Feel the field of Christ consciousness that is now awakening on Earth. Although it may not be easy visible in what you read in the newspaper or what you hear on television, this field is there. A new consciousness is dawning.

I am calling you. I am part of this huge field of consciousness as much as you are. We are one in this field. We are equal, and I am calling you home. You can feel home on planet Earth right now if you remember who you are and are bold enough to show it.

10 - The highest you can give

I am Jeshua. I have been the representative of a new energy on Earth, which is the Christ energy. It is a kind of energy or consciousness that acknowledges the oneness for everything and everyone. It is the energy of connection, which brings oneness back to Earth. My goal was and is to recover the sense of belonging among all creatures that live on Earth, the key to which is the heart. The heart connects. The heart is a place where you can come Home. Feeling at home has to do with being connected, connected to your deepest self. Your deepest self is always connected to the whole.

What the whole is cannot be described with words. You can come up with words such as universe or cosmos, but the whole is neither a thing nor an entity. The whole is the unspeakable source of being, an infinite realm of probabilities. Each individual life has its own specific place within the whole. All of you are part of an infinitely huge entirety that is eternal and at the same time dynamic and variable. Life moves constantly in an endless dance of manifestation and withdrawal, birth and death, creating and letting go. As a human being, you take part in this creative dance in your present form as a man or a woman. At the same time, there is a divine and indestructible core inside you, which is independent of form.

Imagine that you, in your current body, are connected with the incomprehensibly huge entirety. In your mind you cannot reason out how and why you are part of the whole and which place belongs to you. However, you can feel it by heart. You are embedded in the whole, connected with the beating heart of the cosmos, for which you don't have to do anything. It is a fact. It is an inseparable part of who you truly are.

You have a unique place and a unique role within the whole. Finding your place and letting your light shine makes you feel deeply fulfilled. It makes you feel happy and joyful. Being at this unique spot and fulfilling your unique role activates the highest of you that you can give. This is what I am going to talk about today: the highest that you can give.

Many of you wish to be aligned with the source of light that you are at the deepest level, to exist from the Source, to give and to shine in this world. Feel the Source from the inside out, since it flows through all your cells. It connects everything within you, although you cannot see it. Please feel it…feel the living flow that carries you. Life knows which place is meant for you and which role is yours. Feel your desire to embody the highest of you, the angel of light you truly are, independent from time and space. You are here temporarily, in this body, so that you can bring the light that you are to this place. Earth is a place that you love. Feel it. Feel how you are connected with the heart of Earth deep inside.

Let go your thoughts of how difficult it is to live on Earth, how hard it is to cope with the dark aspects of human society. Connect with Earth itself only, with the essence of the planet. Think about the extensive forests on Earth, the oceans and the broad sky. Think about the abundance of animals, trees, plants and flowers. Connect with Earth…and feel how she is embedded in the entirety of the cosmos, within which she takes her own path.

There is a place for you, here and now on Earth. Believe in yourself; know that you are connected with the whole and that there is a path that leads you to the manifestation of your highest self.

How to find this path? And how do you know whether you are developing and manifesting your highest self? I shall mention three aspects by which you can recognize whether you are "giving the highest of you".

The highest that you can give is unique

The first aspect is that the highest of you, the highest that you can give on Earth, is unique to you. Your contribution is a unique combination of characteristics and qualities, with its own vibration and flavor. Essentially, you are giving yourself. The highest you can give is you! What distinguishes you is not what you have learnt from others, such as certain skills or knowledge. The highest that you can give does not come from outside of you. No, you are the decisive link.

Of course you have gained knowledge and information from others, from books and through education. Of course you are formed by your culture and upbringing. However, you have integrated these influences into your nature in your own way. Because of everything you have been through in your life - in this life and in lives before -, you possess a unique charisma. You shine your light on life in your manner. People are attracted to this unique light. It is the light that shines from your place on Earth; it is the light that makes you shine.

Your unique light is a mixture of earthly and heavenly qualities. In this life, you are a man or a woman, who has had a certain upbringing and education. You are formed by the worldview of the society you live in. This is as it should be, for this formation has helped you gain intimate knowledge of human life. Since you have been through all these hard experiences, you have obtained deep insight into how it feels and what emotional ups and downs you might experience as a human being on Earth. Through your own journey of exploration, through darkness and light, you have walked a unique path. Thus, what you have to give to others is also a unique mixture of qualities.

Always maintain your individuality in the area of creativity and work! No matter what you do, as a baker, a teacher, an artist or a spiritual therapist, giving the highest of you corresponds to expressing your individuality and sharing it with the whole world. The world is not complete without you. The universe is waiting for your contribution instead of the copy or reproduction you have made of somebody else's contribution. The universe wants to encourage you to let your unique energy flow. Thus, embodying your highest self refers to being yourself and expressing your individuality.

To give the highest of you is to receive the highest for you

The second aspect is that to give the highest of you always implies that you receive the highest for you. These two flows are in fact inextricably bound up with each other.

When you let your unique light shine, open your heart and give from your heart, you experience deep satisfaction and fulfillment. You are allowing yourself to be yourself completely, to shine your light without reservations. You feel it is right, natural and sincere to do so. When you give yourself so openly and freely, you receive something very special at the same time. The greatest gift you receive is that you come home. In the moment you are truly yourself, you are naturally united with the greater whole, with God. You are at home with you and the universe at the same time. There are no judgments passed either on you or on others. No more judgments that separate. You are Oneness.

By daring to be true to yourself and express your highest self in the outside world, you attract good things to your life. The necessary material things and the right people for you shall appear automatically. The universe will support and nurture you. It will offer you the right circumstances to manifest your soul's energy. In this way, the giving flow is replied by a receiving flow, which fulfils and enriches you in all areas of life. At the deepest level, you have given yourself all of this by having the courage to let your own light shine. Life shall say yes to you whole-heartedly if you say yes to life without any reservations.

The whole of creation, within which we all have a role to play, is like a huge jigsaw puzzle and each of us represents a piece. The puzzle is not complete without you. The moment the jigsaw piece that you are is put in the right place, you contribute something to the puzzle which nobody else is able to add to it. In that very moment, you also receive something very precious: you come home. You feel that you are in harmony with the greater whole, that life is supporting you and that you are safe. You know you are making an essential contribution and you feel received by the whole with joy and appreciation. To give the highest of you is to say yes to yourself in a profound way and to allow yourself to receive everything you need to blossom and shine.

To give the highest of you actually means that you are not separated from the whole anymore. You are not an ego, not a separate individual at that moment. The question "how to balance the two flows of giving and receiving" in fact dissolves in that state of being. The balance is taken care of automatically; it happens naturally. When you express yourself from the sincerest part of you and let your light shine, you are the light and receiving it at the same time. This is the experience of oneness that you all long for.

Now you might ask yourself: how do I do this? How can I become aligned with the highest of me, my unique gift, my true light? This brings me to the third aspect I wish to mention about giving the highest of you.

You give the highest of you if you are able to connect with the lowest of you

You give the highest of you if you are open and willing to connect with the lowest of you. By the lowest I mean the fear, doubt and depression, in brief, the darkness that is in your soul as a result of unresolved pain experiences.

Your highest self shall shine at the moment you welcome the darkest part of you. When you invite the lowest of you to enter your awareness, you let your light shine without judgment on those parts of your soul that have felt rejected and cast out. This is the part of you that has become angry, sad, bitter and lonely due to painful experiences. Please have compassion for this part of you that lives in the darkness and seeks solutions from the darkness, which often take you even farther away from the light.

In the darkness, you develop survival mechanisms which keep you from feeling what is really going on inside you: the fear, despair, depression and loneliness. You turn away from them. In fact, you are often taught to do so by the world around you. "Turn away from negative emotions. Be positive. Do your best. Be useful." This kind of warnings and invocations create fear inside you about your own darkness and they alienate you from your deepest feelings.

You all have a deep desire for light, for the freedom inherent in surrendering to who you truly are. Please realize that you ignite the greatest light inside if you are willing to reach out to the darkest and most neglected parts of you.

I invite you to do so now, at this very moment. Please take a look and see whether there is a negative emotion or thought inside you that shows up constantly and needs your attention. First realize that this dark emotion or thought is part of being human. Imagine that this dark area inside you is a child that has been neglected. You might find him/her hiding in a corner. Is it a boy or a girl?

101

Take a look and see whether you can find him or her, whether you can make contact with the child. Start with eye contact and then stretch out your hand carefully. Look at the child tenderly and see how hard he or she has tried to survive. This child is filled with joy and passion for life. However, he or she had to endure so much that the power of joy and passion has been distorted. The original energy of the child has become trapped in all kinds of masks and survival mechanisms, due to which their life force began to work against itself. But now, the child is allowed to be who he/she truly is. Please stretch out your hand and let your light shine. Welcome the child with your eyes.

Let the child come to you, in his/her own pace. Wait patiently, hold him/her in your arms and press him/her against your heart. What the child needs to relax and recover is to be seen and soothed by you. Observe how you shine with warmth, love and understanding when you are in contact with this helpless and agonized child. Inviting your darkest part in, welcoming it and bringing it home, brings out the lightest part of you. You understand how this child feels. This understanding heals. The child in the dark represents the part of you that has been carrying a lot of pain without being able to understand why. By surrounding this pain with understanding and compassion, you shine your light on areas that used to be the source of negative emotions and thoughts. At the moment you embrace the agonized child inside you, you become a human angel. You bring light into the darkness, which is exactly what humanity needs right now.

Humanity doesn't need saints and guru's who teach from a pulpit or pedestal, but real flesh and blood people who have experienced darkness and light by themselves and are able to embrace both without judgment. You become a human angel at the moment you dare to face and accept your own darkness. This will make your light pure and powerful. Life shall support you. You will be drawn to opportunities and places where you can reveal your highest self in an easy and natural way. You don't have to work for it. You don't have to pretend to be somebody else, since it is your own unique vibration and energy that inspires people and brings joy to them. It is you! You represent the love of God in your unique way, because you are willing and able to face and embrace your own darkness with understanding. People experience openness, tenderness and inspiration in your presence, in the way you listen to them. Whatever you do in expressing and manifesting your highest self on Earth, it will invite people to shine by themselves and believe in their own unique power and talents. To give the highest of you encourages other people to do the same.

11 - The Stone

I am Jeshua. I salute you. You are a being of light. You have come to Earth to spread your light. In doing so, you meet with resistance. You are confronted with darkness. What is this game between light and darkness really about? What is the purpose of the resistance and darkness you have been experiencing?

Being in the light means being in a state of consciousness in which you realize your oneness with all that is. If you are in the light, if you *are* light, you feel completely boundless and free. You know you are part of a greater whole and you feel you are deeply cherished within this infinite web of living consciousness. Light is your connection to the One.

Light is by nature formless. It is not dependent on any material form. It is free from the constraints of time and space. You are not the material form in which your consciousness dwells at this moment. You are not your body, you are not the flesh and blood of which your body is made, nor the gender, nor the characteristics that belong to your present personality. They are part of you, but you are so much more. You are their origin, their divine creator.

Your infinite soul has dwelled in many different life forms and has experienced a great number of lifetimes throughout the universe. These experiences have enriched you in ways you do not yet recognize. Your sometimes arduous journey through incarnation is nothing short of God's way of expanding him/herself. Your journey through form is meaningful, for it allows all of creation to expand and proliferate in new and enriching ways.

I know it often does not feel to you this way. You can become overwhelmed by the lack of light and connectedness on Earth. I know. I am here to ignite a spark of remembrance in your soul. If you remember who you truly are, you realize that your divine core is still whole and unscathed, in spite of all that you have been through. Feeling your wholeness may give you a sense of relief or even a feeling of ecstasy. This is when you know you are hitting upon the truth. You remember the truth of who you are: a divine soul with infinite possibilities. I am here to remind you of who you are, and to inspire you to bring that awareness to your everyday life.

There is no real gap between the human you and the divine you. Your divine self is not somewhere else. It is not located in time and space to begin with. If you want to connect to it right now, you can do so by stepping back for a moment from issues that press on your mind and emotions. Imagine your consciousness to become larger, withdrawing from these issues, and entering a space of open awareness. Within that space, there is no needing or wanting, there is just being. It may seem as if this is not going to help you solve any problems in your life, but I am inviting you to simply try. Can you shift your awareness and just observe yourself in a quiet and detached way? Can you be with yourself without judging or interfering? You will find that doing so makes you calm and more relaxed. If your emotions, thoughts or physical sensations draw you out of this calm space, don't worry. Let it be. Observe what happens. In time you will discover that entering this space of silent awareness is a powerful tool to remember who you are.

This tool is always available to you. You can stay in touch with your wholeness, with the space of freedom within, by always keeping some distance from the things that trouble you, or even excite you in a positive way. By maintaining some distance you keep the awareness alive that these things never define you completely, although they are indeed important in your life. You are more than the emotions and events that transpire in your life. Inside you there is a presence who silently yet intensely observes all of these events and experiences come and go. This presence is indestructible. It is the fountain of life itself.

You chose to temporarily connect your consciousness with a body, a form, in your life on Earth. There is a reason for this choice. The body is very precious. It is a wondrous feat that you can focus your consciousness in such a way that it identifies partially with a body, with the person that you are now, man or woman, with all the talents and characteristics that belong to you. However, please do not make the mistake that you are this package of characteristics. You are the consciousness that experiences them. This awareness can set you free.

The divine you, your beingness stripped to the core, is like a wide, open space, empty and yet full of vitality and potential. This is the part of you that is God. This is Home. If you connect to this part of you, you sense relief, joy and freedom. You feel safe. Being in the dark means that you feel separated from your core, from your connection to the whole. You feel dispelled from the wide inner space which alone can bring you the peace and joy you are searching for. All suffering originates from this sense of disconnection. It is the severest pain your soul can experience.

Understanding the purpose of darkness

Why do souls ever choose to experience separation? The moment you choose to incarnate and live inside a material form, your light gets limited and constrained. Your consciousness gets narrowed down and you lose your sense of infinity. You tend to lose connection with the real you, who is formless, free and unlimited. Especially for young souls, who are in the beginning stage of their incarnation journey, it is easy to forget and to identify themselves with the form they inhabit. It is a sign of maturity when a soul is able to fully inhabit a human body and at the same time realize that that it is not the body but the one who experiences it and gives life to it. As the soul evolves, the awareness is born that there's something transcending the body, the material form focused in time and space. The mature soul opens up to the dimension of formlessness and starts to recognize that its true essence resides there. In doing so, the evolved soul will be able to bring down the awareness of oneness into the realm of material form.

Why would a soul choose to embark on the journey of incarnation? Why did you choose to be confined by material form, by the cycle of birth and death, and all that goes with it? Wouldn't it be much more blissful to stay in a state of unbounded oneness all the time? Ask yourself this question. Some of you would say right away that if possible, you would never incarnate again. You would tell me life on Earth is too harsh, too dark and that you direly long to go Home and stay there forever. Nonetheless, I am telling you that your soul chose to experience this lifetime you are living on Earth, like it chose to experience all of the lifetimes it lived on Earth. There is a part to your soul who loves to dance with matter, and I am telling you this is the most divine, sacred and creative part of you.

God desires to bring light into material form. Spirit (which I use as a synonym for God) created matter for Light to take shape and be experienced by itself. The creation of matter brought into being the dance of consciousness and matter: the dance of spirit and body. The interplay between spirit and body is God's way of creating. You – as a spirit inhabiting a body - are God's creation unfolding. As your soul is evolving and maturing, it is becoming more able to hold the light of Spirit and express it through a body. The art of living in a body is to manifest the freedom of Spirit within the material dimension. Anything in the material dimension that is lighted from within by the awareness of Spirit radiates beauty and vitality and adds something important to life. Embodied light is the most precious light there is. By embodying your soul's light on Earth, in a material form, you are expanding God's creation. You are creating something new, and contributing something to the whole which would not have existed without your unique presence.

The abundance of life forms existing on Earth, in the kingdoms of animal, plant and mineral, reflects Spirit's desire to manifest in a variety of forms. The beauty and variety of life on Earth has evolved out of a dance of spirit and matter, consciousness and form. God longs to express in different forms, because it enriches creation and because it allows all beings to experience beauty, joy and adventure in their life cycles. All beings are sparks of Spirit. Traveling through different forms and getting acquainted with life from many different perspectives brings depth and wisdom to your soul. Even the experience of separation, of darkness, can help to enrich creation.

You are God. You once made the choice to descend into matter and to shine your light while dwelling in a limited form. This is not some punishment you have to endure. It is the result of a sacred choice you made, as part of God. You are truly a Creator. Beneath the resistance you may feel towards your life on Earth right now, there is a deep and enduring desire in your soul to bring light into the dense reality of Earth. Shining your light upon the dark parts of Earth reality, inside and outside, is truly your soul's calling. If you do so you experience a kind of fulfillment that touches your heart more deeply than anything else. Even the vision of being up there in heaven in eternal bliss and peace pales by comparison. This is because it is in your nature as a divine being to dance between spirit and body. It is this dance that constitutes the essence of creativity. You, who sometimes feel discouraged by living in a human body on Earth, will feel joyful again not by discarding the dance altogether, but by knowing how to bring your light into the darkness.

Darkness and density are part of life on Earth. When you experience darkness or density in your life, you feel that the energy is heavy, slow and stuck. You sense a lack of movement, freedom and flow. Always, when there's this type of density, there are negative thoughts or emotions, which betray a sense of disconnection and separation. I said before that feeling disconnected from Spirit, which means feeling separated from your own essence, is the severest pain a soul can experience. How do you remedy this sense of separation, which makes you feel wounded emotionally and doubtful of the meaning of life?

Carrying your light into the darkness

Today, I invite you to meet with the densest part inside you and welcome it with an open heart. In everyday life, you experience the densest part of you in areas of life in which your energy hardly flows. This may be work, relationships, health or any other aspect of your life. In this area, it is most difficult for you to accept yourself or what life offers you. You experience that aspect of life as an encumbrance, as something that should not have existed. You feel blocked, stuck and I invite you to visualize this density as a stone that you carry, just like the proverbial "millstone round the neck".

You may feel that the density you experience is due to outer circumstances. You may feel that it has been caused by the rejection, betrayal or violence of other people. Or you may say: I do not fit in with life on a place that's so dark and dense as Earth is. It is understandable that part of you reacts in this way. It is the bewildered and shocked part of you that has forgotten about the true power inside your being. It is a traumatized inner child speaking to you through these negative thoughts. This child feels a victim, it feels discarded and disconnected. I invite you to recognize the wisest and lightest part of you, whose sole purpose it is to bring that child home. You have one choice to make. Do you identify with the traumatized child inside, or with the bright and unbroken part of you who is able to heal that child?

The origin of your suffering lies not in the density or darkness of outer reality. It is in your felt inability to rise above the densest part inside of you and embrace it with your light and true radiance. Feeling victimized by the dense part, you resent it and want to get rid of it. To cast out a part of you, makes you feel torn inside. Your soul will not be at peace until the lost child has come home.

Imagine that you are carrying a stone around your neck for real. Take a look and see how heavy or large the stone is. Set your imagination free. The stone contains all the emotions you have difficulty with and all your negative beliefs about living on Earth, such as "I am not welcome", "people don't understand me", and so on. The stone carries your fear as well as your resistance to life. It symbolizes what has gotten stuck and blocked inside you. Therefore, the stone also points at your mission in life. It is your soul's mission to bring light to the densest parts of yourself.

It is your life purpose to shine light on the hardened and petrified parts of you. To spread your light on Earth is first and foremost to reach out to the darkness within. As soon as you embrace this journey within, your light will automatically radiate out to others and inspire them to do the same. You do not have to focus on what needs to be remedied in the world. Focus on your own stone. Do you see a picture of it? What color does it have? How does it feel when you pick it up? Say hello to the stone and hold it gently. Allow your consciousness to flow into the stone and sense the energy inside of it. Do you feel anger, or grief, or fear? Allow the stone to tell its story to you.

Remind yourself that you, who are holding the stone, are a being of living light. You are whole and unbroken, safely held within God's arms. Now watch what happens to the stone by just holding it and turning your attention to it in an open and welcoming way. It will transform. As you connect to it from your divine core, surrounding it with acceptance and quiet understanding, you sprinkle it with sparkles of light. The stone is lit from within. Your consciousness brings life and movement into the stone. It is no longer cold and hard. It gradually transforms into a gemstone. The structure of the stone has changed due to your loving attention. Take a good look and see what color and form it takes.

Now ask the stone: "What is your gift to me?" What kind of quality do you feel is present in the gemstone? Feel it from the inside. Is it compassion, endurance, the ability to surrender and trust? Is it tranquility, courage or joy? Receive the gift. This stone first contained stuck and dark energy. After you embrace it with the quiet power of your true nature, it transforms into a treasure. It will not simply be neutralized; it will be transformed into a gemstone, reflecting your inner beauty and wisdom. What was first a millstone round your neck has become a precious jewel. Pick up the stone and see how it sparkles and shines in a color and form that reflect your unique energy. Allow the gemstone to enter your body and see where it goes naturally. To what part of your body does the stone go spontaneously? What effect does it have on you? It will have healing effect on your body and spirit.

Life continuously invites you to turn to the dense, dark and stuck parts of you. The dance between spirit and body is like a dance between light and dark. As soon as you recognize your true nature, the dance becomes less of a struggle. It becomes a joy. As you become aware of the transformational power of the divine you and invite darkness to come out into the open, the dance of light and dark brings forth precious jewels which show how light can travel into the densest part of reality. The gemstone is the result of the integration of consciousness and matter, the fruit of the dance between spirit and body. Life invites you to perform this dance again and again. Whenever you feel negativity or darkness in your life, please don't judge. Bring the stone into your imagination. Welcome it and connect to the part of you that is not yet lighted by your divine awareness. Take care of the stone. Your loving attention is the key to enlighten the stone from the inside. By shining your light upon the dense and dark parts within you, you embrace the dance of creation and God is born on Earth through you.

12 - The way of the lightworker

I am Jeshua. I am closely connected to you from my heart. We are deeply related and there is a level at which we are one. The one, undivided consciousness that unites us can be sensed as an energy of freedom, creativity, kindness and joy. This is your true origin and home. You have now manifested in bodily form, located in time and space, but there is so much more to who you are. I ask you to now feel this grand and unlimited consciousness that you are part of. Feel God within and feel how simple this energy is. God is not at the top of some hierarchy looking down at you. God is the flow of energy that runs through everything: through you, through all living beings on Earth and even through what seem to be inanimate things in your material environment. God is everywhere.

God is not limited by forms. God is pure, creative consciousness, connecting with material forms in time and space to experience life in a myriad of ways. Now feel who you are in this great, divine flow: one spark of light within an ocean of living awareness, but an indestructible spark who offers a unique contribution to the whole. Feel the indestructible force within you, it is there forever. You are part of God.

Your consciousness is divinely creative. You choose your life path and experiences. Even though it often does not feel that way to you as a human, deep down inside there is a creative force in you that designs certain pivotal happenings in your life and attracts the experiences that you wish to go through in order to understand, grow and expand. Essentially, you are never a victim of this world. At the core of who you are, you are never truly powerless or devastated. Because in that core is the spark of God who says "yes" to the experiences you go through in bodily form, and who knows that you are able to learn from it so that your consciousness becomes even wider and more compassionate.

Embrace this creative power within, which attracted to you the life that you now experience. Embrace your life with all the ups and down. You have the power to live it well. The greatest fulfillment you'll find is when you remember who you are while you are in form, caught up in the demands and challenges of life on Earth. Remembering who you are allows the spark of divine light to connect fully with your human self. Surrendering to this spark of unlimited, creative light inside will change your life and it will change the lives of other people as well.

You who are reading this, and who feel drawn to the Christ energy, are someone who longs to shine your inner light out into the world. You long to manifest as a lightworker, meaning that you feel the desire to spread light and raise awareness on Earth. Your passion is pure and real; it comes from the core of who you are, from your soul. It is the spark of God within you which leads you to this desire, for it is natural for God to want to share joy, light and compassion. Whenever you feel happy in expressing who you really are, you are feeling God's happiness too, for you and God are one at heart!

You often wonder what light work is really about. What does it mean to spread light, or to offer healing to other people? This is the question I'd like to address today. First of all, we need to take a closer look at the relationship between people when one is helping the other. I would like to point out that something strange is going on with the distinction between healthy and sick, or between whole and broken, as it is used in your society. When you go to the doctor with a medical problem, you are a "sick person in need of treatment". Doctors are supposed to know something you do not. They are the expert and you easily get the feeling that your health is in their hands. It is not so much different when you suffer from mental or emotional problems. If people see a therapist, psychologist or a healer, they silently presuppose that these experts have some superior knowledge or skill which can help them solve their issues. By the very way the relationship between patient and doctor, or client and therapist, is defined, something happens to the self perception of both parties involved.

By framing this relationship in terms of one having more knowledge and insight than the other, it is suggested that the client needs the therapist/healer/doctor to receive something that they themselves lack and cannot give to themselves. It is assumed that the therapist is whole and healthy, offering light and healing to the one who is ill and/or broken. From this viewpoint, the therapist or healer is ahead of the patient, and is in possession of something that they hand to the one who is lacking this knowledge or ability.

From a spiritual perspective, this viewpoint is false and distorted. It starts you on the wrong foot right away. However, it is deeply ingrained in your society, in both physical and mental health care. Notice how easy it is to feel smaller than the person you are seeing for medical or spiritual advice. You are the one with the problem; they are the one with the solution. It's a common pitfall for people who help other people on a daily basis to identify so much with their role of helper, that they cannot let go of this role. They define themselves by it and this makes them dependent on their clients or patients, as much as the other way around. The client may feel they need the helper to cure or heal them, but the helper needs the client as well to sustain their image of being the helper: the knowledgeable, bigger person who is willing to share their achievements with the ones in need. It is easy now for unbalanced relationships to arise, which center around power and dependency.

Light work is something very different. To understand what light work or spiritual healing is truly about, you need to let go of the traditional image of "therapist helping client" or "doctor curing patient". You need to let go of the very idea that helping is about giving something to someone else. The very notion that the other person is lacking something is detrimental to their healing process. The truth is that the only way to help someone is to make them aware of their own power and ability to heal themselves. It is the mark of a good teacher that they make themselves small rather than big. Real teachers invite you to take back your inner power and they do not buy into the suggestion that you are small, needy and dependent upon someone else. Real teachers never present themselves as authorities. It is a silly thing to do. The true gift of a healer is to make the other person aware of their own inner authority, the fact that they are a spark of God and have all the knowledge available to them that they need.

True healing is very simple. It does not require elaborate methods or knowledge. I am speaking here of healing for the soul. Of course, physical problems may need to be attended by medical experts which have very specific knowledge and skills. Healing that affects the soul, however, is very simple. If you go to the root core of mental as well as physical problems in people, you will somehow encounter the belief that they are powerless, unworthy, unlovable, lonely and doomed.

The root cause is that people feel disconnected from their true being, the spark of divine light that they really are. To offer healing to people is to open up their memory of Home, to remind them of their perfect beauty, strength and innocence.

How do you do this? First of all, there is no fixed method or medicine. It is not a mechanical procedure. It is an energy transmission which can happen in a variety of way. I'll get back to this. Second, no one heals unless they decide to open up to healing. You cannot force healing upon anyone. It is their decision. In fact, real healing is something of a miracle: it is the birth of a new consciousness in the soul. It is their creation and it cannot be predicted ahead. In everyone's life there are moments in which you face the choice between dark and light. The dark represents giving in to self-judgment, self-hatred, negative thinking and fear. The light represents opening up to the kindness, forgiveness, joy and abundance that is truly the mark of divinity. It is up to you to choose. Even if the most beautiful angel is beckoning you to let go of the past and enter the kingdom of God, meaning to merge again with the spark of light that you are, it is up to you to decide. If you are still immersed in deeply negative pictures of yourself or other people, if you are in the thralls of fear and anger, you may not even notice the angel. In truth, the angel of healing is always near you. It is your higher or true self, your divinity trying to remind you of who you are. Sometimes, in your life, you meet with people who play the role of healing angel for a while. They may not even be aware of it, but they remind you of who you really are. By the way they listen to you or speak with you, a spark of the true you suddenly enters your awareness and you feel joyful and inspired after having been with them. This may inspire you to choose for the light, to make decisions in your life that serve your higher self, your true passion and love of life. The presence of the angel may serve as a reminder, and it may be the key to changing your life, but even then, it is your decision to trust and take the leap of faith. Only you can make the miracle happen!

You may have encountered angels of healing in your life and you probably have been an angel of healing for others on several occasions, even if you did not know. My point here is that this is what light work is about. It is not about curing or fixing people, it is not about offering solutions to their problems. It is not about teaching them certain skills, or knowledge or ethical rules. All of these actions presuppose they are lacking something, that they are small and helpless. Spiritual healing turns this picture upside down. What you offer someone else if you mean to offer spiritual healing is really a change of perception. Instead of focusing on their problems, their issues and their feelings of disempowerment, you focus on their essence, their wholeness, their radiant beauty. If there's anything to give by the spiritual healer, it is the gift of the true vision. If you are able to look beyond someone's pain, anger, fear and self-destructive behavior, and see the angel of light in their face, you offer them something very precious. By seeing their true essence, you are gently summoning it and beckoning it to come forward. Perceiving someone else's true power and inner light, even if they don't show it on the surface, is like calling someone by their true name. Nothing is as powerful as being called by your true name.

What I did when I performed so-called miraculous healings in my life on Earth as Jesus, was that I got in touch with the divine essence of someone. By seeing and feeling the spark of the divine in someone, it became awake and it was their divine essence that performed the healing, not I. It was their self-remembrance that restored mental and even physical health to them. Not always did such a meeting result in healing, for it would always depend on whether the other person decided to open up to healing. The miracle was upon them, and this is important to remember whenever you work with people for the purpose of spiritual healing.

All spiritual healing comes from within. You are not healing anyone as a lightworker. You are creating a space of openness, of being without judgment, which invites the other person to look at themselves with openness and compassion. Instead of trying to solve any problems on the outside, you are connecting to the other person's soul and you are holding a vision of trust and clarity for them. This is the way of the lightworker. You are trying to return to the other person their greatness, instead of focusing on their smallness. Working with someone on the soul level means that you show them their responsibility for their own life. Because you do this lovingly and without judgment, this responsibility will not feel as a burden. It will feel empowering and liberating to take responsibility. By really believing in the creative powers of the other person, you mirror their own strength back to them through your eyes and words. By focusing on what is whole and untainted in them, you reinforce it.

You can only do so if you truly believe it. If you doubt at some level that they can do it, you affirm their sense of weakness instead of invoking their

117

strength. You are most powerful as a healer if you completely trust the other person's ability to solve the problems and let go of any notion of them being dependent on you. Many of you feel that returning responsibility to people in this way means to abandon them or to tell them to solve the issue all by themselves. However, to release all ties of dependency does not mean you are not there for them anymore. You are still there, holding your faith in their true strength and inner power, encouraging them to go beyond their self-imposed limitations and be all that they can be. It will be their choice what to do with the healing space you offer.

I know that many of you have a very hard time watching other people suffer, especially if they are loved ones. It may seem impossible to stop "helping them", to let go and put your energy elsewhere. But, please take a moment and consider if you are really helping them by holding on. If they are dependent on your energy of kindness and support to feel good, how will they ever face up to their own lack of kindness and support towards themselves? From the soul level, you may be reinforcing their weakness instead of awakening their true inner power. This affects both of you negatively.

Being a lightworker or spiritual healer means that you seek to connect with someone from soul to soul. On the soul level, every being is equal and no one is ahead of anyone else. You are all sparks of the divine beingness you call God. It may seem on the human level that one person is more knowledgeable, evolved or wise than another person. However, if you look at it from the perspective of the soul, this kind of judgment becomes obsolete. All souls are travelling through the infinite universe and go through various cycles of experience and growth. It may be that you are helping someone who is suffering from severe emotional imbalance due to very difficult circumstances they encountered in their life. You may be the one offering assistance at this point of time. But later on, once the suffering one has regained their strength, they may become your teacher and show you a depth of wisdom and compassion that will blow you away.

To offer spiritual healing or be a lightworker, it is important to always remember you are equal to the other person on the soul level. It is essential that you recognize your own humanness and that you are really in the same boat as the other person. You may be holding a space of light and compassion for someone, but that does not make you different from them, in the sense of "being higher" or "above" them. Don't identify yourself with being a lightworker. If you feel drawn to helping people discovering their true inner power, follow your passion and do whatever you love to do. Light work may take all kinds of forms; it is certainly not limited to offering therapy. Generally, if you do what you really love to do, you will see that you inspire others to do the same. Being one with the God spark in your heart will naturally lead you to the right type of work, or relationship or place to live. Living from the heart is really very simple. It is about connecting to your heart's desire, your true joy, and daring to act upon it. Doing this will make you a lightworker and not necessarily because you are "helping other people". It is because you are bringing your soul's unique song to the world that you will inspire other people to also believe in themselves and bring out the best in them. Light naturally radiates outward. You don't have to focus on the question on how to spread light in the world. Don't try to be good and helpful. Try to live according to your own unique and divine nature, and the world will be a better place because of it.

13 - Lightworkers bonding in the new era

Many of you share a deep desire to meet with your soul family. Many of you have known loneliness in your lives, a sense of alienation that makes it hard to feel at home in a group or even in one-on-one relationships. At birth, your inner tuning often was not on the same wavelength as your family's energetic vibration. This meant that from early on, you felt a lack of connection with the world around you. You were different, you experienced your feelings more intensely and would react with more vigor to injustice and suffering and you needed to retreat from the world in order to get back in touch yourself. These are characteristics of your particular soul group.

You are lightworkers. You are here to create light and awareness where fear, power and negative beliefs have obscured the natural bliss of all that is. The veil that hides this bliss is the veil of ignorance that keeps people away from their true destiny: to live in love and harmony with Earth and each other. You are the ones who have come to lift that veil, to bring change and awareness. You are departing from traditional ways of thinking that have become part of the collective human mind. You are not alone in this. As a group, you have all come a long way. You have been pursuing this mission on Earth over the span of many lifetimes. As a group, you have sought each other's company time and time again, in a variety of previous lives on Earth and beyond. There is a spark of recognition when you meet – sometimes at first sight. This bond has been forged by your common mission and by the numerous individual encounters you've had in previous lives.

Something magical occurs when like souls meet. Because the mutual recognition goes beyond the personal – your individual background and personality in this lifetime – it sparks the awakening of the soul, which in turn accelerates your inner growth and return to wholeness. There is nothing as comforting and inspiring for the soul as being recognized by a kindred spirit, a brother or sister on the spiritual path. Often such a meeting will enable your soul to express itself more profoundly and to be grounded with more intensity and richness. To be welcomed by a kindred spirit is balm to the soul.

In this channeling, I will talk about the role of these meetings with soul mates. I would like to talk about the role spiritual groups or communities have in the New Era. The dawn of the New Era on Earth aligns with the reunion of you with your soul mates, albeit in a way that differs from the past. Therefore I will first talk about your past, your origins.

Spiritual groups and communities throughout history

In the history of spirituality there is a distinction between the *esoteric* and the *exoteric* traditions. The esoteric tradition points at inner spirituality, the quality that makes an individual feel directly connected to God, the Source, the One. Throughout all of history there have been people who, by means of an intense inner quest for purpose and meaning, have penetrated a dimension of being that is beyond form and matter. They entered the realm of the unknown by pushing aside all that was handed to them from the outside. Their thirst for the living truth was so intense that they did not occupy themselves with what authorities dictated, seeking instead their own personal connection with God. Through this connection they experienced a love and liberation that enlightened them. Some tried to name this experience and hand it down to other seekers. The naming of enlightenment, the mystic experience of deeper knowing, is a precarious undertaking. In its essence, this state of being and the knowing that comes from it, cannot be defined. Words fall short. It is often by the mystic's presence that the true meaning is conveyed of what the words try to say. So, people can be touched by the energy of such a teacher and if they are, they understand that the words and concepts handed to them are just means to an end, tools that point at something which is unnameable. They look beyond the words and are touched by the purity of love, which belongs to all people, and can be put into many different words. Such followers or disciples have "the ear that hears", as the Bible says.

However, if people focus on the words rather than the spirit of a teaching, they tend to take the words too literally and build spiritual teachings upon them that lose touch with the inspiration that lies beneath the words. Such teachings devolve into a set of rules and regulations that do not take into account the uniqueness of new situations. Little by little the teachings become rigid and fossilized, far removed from the living reality of everyday life.

When such a system of rules and regulations becomes the foundation of an organized religion, an *exoteric* tradition is born. An exoteric tradition is one of organized, institutionalized religion, such as the Catholic church. In such traditions, religion is always taken over by power, because the organization becomes a means unto itself and vested interests emerge that have little affiliation with the original source of spirituality.

In the exoteric tradition, the original spiritual pulse is often watered down to a set of rules and dogmas dictated by the authorities to the common people. In the past, esoteric, inner spirituality was found in the mystical branches of all mainstream religious traditions. In the writings of individual seekers you can see the original quest for truth and meaning, untainted by the desire for worldly power or the need to preserve the organisation. Some of these individual mystics became recognized or tolerated by the exoteric tradition, others were rejected and persecuted for their non-conformist ideas.

All of you to whom I speak and who feel attracted to my words, have in some lifetimes been part of the esoteric tradition. You have repeatedly felt drawn to a living form of spirituality that relinquished power and wanted to reinstate the purity of the original beginnings. This often attracted you to groups and ideas which were progressive and rebellious. You proclaimed new spiritual teachings that called for a return to the living spiritual source, the common man, and everyday reality. You often turned away from established authorities such as the Church, and doing so has often cost you dearly.

You often had a very ambiguous relationship with the exoteric tradition. You sought to connect with existing organizations and institutions because, by nature, you were interested in spirituality. As children in those lives, you were often dreamers, highly sensitive and idealistic. There was a yearning in you to preoccupy yourselves with life's big questions, higher awareness and holistic forms of healing. You often felt a spiritual calling in your lifetimes after Atlantis, when your heart chakra had opened and you returned to Earth as a lightworker. (See chapter 2 for elucidation). You often withdrew to temples, monasteries and convents because you didn't fit in very well with society. In those places you became involved with religious traditions that didn't necessarily tally with your notion of the spiritual. Many of you felt alienated within the walls of such institutions. The exoteric kind of spirituality intertwined with worldly power did not leave much room for the type of inner spirituality that you felt drawn to.

True spirituality is at odds with power, authority and hierarchy. Within exoteric structures, the original energy and legacy of a teacher wither and die. Just look at what happened to my legacy. I set out to remind you of your inner light, which is your own and for which you do not depend on anyone else. The essence of what I wanted to transmit can barely be captured into words, but each one of you who has been touched by my energy knows what it is about. The emotion many of you feel when you connect to me is in fact the Christ energy awakening in your own heart. Throughout many lives, you have been eager to establish the energy of the awakened heart on Earth, but it wasn't welcome within the structure of the Church, that wanted to restrain my energy through dogma and fear.

The history of the Church has become an exoteric tradition of power and authority. During the lives you've lived after Christ, you have often struggled with the question of how to express your heartfelt inner spirituality within society? You sought a fertile place on Earth to seed your inspiration. However, getting involved with organizations that proclaimed to be spiritual often curtailed your momentum – even drove you to exile. And whenever you associated yourself with like-minded people who like you sought spiritual rejuvenation, you found yourself in a dangerous position. All too often you were persecuted for blasphemy and submitted to violent treatment – if not killed outright.

You still carry traces of this tradition within you, namely in your fear of coming out in the open with your motivation and inspiration. You have become reluctant to voice your spirituality. This reluctance has blocked the free flow of your soul energy on Earth, and consequently your ability to find work that truly inspires. You have also grown mistrustful of groups and organizations. You have become loners, solo players who carve their own path in life, unbound and independent from groups, family or society.

All this has not been in vain. The isolation in many lives, the rejection by society, or the feeling of alienation within a group, were all indicators of the nature of your true path. I will explain that first before going into the question of how to connect now with fellow lightworkers, with your soul mates.

The trauma of rejection and the birth of individuality

In the ancient time of Atlantis, you operated more or less as a group. You belonged to the elite of society (see chapter 2). Your powerful mental abilities afforded you prestigious social positions. Your attitude contained an element of arrogance and haughtiness. You felt superior to the lower classes in the sense that you thought you had a better grasp on the truth than they did. You did not question your role and purpose in society. You often had positions of governmental and/or spiritual leadership, and even though you often felt trapped and alone in these roles, you had a strong sense of confidence about your abilities and the value of your role within society as a whole.

The fall of Atlantis brought an end to this status. The destruction of this old civilization didn't just end a grand and profound experiment in awareness, it also caused your natural self-confidence to collapse. The fall of Atlantis created a shock wave in your consciousness. You started to realize that the purpose of your incarnation on Earth wasn't to dominate and manipulate life. In Atlantis, you had developed a technology that was geared towards the mastery of life on the biological level. You had a vision of becoming your own creator of life, enabling you to steer it your own way. This is *hubris*, as the old Greeks named it: a proud and over-confident attitude that goes against nature and eventually evokes counter forces that are beyond man's ability to contain. On the spiritual level, you were highly developed in the sense that you knew how to handle psychic and energetic forces in ways still unmatched by modern technology. However, the real purpose of your incarnation on Earth was to understand that true creation can only originate from the heart.

In Atlantis you created in a technological manner, from the head, and Mother Earth destroyed your creations. This startled you. You truly believed in this experiment and were deeply disappointed by the collapse of the ancient and deep-rooted civilization of Atlantis. It caused a huge shift in your self-image. It pulled the rug from under many certainties that you had, and it's exactly this shock that sparked an inner awakening in your heart. As a consequence, you opened yourself up to forces that work in ways quite different from willpower and mental manipulation. You started to understand something about the creational force of love. It was love's power that shook Earth's foundation when Atlantis collapsed. Earth's heart, supported by cosmic forces, intervened from a natural tendency towards balance. This intervention shook your foundation as well. You knew you were entering a new chapter,

125

one without vested certainties or privileges. Naked and vulnerable, you set foot in heart-based awareness and re-acquainted yourself with Earth's reality in new ways.

When you reincarnated, the memory of Atlantis had been erased from your worldly consciousness. Yet you had a notion of certain talents and abilities within you, which you better kept to yourself. You retained a feeling of shame and guilt about the way you embodied your power in Atlantis. This karmic burden weighed on you when you came back. Due to the guilt and shame inside, you attracted lifetimes in which you fell prey to oppressive social powers and became a victim of power. While you were taking your first precarious steps in the ways of heart-centered living, the world around you didn't seem very welcoming. It often failed to understand your attempts to introduce a new heart-based consciousness, and you were often persecuted for being different.

You witnessed the other side of the karmic cycle. You went through the experience of being the loner who couldn't conform to the existing order, who fell to the wayside or was cast aside violently. Often there was not a single group or community where you truly felt at home. And even if such gatherings existed, the people in it were often persecuted and exiled by the authorities. You have experienced the depths of loneliness and self-doubt in a series of lives as victim of power.

Yet, being thrown back onto your naked self enabled the birth of an invaluable type of individuality, no matter how painful the birthing process was. You were forced to go deep within and reach for the core of your being: a divine, independent, creative entity. The collapse of groups of like-minded people around you had a purpose. It invited you to really begin to discover who you are independent of social structures or obvious roles that were handed down to you from the outside. All this history prepared you for what is happening within you now: the *individual* awakening of Christ consciousness in every soul. No longer presented as a dogma from above, no longer handed to you by a guru or group, Christ consciousness now rises as the free, independent heart energy that it essentially is.

The energy of the New Era is born out of the individual awakening of heart based consciousness in people. When it has awakened in the individual, like-minded individuals can connect and share the joy of mutual recognition. They can inspire and strengthen each other's inner growth. The sequence is: *first the individual, then the group*. A connection between kindred spirits is possible only when the individual first ignites their own inner light of love and self-acceptance. When someone's heart is opened to the Christ within, they radiate a magnetic type of energy towards kindred souls; their attraction is obvious and effortless.

In these times, awakening does not require affiliation with a group, community or leader. Once awakened you meet others who resonate with your energy. It is not necessary to form a group with a common goal. This is not the time for organizations and congregations, rather it is a time for open-ended networks of individuals, connected in flexible ways. They joyfully complement and support each other with their individual skills, each carrying out a specific aspect of the shared ideal of heart-centered living.

Spiritual networks in the New Era

In the days running up to the New Era, spiritual families will gather from the grass roots up. Instead of the traditional pyramid model with its all-powerful leadership on top and executive layer at the bottom, a network model of bonding will arise. There will be free and open relationships between independent individuals. There will no longer be a core entity that regulates everything. When a mutual goal is to be accomplished, nobody will have leadership in the traditional sense. All will contribute in a way that matches them personally. This will be a different, fluid and flexible way of cooperating, which lacks hierarchy in the traditional sense.

This type of bonding and cooperating, flexible and open, fits well with the esoteric tradition. In these times, the knowledge and wisdom of the esoteric traditions are sought after by a great variety of people. In the past, this kind of spirituality could often only be practiced in seclusion, and was all but killed by overly structured religious organizations. Now, however, there is a widely felt need in people for spirituality that comes from the heart and has direct bearing on everyday reality. In these times, the exoteric tradition is ever more exposed as power and fear based and the demand for true, heart-felt spirituality rises.

The inner knowledge you carry within as a lightworker is now welcome in the world, and as you gather the courage to live according to this knowledge, you will meet like-minded people who desire the same. When lightworkers reunite, they will gather in a way that is neither elitist nor isolated. They will fully participate in the world and bring their knowledge and love into society. This sounds incredible, but the time is right. When you bring your energies together, it will no longer be necessary to use traditionally structured organizations.

Honor the esoteric tradition you stem from! Let go of mind-based organization and open yourselves to the possibility of heart-based organization. When you connect with someone from the heart and without expectations, you trigger a surge of inspiration between the two of you. From that surge you can get a sense of the mutual creativity that is possible. If the potential is there, you will attract situations on your path that will support you in your efforts to bring that creativity to fruition. You will be guided by a flow of inspiration that is bigger than your personality's singular wishes. You will be elevated by the energy of your heart combined with the supportive powers of Earth and cosmos. Wherever two or more individuals gather their energies with the intention of tuning into this greater flow, things happen easily and effortlessly. There will be synchronicity – pieces of the puzzle falling into place at the right time and place. This is the way of the future, this is the way of the heart.

Because of your painful experiences in the past, you all have to some degree become reluctant to participate in groups or organizations. You have become acutely aware of how power structures within organizations can go awry. The exoteric tradition has spat you out, and from that you developed a critical, reserved and even suspicious attitude towards groups. This attitude has bred important qualities in you, such as independence and a kind of rugged individuality. However, these traits have become mixed with pain and fear of showing your vision, your passion. This is regrettable, because now is not the time to withdraw from the world. The world is, now more than ever, ready for your contribution. When you say "yes", there will be people and possibilities waiting for you. Meeting kindred souls is one of the most precious gifts you can receive in these times. I am asking you to trust the possibilities that await you, and at the same time to keep using your sense of discernment. I will now elaborate on this by talking about the emotional pitfalls one might encounter in meeting with soul mates.

Emotional pitfalls in the reunion with soul mates

Meeting with kindred spirits can bring a lot of joy. Relationships based on connection and recognition on the soul level are often sources of great inspiration and healing. Such relationships can also stimulate the awakening of heart-centered consciousness on Earth in a much broader way. Nevertheless, there are some pitfalls on the road of joining with soul mates. We'll discuss two of them.

The pitfall of emotional dependence

All of you have a deep yearning for oneness and transcendence. There's a memory inside you of being part of a field of consciousness in which you were loved unconditionally. In previous channelings I have talked about the "cosmic birthing pain" you all carry within, which is the pain of separation that arose when you departed from this field and began your journey as an individual soul. (see *The Jeshua Channelings*). This old wound, which you have carried along throughout all your incarnations, is the biggest cause of emotional imbalance in relationships. When the pain of being on your own, being torn away from Home, is overlooked or not recognized, it develops a life of its own. It will manifest as a hunger for absolute love in relationships with others. Although the cosmic birth pain can only be healed by you, you could continue to believe that there is something outside of you – a lover, community or god – that will make you whole. This is, in short, the pitfall of emotional dependency, of needing something outside yourself to feel whole and loved. This pitfall is just around the corner whenever you connect with soul mates and have not healed the wound within. When you feel lonely and eager to belong to someone, this creates emotional dependency before you have even started the relationship.

Especially because meeting someone at the soul level stirs deep emotions, it is important to be aware of your motivation, and the expectations you bring into the relationship. High strung expectations will sooner or later turn against you. It may lead to a sense of suffocation, possessiveness and dependency in either one of the partners. The promise of unconditional love and belonging, of *coming home to yourself*, can be fulfilled by nobody but yourself. The key to paradise is held by you only. Paradise is unconditional acceptance and appreciation of who you are. When you have unlocked that paradise in your own heart, you will bring a loving and caring energy into any relationship, and it will not be something you need or expect from the other. This will give your relationships a much more balanced energy. It opens you up to the experience of joy and connection without losing yourself and becoming dependent on the other's approval. This is the blueprint for a mature relationship, personally as well as professionally.

In the past, spiritual congregations and communities were often breeding grounds for emotional dependency. Individuals were encouraged to sacrifice their personal interests, desires and gifts in favour of the greater whole. To this day, many lightworkers still have difficulty appreciating their emotions and embracing their humanness. You were taught to "rise above your humanness" and denounce yourself in favour of the group, often held together by an authoritarian figure or guru. There was a sense of oneness in such groups, but it was based on suppression of the individual and the need to make individuals emotionally dependent on the whole. This is quite opposed to the joyful sense of oneness that arises from a free gathering of independent individuals.

Not all spiritual gurus have ill intentions. A significant portion of them starts out with an honest desire to share their spiritual findings with others, but they ignore the pitfall of emotional dependency. They underestimate the degree to which their followers will project images of perfection and godliness upon them, and they fall into the trap of regarding themselves as spiritually superior. This belief in their superiority makes them lose sight of their humanity. This shows that they themselves haven't yet solved the problem of emotional dependency, as they in turn become dependent on the admiration and recognition of their followers.

In many cases, the followers of this type of spiritual guru are left traumatized. Even if they manage to liberate themselves from the group to which they often sacrificed themselves completely, the hypnotic suggestion that they should relinquish their individuality to some higher good lingers on. The psychological traces coming from this false sense of oneness are still present in many lightworkers. You have learned to distance yourself from your own individual human needs and desires, and you think it is spiritual to denounce them. You have a hard time accepting that inner growth and the rise of awareness happen *in cooperation with your emotions*. Your humanness it to be embraced, ni transcended. By ignoring the importance of individual emotions, you miss the key that can open the door to your heart. The door to your heart is unlocked by consciously integrating your emotions, by listening to what they have to say and embracing the pain and fear they may hold. This is a personal path, one on which you may occasionally find help from a teacher, therapist or close friend. In the end, however, it's about your individual journey, your choices, your path.

Check with yourself if you feel the need to join a group because you "want to belong" or because you feel small, insignificant and lonely on your own. Sacrificing your individuality in favor of a guru, a spiritual teaching or – on a more worldly level – a life partner or an employer, can never create heart-based relationships. Relationships which are emotionally balanced, the personal as well as the professional ones, can only be created by independent humans who have a deeply compassionate understanding of human nature. They have taken responsibility for their own unsolved emotional trauma. They love to connect with others and celebrate their kinship if they are soul mates, but they do not project immature notions of oneness onto the other human being. If you no longer depend on anything outside you to make you feel whole and loved, this will open the possibility of relationships which are inspiring, deeply joyful and rich.

The pitfall of "us against them"

In the past, spiritual communities were often buffers against a harsh and materialistic world. In past lives, many of you joined convents and monasteries because those were the only places you felt kinship with in view of your spiritual interests and you sensitivity. Many of you were in one or more lifetimes also involved with radical groups that revolted against the existing religious or political structures. In both cases you participated in a community that kept its distance from society and that had a lifestyle all its own. You are familiar with the feeling of not belonging or being an outsider from past lives, and this might create a false motivation in you for joining with soul mates in a spiritual group in current times. I call this motivation, bluntly put, the pitfall of "us against them". It manifests itself in a desire to withdraw from the world, in individual isolation or as a group, and to no longer participate in society. This often happens against a background of frustration and disappointment.

These times call for integrated spirituality: a type of spirituality where heaven and Earth come together and complement each other. The days when

131

spirituality was dominated by certain organizations or authorities – the organized religions – are over. The birth of Christ energy on the individual level causes it to rise person by person, from the grass roots up, rather than be stipulated by an organization or authority. Now it is possible for lightworkers to express their inner spirituality in the world: no longer is it necessary to withdraw from society in order to live your deepest inspiration.

You possibly still experience society as harsh and materialistic. But changes are underway, and you will be surprised – at least if you're receptive. There are many who are searching for that what you already have. You, the sensitive dreamer and pioneer, who thought you had to protect yourself from the hammer of society, are welcome on Earth now more than ever before. This doesn't mean you have to hurry to claim a certain rank in society. It is first about you welcoming yourself on Earth, realizing what a valuable contribution you can make, and that it is no longer necessary to abandon society and isolate yourself. Now you can connect and live your life "in the world". You'll probably still feel different and have a non-conforming lifestyle – but that's fine. It is no longer needed to join a separatist group of like-minded people who form a buffer against society.

Connecting with the like-minded to protect yourself from the world, turning your back on the world out of resentment or frustration – these are false motives for bonding with fellow lightworkers. This is not a time for isolation but for participation. This doesn't mean "running with the pack"; what it means is that the time has come for the spiritual and the worldly to fully mingle and interact. Not only can you engage fully with the world through your work and relationships, a deep connection between your spiritual and your emotional self, between your higher and your lower chakras, between your knowing and your feeling, is possible and desirable. That is the true meaning of participation: unifying the spiritual and the worldly *within yourself*. Enjoying earthly pleasures, welcoming your emotions as valued messengers, and trusting that there is a place on Earth for you to blossom – *that* is participation.

When this is your approach, like-minded people will cross your path automatically. The relationships you then enter into will no longer be places of refuge or safe harbors in a hostile world. They will enrich you and be sources of inspiration, helping your soul to manifest itself even more profoundly in this world.

Characteristics of mature relationships between soul mates

Mature relationships can be recognized by the following characteristics:

Joy, appreciation, inspiration

The basic vibe of a mature relationship is one of joy, ease and mutual inspiration. There is a remarkable quality of intimacy and affection towards each other. You're not trying to change the other person; you accept their nature. Differences in opinion as well as miscommunication can occur, but they don't fundamentally disable the relationship. Both individuals take responsibility for themselves and consciously try not to project expectations that stem from old, emotional pain onto each other. Emotional conflicts are discussed. Pain that's encountered whilst relating to each other is recognized and put in context, creating a bridge to the other rather than an obstacle to the relationship.

Being realistic

Mature relationships are loving but not perfect. The initial infatuation when you meet one another can hold the promise of total recognition and mutual understanding. But even soul mates have to tweak this ideal towards a more realistic concept of relationships. Even when you complement one another well and understand each other on a deep level, your individuality remains in place. Maintaining togetherness will therefore require continued focus and fine-tuning. It will require empathy with, and sympathy for, your partner's imperfections. Everybody has imperfections. It's important to recognize and accept these in each other. This will keep them from creating a rift between the two of you. Harmony between kindred spirits doesn't exist by the grace of eternal infatuation or total unification of energies, as is sometimes imagined in spiritual fantasies about the ideal partner (called twin soul, a hazardous concept in view of the pitfalls mentioned). The idealizing or romanticizing of relationships leads to unrealistic expectations, and in the end is one of the main causes of emotional alienation and mutual blame. Harmony amongst the like-minded stems from a profound inner accord, a compassionate understanding of each other's imperfections, and the ability to let go and forgive.

Cooperating without power structures

When lightworkers and kindred spirits meet and engage in a mature relationship, many types of partnership can come into being. There could be a romantic relationship, a friendship, or a creative partnership that has as its goal bringing certain spiritual qualities into this world. Such creative partnerships between several persons may need some level of organization. These organizations are shouldered by aware, independent individuals. Everyone contributes their own particular talents in an equal manner, and these are merged in a way that creates *synergy*: the whole is more than the sum of the parts. Such networks don't have a power structure in which leadership is assigned to a single person. Of course there can be a single person who acts as the organizer of certain activities, but there's no absolute leader. The communal energy is not directed from a single point, but gains impetus from the combined inspiration of all persons involved: there is *synchronicity*. It is this flow of inspiration that enables a type of cooperation that does not rely on power structures.

All of you long for the joy and inspiration the bonding with fellow lightworkers brings. In these times this bonding can happen in a way that aligns with the esoteric tradition of spirituality: free, open and flexible. Also, these times challenge lightworkers to function within society, not outside of it. You are not meant to isolate yourself and renounce your humanness. Once you recognize and avoid the pitfall of emotional dependence and the pitfall of "us against them", your connection with other lightworkers will gain momentum and make a difference in the world. You will help the awakening of heart-centered living on Earth, leading by example. You will join with fellow lightworkers without losing your emotional balance and without wanting to leave society. You will create loving relationships, both personally and work related, which will inspire other people to do the same. This is how the Christ energy awakens in society from the bottom up.

I am a fellow lightworker, I am your family. I am bonding with you to lift your spirits and make you feel hopeful again. In the deepest way possible, we are one. I live in your heart as the Christ energy that is now being born in you.

14 - Expressing your soul's light

I am here, I am among you, I am Jeshua. You know me, I am your friend and your brother. I know what it is like to be human, I am very close to you at heart. And you all are close to each other, for all of you present here or reading this are souls who have come to Earth time and again, inspired by the Light, by the desire to change consciousness on Earth.

Deep in your heart, you love Earth so much. Of course a part of you has become very disappointed. You have experienced rejection in your lives on Earth. This has caused pain in your heart, but you have returned, time and again, and at this time of history something is happening. You can feel it in yourself, in your own body. There is a movement in your soul; your soul feels drawn to really expressing all of its light. Consciousness on Earth is now ready for a change, and I know that all of you want to express your soul, this lifetime on Earth. I praise your courage. There's both a dark and a light part to you. In the dark part you can feel very disempowered; you can feel discouraged, and you want to return home. But I tell you: now is the time to truly show the world who you are. Don't be too much impressed by the fear and aggression in this world. You are needed, right now!

How do you connect with your soul and express your soul's light? You all have feelings, inspirations, desires: they are the language of your soul. As a child, many of you had dreams and visions of another kind of reality. During your upbringing, you may have been told that you shouldn't be naive, that you should be realistic; you were discouraged to be different, to follow an alternative way. That's why it's difficult now to trust the dreams and visions you have in your heart. Yet it is time to connect again to the calling of your heart. Your soul gives you messages all the time. These messages come to you through your emotions and through your body.

For instance, in the area of work, or in the area of relationships, you often sense that you cannot truly express yourself or that your energy is not truly appreciated. You are very able to sense, to feel, if your energy is received well or not. Be honest about it to yourself. The emotions you feel, which may have turned into physical complaints, are messages from your soul that you are not truly honoring yourself. You have fear of letting go of the old, the familiar. However, your soul often wants to guide you beyond the familiar, into the new.

I now ask you to imagine with me that there is an open space in your heart. You can visualise it as a bowl or a vase, and in it there is still water. Imagine this place in your heart, and see how flowers are falling into this vase or bowl, and look at the flowers, feel their energy..... this is your soul's energy. Remember what it was like to be a child and feel completely free, free to dream and envisage any future you wanted. Now marvel at the beauty of this flower.....and perhaps you receive a message from it, telling you about where life wants to guide you to. Let this flower speak to you, and it doesn't need to be in words; you can simply sense its energy.

Now it is one thing to *feel* the energy of your soul, like you just did, and another thing *to put it out into the world*. To do so, you have to receive the energy of your soul not just in your heart and in your mind, but also deeper within, in your belly. What often happens to you is that you feel inspiration in your heart, and you start thinking and worrying about it: "How am I going to put this out into the world?", or "How can I make a living out of it?" Your mind starts racing, but the art of receiving your soul's messages is to receive them fully, which means *way down into your belly*. Why is this important? The belly holds your deepest emotions. To ground your soul's inspiration, you have to let the light of your soul shine on the darkest emotions that are part of you. The area of your belly holds old fears, the remnants of deep emotional pain and sadness, and you have to address these in order to be able to express your light. It is only when your soul's light is allowed to shine on the darkest corner of yourself, that inner transformation and liberation takes place.

This kind of *inner* transformation is the key to attracting - on the outer level - the work and the relationships that resonate with you. So to express your soul's light in this world, you need to merge fully with your soul, which means you allow your soul's energy to go all the way down into your belly. This is really the hard work. It is one thing to feel the inspiration in your heart, a clear memory of oneness and light, but it is another step to reach out from that place of oneness to the parts of you who feel very alone and discouraged. When that happens, you arrive at Christ consciousness, and you feel deep peace within. Christ consciousness reaches out to both light and dark. It understands darkness from within. There is no judgement, no struggle between light and dark from the perspective of Christ-awareness. There is deep acceptance of life as it is.

To connect with the darkest parts of yourself, see them as children who need help. From the soul level, you are their guide and their parent, and it is by embracing your lost inner children that you become whole. That is how your soul becomes fully grounded and present on Earth. The way of the lightworker is not to preach about a better world; it is not so much about *doing* anything anyway. It is about turning inward, on all levels, and truly loving and understanding yourself. When you receive the gift of love, you will automatically give it to others. You have become a lightworker even if you don't do anything specifically with it. You will bring change into the world, simply by being yourself.

I invite you to make a connection between the lightest part and the darkest, most traumatized part of you. Don't think about it, just feel it. See yourself as an angel, radiant with light and unconditional love. That is who you truly are! Now see a small child approaching this angel. This child feels desolate and alone. Can you receive her or him in your arms? The child is a part of you and wants to come home to you. This is what light work is truly about. Once you make peace with that child, and embrace it, you can feel it in your belly: the child will give you passion and life energy, and you will become a *human* angel. Your soul's light will be expressed easily in the outside world and without thinking too much, you will attract what resonates with you in the area of work and relationships. All things on the outer level will fall into place. Expressing your soul's light begins within and from this inner work all else will follow effortlessly.

PART II

REBIRTH OF THE FEMININE ENERGY

Messages from Mary

Messages from Earth

Message from Mary Magdalene

Messages from Mary

15 - Spiritual motherhood

I am here with much joy and an open heart to all of you. I am Mary. I have been the mother of Jeshua. I represent the female aspect of the Christ energy that is now being born on Earth in greater and greater measures. The female energy has long been repressed in your society, and in your hearts as well.

The female energy is a primal force of creation, a fundamental part of All That Is. She brings forth life and flows through everyone. Without her, you would not exist, either as a soul or as a human being. The female flow of energy also carries magic at this time and wants to lighten the darkness of this December month as well as your inner struggles and heavier moods.

You sometimes wonder what it is all good for, this life of yours on planet Earth. I tell you it is valuable and serves a purpose. You are doing important work here. Your presence has an influence on all life around you; you are bringing change to the world. However, that need not be the focus of your attention. You need not focus on others at all, to make the difference. The secret is that you need to focus solely on yourself and the integrity of your being. As you fill yourself with a loving consciousness, an acceptance of who you are in all your facets, you create a channel through which light easily comes to you and automatically flows out to others as well. You really only need to pay attention to yourself, to fulfill your mission here on Earth.

In this context I would like to speak today about how you can be a spiritual mother to yourself. I represent the mother energy in the Christian tradition. But what does that really mean? Motherhood is a crucial aspect of the female energy: the mother is seen as the life giving, nurturing and caring aspect of nature. But is this image complete? In the images that were conjured up about me in the course of history, much has become distorted and misrepresented. I therefore would like to tell you a little more about my life on Earth, when I was mother of Jeshua.

I have often been portrayed as a saint, but I surely wasn't one during my life back then. I was an ordinary woman of flesh and blood, I knew great emotional turmoil and I am familiar with all that you are going through in your lives. In the family I was born, I was a latecomer, the seventh and last child with many brothers and sisters above me. I was a fairly strong headed child. As a little one, I learned early on that I had to take care of myself and not rely on others. My parents were there for me, but I was not in the center of their attention. This however did fit my nature to some extent, for I loved being in my own fantasy world and go out on my own.

For a girl I was quite stout and adventurous. I also had a strong inner sense about things and I would not deviate from that guidance easily. I wasn't too concerned about what others thought of me. I had elder brothers who teased me every now and then, and therefore I realized early on that it was necessary to build my own pride and self esteem, so that I could be who I was. I was a little different. I could sense energies and I had a tendency to "look through" people. Often, as they were chitchatting, I could feel they were hiding things, emotions that were violent or heavy, while their behavior was calm and collected on the surface. This confused me as a child. I sensed something was wrong and I wondered why, but no one explained it to me. I was therefore also a lonely child at times, I often felt misunderstood. I loved to be out in nature and I was fond of the animals around the house.

The worst thing that happened to me in my childhood was the death of my mother. This happened as I was still quite young, a teenager; my mother was relatively old as I had been a latecomer. Her death was the first confrontation with loss for me. It was a deeply painful experience and I felt shattered and abandoned. As I sat next to her on her death bed, it felt like I lost a piece of me. A part of me seemed to fade away irrevocably. And I could not hold on to it, I had to let go. This in fact would turn out to be the greatest lesson I had to learn in my lifetime: letting go.

I now take a great leap forward, to the time when my son Jeshua was born. Just like any mom, I adored my little baby and wanted to shield it from harm. In the beginning, I did not so much realize that there was something special about Jeshua. What I did know – all my life – was that there is an invisible hand guiding our lives. I sensed something bigger was working through our lives, something we cannot bend to our will, to our human needs and desires. I also knew that this greater power was benign and wise. There is a wisdom to it that we often cannot grasp with our human minds. It is only afterwards that we realize that life brings us exactly what we need. When it is actually happening, it may seem cruel and unjust.

And that is how seemed to me as I raised Jeshua. When he grew up, it soon became clear that there was something special about him. He had remarkable gifts and talents and was strong headed just as I had been as a girl. I recognized that special energy in him quite well on the one hand, but on the other hand I found this very difficult. As a mother, you wish to protect your child for the bad powers in the world. But my son did not want to be shielded, he wanted to speak up and shine his light openly into the world. He was propelled by an inner mission, a greater power, that guided him to follow his very own path of bringing change into the world. It took me many years and much anguish to accept that. For his appearance raised distrust with the established order and he was running risks. He violated certain rules and boundaries and therefore he was challenged and even threatened. I gradually had to let go of my fear and the need to control him, and make room for the unique light that he came to bring here.

In your Earthly terms, one might say I had to let go of my motherhood. The part of me that tended to be anxious, overbearing and controlling, I had to release. Until finally I realized that he was not my child. Yes, he had been born though me, through my body, but he was not mine. He was a mature soul in his own right, wanting to shape and create his life in his very own way. Moreover, he was supported in this by heavenly powers that supported a special path for him. But isn't this true for all of us? For every child that comes to the Earth, there is a special path, his or her path, chosen by this soul. This you have to realize as a mother, and respect it. As soon as a child comes out of your womb, one has to learn to let them be and trust their innate strength and capacities to solve the issues they will encounter during their life.

Eventually, it was Jeshua's choice to die at the cross. He allowed this to happen. I had to come clean with the fact that this was his decision, that it belonged to the path of his soul and that therefore it was appropriate. I cried bitter tears and my heart was filled with darkness and despair as I watched him die. Do not think that I could transcend my suffering easily and have peace with what took place. I was not a saint. I was devastated by it and indeed it was my "dark night of the soul". At the same time, this experience taught me great truth and eventually it brought me enormous liberation. But this came afterwards. Jeshua's presence in my life lifted me and in the end I allowed myself to be lifted; this was my most courageous act in that lifetime. The Christ energy that came through Jeshua challenged me to see him die at the hands of brutal killers and yet trust that greater power, that higher wisdom guiding us all.

Surrendering myself and my grief to this higher source of wisdom awakened me at deep levels. It awakened my higher self and made it come forward during that Earthly life back then. I started to truly realize then that inner peace and freedom, that which you all so long for, can never be attained by wanting to take control of life. However, motherhood has in your culture become associated with clasping and controlling. A good mother, it is said, goes through fire and water for her children and never stops to fight for them. Although unconditional love sometimes takes the form of perseverance and implacability, for me true motherhood meant that I let go of my fears and expectations about Jeshua. My greatest achievement was that I released Jeshua and let him be who he was. Only then could I sense the overwhelming beauty and purity of who he was and what he represented. Only then could I truly be there for him, as an equal, a soul mate, as a mother in the spiritual sense of the word. This was my heaviest assignment: to learn to be a spiritual mother and to let go of the emotions of the Earthly mother.

When I died in that lifetime and passed over to this realm, I was tired and worn out on the one hand. I had experienced so much, went through so many emotional ups and downs. But on the other hand, I felt deeply enriched. A great light had touched me and through it, my higher self was able to come through and manifest itself on Earth. I had released, I had accepted ultimately that things were as they were. I let go of my earthly motherhood (in the sense of a worrisome, controlling motherhood) and became a mother in the spiritual sense.

You are all invited to become a spiritual mother to yourself. You all are struggling intensely with certain negative parts of you. These are emotional blockages or negative beliefs about yourself. Try to look at it with the eye of a spiritual mother: not a mother who wants to solve it all, but a mother who sees you, who recognizes your unique energy. A mother who does not want to change you but who honors you for who you are. Feel that kind of mother energy for a while. You can sense this energy as something that radiates from me, but it is not mine. I do not own it. It is more like a vibration or level of consciousness to which I had to rise up to liberate myself. It is universal and accessible to all of you. It is your heritage, for you are all meant to become spiritual mothers to the Christ child within.

You can access the energy of spiritual motherhood by stopping to try to solve your problems for a moment and just looking at them, letting them be for a while. Can you muster a sense of love and appreciation for yourself, while you are having this problem? That's a start.

Remember how a mother looks at her newborn child. On the one hand, there's the intimacy of being physically so close and on the other hand it is as though you look at the child from a great distance, because you are filled by reverence and awe for the very miracle of its being.

Such a tiny creature, and yet whole and complete, not just physically, but spiritually as well. A mature soul who is to follow his or her very own path in life. What a miracle!

Now dare to look at yourself in this way. Create some distance toward yourself and realize how you have been walking your very own path, all of your life, and how you have always tried to build a satisfactory reality for yourself. Even when you make mistakes, as you call them, you are trying your very best, to create happiness or to find a way out of pain and despair. Give yourself a break for a while and generously allow yourself these mistakes. You are not here to be perfect. That would become quite boring actually. You are here to live, to experience and to move through your experiences with a sense of wonder, even if they are negative.

The worst thing that can happen to you as a human being is when you are not moving anymore, when you are not open to new experience anymore. This happens when you get completely stuck inside a problem or a belief system. Whenever you feel completely stuck and you do not seem to have any other choice but to passively endure the misery in your life, then you are spiritually dead. There is no space anymore, no air to breath, no sense of wonder in your life.

If such is the case, try and create some distance from the situation or problem. Try to breath around it. Imagine that the problem has a place in your body, for instance where it feels tense or painful, and let your breath easily flow towards that place and surround it with space. Feel the soft breeze of the air, surrounding the tense and cramped energy, and recognize the original sparkle of your soul in it. It is pure consciousness and a sense of wonder. Remember that your stay here is just temporary, you do not have to take it that seriously! It is a game, a grand game, and in a twinkling of the eye you are back on the other side, and you remember. You need not make it all so heavy, this is just one moment in time, breathe in space again and widen yourself, open yourself up and rise above that particular problem. You are much grander than that. Feel how things can start to move again in the space you create with your breath.

If it feels downright impossible to find space within, try to move physically. Do anything but think about the problem. Go outside, take a walk, focus your attention on something else, just to get the energy moving, to again connect to the flow of breathing, the sense of wonder, the Light that is you. Taking your mind off it will bring you new answers, new perspectives. Answers never come from your will or your mind. If you insist that "I have to find out now what I need to do", then you put pressure on yourself and you get yourself stuck. The answer always comes from making your consciousness wider and more open, not from narrowing it down and focusing hard. And if your mind is obsessive and restless, and you seem unable to let go, move physically – go running, walking or swimming, it does not matter what. Physical movement calms down the energy in your head.

By connecting with the spiritual mother within, you can give yourself some space again. You take one step back, you let go of self judgment and that creates new room to Be. The negative things are given room as well, as the mother in you realizes that they are there for a reason and have a definite cause in the past. When you feel very sad and disillusioned, imagine the hand of a mother on your shoulder. Feel her slight yet comforting touch. A genuine mother merely has to look at you, and see through you with a glance, to console you. Let this consolation be with you, descending from heaven and ascending from deep within you. Reassure yourself, know that you are well: you are doing the best you can and it is okay to make mistakes. Mistakes are part of this game. Give yourself some leeway to live: to make choices, make mistakes and then make some new choices. That is what living is about. Continual movement and growth and discovery and a sense of wonder that accompanies it all. The art of living is to find room for choice in everything that occurs to you. If you find that space in which you have the freedom to choose the way you experience something, you are a master of life on Earth. Things will loosen up, even in dire circumstances, and answers will come to you that you (your mind) would not have expected. You let the magic of life take over.

I am now residing in a realm of freedom and creative joy. The burdens of Earthly life are not upon me anymore and I enjoy being here as a visitor, connecting with you from the heart. I wish to impress upon you that you can share in that same freedom and joy, even while on Earth, in your own unique way. Freedom is available to all of you now, if you dare to let go and trust the hand of Love that guides you. It is time now to celebrate life. Allow light, air and space into your life so that it may flow again according to the rhythm of your divine soul.

16 - Guiding our children

I am here. I am Mary. Before I say anything about today's subject matter, which is about the new generation of children, I wish to draw attention to you. Each and every day, you try to embody more of your light and inner being on Earth. You often experience heaviness in your lives and it seems sometimes like you are imprisoned in your body or in moods and emotions that suffocate you. We – me and my friends - would like to tell you that we trust and respect you for all that you go through and accomplish in your lives. We love you just as you are and we wish that you would have more respect for yourself and all that you have already accomplished in your life so far. By staying hopeful, cherishing your dreams even when you have to deal with setbacks, you show your greatness and strength. You are planting seeds of light on Earth and these will bear fruit. Thanks to your inner work, you have created a bridge for a newly incarnating generation of souls who wish to shine their light on Earth. It is about these souls we wish to speak today.

Before we talk of them directly, I ask you to go back in time and feel who you were when you entered the realm of Earth as a newborn. Feel the innocence and beauty of your energy. Sense the sincerity of your intentions and the delicacy of your energy. Ah, you have been connected to Earth for so long! So many times you have plunged into the deep as a small babe. Now feel what your intention was this time. You probably carried some personal baggage that you wished to solve in this lifetime. There may have been wounds deep in your soul that you wanted to heal and overcome. But apart from that, you were also guided by a vaster and more universal ideal, which is to enhance spiritual awareness and growth on Earth. You knew you were going to be born in an age of transition, an age of crisis as well as opportunity. You knew there was "work to be done", work on the inner level that would open up new pathways in thinking and feeling. You felt a connection with this great global transformation on Earth and you were prepared to take the plunge into the deep once again to help make true this old vision of a peaceful Earth:

a new consciousness of unity among men and a renewed harmony between all living beings on the planet.

Time and time again you have broken through old boundaries of thinking and feeling. Every time you felt suffocated in traditional structures and rules, knowing deep inside that your soul could not flourish in a fear dominated environment or relationship, you have felt the necessity to break free. It has been painful at times, to say goodbye and travel new roads, yes difficult and very heavy, but you had to stay true to your sense that something wasn't right, that it did not make sense to you or that something was missing. This nagging sense reminded you of the original intentions and goals of your soul. You have not been able to become well adjusted to the demands and ways of society, because they did not correspond with what you as a soul wanted to live by on Earth. You were destined to be "different", not because God or any other external authority planned that for you, but because you are who you are. You have, at some point of your soul history, become inspired by a new consciousness, that we may call Christ consciousness, awareness from the heart, or love. It is not so important how you call it. What matters is that you have been touched by it, that you have been hit by a sparkle of inspiration that has ever since propelled you to go on searching, dreaming and expanding your consciousness. The sparkle that is kindling a new consciousness on Earth is now hitting many. For that reason, the "children of the new era" feel called to come. For that reason, they have been incarnating on Earth for several decades now in great numbers. They are here to complete what you have started.

You who belong to the previous generation of lightworkers, roughly born before 1980, were the forerunners and trailblazers. You were inspired by the same ideal as the "new children" now; it was the same calling of the soul. But the grounds that were opened up by you, especially in the sixties and seventies of the 20th century, were much more marked by conventional beliefs and deep-seated fears about freedom of self expression, emotions, creativity and sexuality. When you go back forty of fifty years in time, the collective energy field of Earth looked much different from now. It was less transparent, more dense and clouded and therefore less accessible to the loving and clear energies that are now finding their way to Earth. One of the things that have enhanced this gain in love and clarity is the rise of equal rights for women (starting at the beginning of the 20th century) or in other words, the growing awareness of the equality and unique qualities of the female energy. The badly needed rehabilitation of the female energy has supported a growing awareness and validation of the dimension of feeling in life. During the sixties and seventies of the last century, much has opened up in the area of emotion, intuition and creativity.

Much work has been done by the older generation of lightworkers and it has cost them much, for they have crossed the inner valleys of self doubt and loneliness, before they could open up a new horizon for the generations to come. If you are part of that older generation, know that you have set a beacon of light for the ones after you.

Now you are passing on the torch to a new generation. And as you are passing it on, you can provide them with support and encouragement, while they can inspire you by their passion and the purity of their hearts. They are "different" to an even larger extent than you were. While you could temporarily or partly adapt yourself to an environment that didn't truly resonate with you, they are unable to do so even at the level of outer behavior. In other words, they cannot even fake it for a bit. Their emotions and their physical body protest at a deep level as they are confronted with the limiting energies of many traditional education systems or ways of raising children. Adaptation is not an option for many of these children. Especially the most sensitive among them will physically and emotionally crash in an old energy environment and their behavior will become so problematic that the environment has to respond and change. Repressing or ignoring the problems is not possible anymore. The children that come in now will force society to deeply reflect upon its own assumptions about children and about life in general.

The children who are being born now (and have been incarnating on Earth for some decades) carry a larger part of their full soul consciousness into the Earth realm than most of you did. As you enter the Earth realm, you go through a "veil of ignorance", which keeps you separate from the dimension from which I presently speak. This veil is like a pair of glasses which, once you wear it, makes you believe you are a separate I, locked into your body. In fact, the veil of ignorance enables you to experience duality on Earth, so it has its value, but at this moment the time is ripe for the veil to become more transparent and allow more communication from one side to the other. There are more and more people who reach through the veil and who realize they are one with something bigger than just "this body" and "this personality". The more people do this, the more a channel is formed through which loving cosmic energy pours into the dimension of Earth. On this wave of cosmic energy the new children ride in.

Try to feel the energy of these children for a moment. Sense the wave of cosmic energy they are riding. Don't think about it, just open your heart and allow the sensations to come through you. They vibrate at a higher level. Their energy may feel playful, light and butterfly-like but at the same time uncommonly wise and deep. They choose very consciously to embody a greater part of their soul, their divine self, on Earth. They do this as they want to contribute to the transformation of consciousness on Earth and they fully realize it might get them into trouble. At the level of their higher self, the most aware part of them, they have consciously made that choice. But on the level of the emotional self (or "inner child") they might get traumatized by the clash they experience with the reality of Earth. They run the very real risk of getting lost and troubled in the realm of Earth, as they cannot switch off their sensitivity and higher vibration when they are in a less developed environment. Thus, they will have to either find a space on Earth to express their energy safely and freely, or they will have to cope with intense doubts and frustrations inside. You can see how courageous and loving these souls are, running the risks they do. The same courage and power of love were displayed by you, when you incarnated on Earth.

I will now go into some of the characteristics of this new generation of children. Not all children are the same of course, and some children display these characteristics more than others. There is a sense in which all children are "different" nowadays. They enter through a different (thinner) veil and with the intention to express more of their soul into matter than ever. But every soul has its own development and within the new generation of children there are the extraordinary sensitive ones, which are more different than the rest and which are often called "the children of the new era" or simply "the new children". I will now list some of the most important characteristics of this specific group of children, and bear in mind that these characteristics also apply to a lesser degree to all children nowadays. Actually, by the development of consciousness on a collective scale, a "new human" is arising on Earth. An evolution is taking place towards a socially and spiritually more intelligent human species, capable of living in harmony with nature and connected to its fellow humans by a sense of unity and respect. The development towards this "new human" is foreshadowed by the children.

Characteristics of the new children

- The new children are increasingly clairsentient, empathic and telepathic. They easily absorb other people's moods and emotions. The boundary between the world perceived by the five senses and the invisible world of feelings and energies is very fluent for them. They perceive the inner side of things often as easily as the outer (physical) side. They are not misled by outer behavior that does not truly mirror what is going on within. Their intuitive perception is astute.

- The new children are peacemakers. They feel the impulse to bring together opposing parties and appease conflicts. Together with their intuitive abilities this often means that they mature early and are wise beyond their age. They often understand their parents at a deeper level than the parents understand themselves or each other. They try to help them or build a bridge of understanding between them. They easily become the "parent of their parents" and this may take away from their spontaneous, uninhibited, childlike part. When they identify strongly with the role of helper they may carry too great a burden of responsibility.

- The new children are idealists. They are spiritual, philosophical and imaginative. They are inspired by ideals such as equality, fraternity and respect for nature. In their aura you can often notice that the upper two chakras are wide open. Through these higher energy centers they often receive plenty of inspiration, insight and enthusiasm. But on the other hand they can easily get restless, overly dreamy and unrealistic because of these widely opened higher chakras. Their energy has not become fully grounded yet; it still has to connect fully to the body and the Earthly plane of reality.

- The new children are feelers more than thinkers. They have trouble adjusting to preset structures and rules that leave little room for intuition, unpredictability and individuality. They are actually here to teach us how to break free from a tradition in which thinking and analyzing was overemphasized. All children are to some extent feelers rather than thinkers. But what distinguishes the more sensitive new children is that for them it is physically and emotionally impossible to adjust to a rigid and overly structured environment. They become sick or display severe behavioral disturbances. They are already anchored into a heart-based consciousness to such an extent that they cannot go back anymore.

- Because of their strong intuitive awareness and their inability to adapt, these children may be viewed as obstinate, rebellious and "different". It is actually not their intention to be rebellious. They just want to be themselves. But if they feel there is no room for that, they can become isolated and even drop-outs living at the edge of society. As they are less driven by fear and the need for self-preservation, they are less responsive to discipline and authority. Yet they can suffer intensely and be confused by the lack of understanding they encounter. They can feel alienated and lonely because of that and wonder what is the meaning of their presence on Earth. If they do however find their way in life and start to express their creative and spiritual energy in material form, they will flourish and many people will be touched by the profundity of their ideas and by their gentle, non-competitive way of dealing with people.

Problems faced by the new children

Summing up these characteristics already shows what problems the new children may run into. The biggest problem is that their specific energy is not recognized and understood by the people around them. When they are not given the means or opportunity to express their feelings and there is a lack of real communication, several "behavioral disturbances" may arise.

Children may become rebellious, hot-tempered and hard to handle. They feel misunderstood and mistreated, and they really want to say "no" to that, but they do not know how. They do not have the right expression and communication skills yet. What happens after a while is that they themselves do not understand anymore what is going on inside. When their inner life is not mirrored back to them by an understanding parent or teacher who gives a name to their feelings and listens with an open heart, they can get locked inside themselves and act out in ways that seem unmanageable and irrational. At that point it requires a lot of attention and a deeply attuned awareness to understand what is moving these children, as they themselves have lost touch with their feelings.

It can also be the case that children, feeling not welcome or misunderstood, withdraw and disconnect from the environment. They do not vent their emotions through aggressive or unruly behavior. They are locked into their own little world and it is difficult to get through to them. Often these children are extremely sensitive, reacting strongly to discordant energies around them. As it is hard to imagine what it is like to be so sensitive, their boundaries are easily overstepped, and to survive emotionally they shut down their feeling center. This survival mechanism is generally called "autism". It is a paradox that autistic children are called non-empathic (i.e. not able to see things from another person's perspective) because they are extremely sensitive. One might say that they have so much trouble holding onto their own boundaries, that they cannot allow themselves to reach out to others, to expand their consciousness in such a way that it includes the other. They feel their world would break down if they do so, and they would be swallowed by chaos. The non-empathic behavior of the autistic child therefore stems from an enormous impressionability regarding the energy of others. It is in dealing with this overwhelming sensitivity that the autistic child seeks to protect itself and shuts down emotionally. The non-empathic or non-social behavior of autistic children is a survival mechanism and not an essential characteristic of the soul.

Children who try to solve their problems in an extraverted way (rebelliousness, agitation, lack of concentration) as well as children who seek an introvert solution (withdrawing and shutting down emotionally) share a number of common features.

- They feel unwelcome, unrecognized or not truly appreciated for who they are.

- They are not firmly rooted or grounded in their physical bodies. This you can literally perceive in their aura which often does not fully connect to Earth at the underside. Practically it means that they lack an emotional foundation or anchor of safety inside from which to explore the world in a relaxed and open way. There is a basic "not feeling at ease" which makes it difficult for them to "just be" in a carefree way.

- As a result, they may display physical symptoms and disorders and/or react strongly to certain foods or substances.

- As they grow up and become teenagers, it can be difficult for them to find their place in society (by finding the right form of education or a job that suits them).

I would like to say a little more about the ways in which these children and teenagers can be supported to feel more welcome and find proper ways of self-expression. But first I wish to emphasize that it is very important not to think in terms of guilt as we speak about the causes of the problems the new children experience. The parents of these children often do their utmost to support and take care of them. A number of parents are very aware of the special qualities of their child and are getting more and more intuitively tuned into them. By their openness and willingness, an enormous learning process takes place. It is these parents who, together with their children, will pave the way in society and prepare the road for new ways of dealing with children.

The sometimes painful confrontation the new children experience with the reality of Earth has been consciously chosen. They come to bring something new and they know this in their heart. This puts their difficulties in a different perspective. At the soul level, they take responsibility for what they encounter in their life; they accept the setbacks and obstacles. Society is not "against them". Society is sleeping in many respects. It is the sleep of old habit and the coming of the new children is a wake-up call. Yes, they are a bit like you, can you feel it?! The previous generation of lightworkers has gone through the same dilemmas as these children, with the difference that in the current age things are gaining momentum and reaching a turning point. The new children are both cause and effect of this acceleration.

Guiding the new children

In guiding the new children, as their parent, teacher or therapist, the starting point is always an inner connection to that individual child's reality. The foundation of all real help is the willingness to open up to the child's way of experiencing life and the ability to tune into what it communicates to you verbally or non-verbally. The most important quality one can possess if one want to coach these children is the ability to listen and be open to something new.

It is less relevant whether you have specific knowledge or skills. These can even be in the way. Theories about (new age) children often depart from general classifications of outer behavior. Syndromes and diagnoses are based on externally observable symptoms. But what's missing here and what's vital for successfully reaching out to these children is that an inner connection is made to what the child is experiencing: the feelings and emotions that give rise to the outer behavior.

To look at someone in an open and unbiased way, one has to let go of preconceived notions and expectations. You can only genuinely connect to someone else (whoever they may be) if you first release everything you think you know about the other. Only then is there room for being present in the now in a truly sensitive and intuitive way. This also is a beautiful way of welcoming someone, for you are now allowing yourself to be touched by their very soul's energy.

From such a fundamentally open attitude, which is feeling in nature rather than thinking, you can enter into a communication with the other person that is beneficial and enriching to both. The interaction with a child is never one-way traffic. In the relationship the both of you are teacher at some points and student at others. This is what characterizes all spiritual meaningful relationships.

When the relationship between guide and child is defined in such a clear and transparent way, there are many possibilities for supporting the child in its development. I will indicate some ways in a general fashion, which does not pretend to be complete but rather to point to a certain overall direction.

- Positive appraisal for their unique qualities (which make them "different")

Help them remember who they are. Help them realize that their high sensitivity and idealism belong to the most beautiful qualities they possess. Let them articulate themselves in what respects they feel "different" and encourage them to find out how these qualities enrich and contribute to the world. Find creative ways of expressing their (high) sensitivity so that they can experience joy in it. Bring them together and let them exchange experiences and share their energies.

- Intuitive development

To train their intuitive skills in a playful way, helping them to connect to their body and their emotions, reinforces their self awareness. Grounding oneself, knowing your boundaries from within and using your intuition to find out what is good for you, are skills that these sensitive children can easily learn when they are young and unrestrained. When they are older, they may feel more inhibited regarding their natural tendency to feel, imagine and fantasize. If that's the case, it is important to first help them become aware of the emotions or limiting beliefs that block the flow of their intuition. If there are problems in this respect, almost always the energy flow in the lower three chakras has become blocked. There are fears, frustrations and disappointments in these children as a result of which they may feel insecure, depressed or even wanting to die.

- Respect their maturity as a soul

Know that their high sensitivity and "being different" has been a conscious choice on their part and trust their inherent capacity to solve their problems. Do not treat them like victims. Appeal to their gifts and talents and, as much as possible, let them find their own answers and solutions. Encourage them to get in touch with their passion and inspiration and help them find out how to express and manifest their inspirational energy on Earth in a practical way.

- Make room for self expression

The energy of the new children or teenagers can be so ethereal and idealistic that it may seem intangible. It is important for these children to express themselves in material form. This may be a creative form such as painting or making music, or it can be through sports or games. What matters is that they know how to ground their energy and make it visible to others. In that way they channel their energy to Earth. In all of these things, the starting point should be that they enjoy expressing themselves in material form. When they are encouraged to freely explore and experiment, they will find the forms that suit them on their own.

- Alternative medicine

Gentle, holistic forms of treatment such as reading, healing and alternative medication can be very helpful in dealing with physical symptoms in these children which are related to their overall energy and psychological condition. As they are so sensitive toward energy, these children respond easily to ways of treatment which are focused primarily at the energetic level (the psyche) and only secondarily at the body. It is however important here also that one does not choose a treatment or medicine based solely on external symptoms but that one makes an inner connection with the unique situation of a particular child. As a parent or therapist one can ask the child on the inner level whether the treatment is beneficial for them. And once it is old enough, the child can be involved in the choice themselves.

- Education

Enlightened forms of education take the child and their inner world as their starting point. In the past, knowledge has often been "poured into" children in a top-down fashion. They were considered to be empty vessels which needed to be filled with useful knowledge and skills. However, if one regards the child as a mature soul with their own interests and goals, education takes on a very different form. The challenge is not so much to make something out of nothing, but to awaken and liberate something that is already present within the child: their natural soul energy that wants to manifest and express itself in the material world. There is a natural tendency in the child to want to learn, to explore and find out about the world. It is only when they are systematically forced to take in knowledge that is not related to the way they experience things that they become reluctant and unwilling to learn. Preserving and working with the natural eagerness in a child to learn is the foundation of new education. In this approach, the role of the teacher is very different. What is asked of them first and foremost is to be present with the child in an open and intuitive way. The teacher starts from the assumption that one can trust the natural and unique abilities of each child. They allow the child to lead the way, supporting it by supplying the knowledge and materials they need to attain their goals.

Dealing with the suffering of your child

When you are the parent of a sensitive child and you notice the hardships they have to go through in dealing with the world, you dearly want to protect or save them from harm. Unnoticed, you may begin to view the outside world as the enemy and your child as the vulnerable victim. You may be afraid and wonder whether your child will ever make it without you. Watching your child suffer can throw you back on your own deepest fears, sorrows and disappointments. Nonetheless, the presence of this particular child in your life always has a hidden logic to it. There is a deeper meaning with a positive intent. One way of unveiling that logic and meaning is to look at the child with different eyes. To not see it as a helpless little being but as a teacher – an angel if you want – who has come to bring you a message. I invite you to go along with me in the following meditation. If you do not have a child yourself, you can simply invite an imaginary child to come to you.

Imagine you are walking through a lovely garden. Open your heart to this world of peace and serenity and let your gaze wander around. There are many plants and flowers in the garden. Feel the rhythm of the seasons, cycles in time which alternate gently and slowly all by themselves.

Now you look to the side and you notice that a child is walking next to you. Take the first child that comes up in your imagination. He or she silently takes your hand and together you walk through the garden, taking in the beauty of nature.

After a while you notice an inviting place to sit down, it may be a little bench or an open spot on the ground. You both sit down. Now you take a better look at the child. See her or his little face and look deeply into their eyes. After a while you observe a transformation taking place. Slowly the face of the child changes into that of an angel. You see how the child gets a shining radiance and becomes more ethereal, belonging to a different world. Perhaps you notice colors surrounding the angel-child.

Quietly you watch this angel and you are in awe of its appearance. You feel yourself becoming smaller, like a child again. Release the burden of being a grown-up for a moment and feel that sense of wonder again that is so natural for a child. With wide eyes you look at that magnificent angel facing you and then you sense that she (or he) wants to say something to you. This he or she does first by conveying an energy to you through their eyes. You take in that energy and feel the essence of it.

Then you ask a question to the angel. "Why did you come to Earth?" you ask, "What is the gift you are bringing?" You let the angel speak. It does not have to be in words – they can also speak through feelings. Then you suddenly know, without words or images intervening.

When you have received the answer, let the angel know and ask: "What is the highest thing I can do for you? How can I best support you in your mission, your endeavors?"

Let the angel-child tell you, in words or in feelings.

Then say goodbye while you feel that a lasting connection has been made between you from heart to heart.

Often, the thing the child needs from you most is the thing that helps you too. The character trait or energy that is needed most to support the child is often exactly the character trait or energy that you on the soul level wish to develop and master for yourself. Let me give some examples.

It may be the case that you have an introverted child that hides their feelings and is hard to communicate with. What this asks of you is that you learn to intuitively tune into them, be patient, and be willing to look at your own feelings in depth. This helps the child. Very often, to develop the qualities that are helpful to the child is exactly right for you as well, regarding your own inner development. Perhaps you are someone who has strong beliefs about a lot of things, or someone who is very practical and efficient, and you have never explored the realm of emotion and feeling that much. Your child invites you to restore that balance. So although superficially, the child seems to present you with a problem only, there is a deeper meaning hidden inside the problem: the challenge for you to develop certain qualities which fit very well into your own specific path of inner growth.

Another possibility is that you have a very lively and strong-willed child who easily crosses your boundaries and forces you to speak up and clearly indicate what you do and don't accept. This child may frequently upset you and you may feel overwhelmed at times by their presence. What this child asks of you is that you get clear about what your boundaries are, so that you can communicate your needs and wants in a resolute and self-conscious way. If there's a lot of struggle between you, it generally indicates that you haven't made up your mind yet about what you do and don't tolerate. Your child invites you to define your own space clearly and to determine where you stand in the relationship to them - and very often this also throws light on all your other relationships. The behavior of the child (and your reaction to it) magnifies a problem that was already there. Very likely you already had a problem with assertiveness before your child was born. Now the child asks of you to become truly aware of who you are and to stand by yourself, and this is precisely what you need on your own path of inner development.

When you develop the qualities that support the child, you are helping the both of you. By your added understanding, love, independence and self-awareness, you can become a role model for the child, a beacon of light. In that fashion, in a mutually inspiring process of growth and healing, a new energy is being born on Earth. A torch of light is being passed on from generation to generation, and it is shining ever more brightly.

We praise you for your dedication, love and commitment. We wish that you experience joy and fun on this journey of exploration that you and the new children are undertaking. We hope you have compassion for them but especially for yourselves as you will surely make mistakes. (Remember that mistakes are always the most important learning tools). We trust that your torch will keep on burning and will spread many sparkles to the torchbearers who come after you. But whatever you do, whether you experience joy or despair, whether you have compassion or are judgmental, whether you are open and trustful or down and depressed, we love you and will keep on offering you our support and encouragement. You are welcome. Always.

Questions and answers

After the channeling, there was room for questions and answers. Some of them have been listed here.

What can I do for my autistic daughter who is 6 years old?

First I would like to say that you love your daughter immensely and that your love is very palpable for her. With this, the most important thing has already been said. Your love cloaks her in a constant, silent embrace. That doesn't take away the problems she has, and the difficulties you experience in relation to her, but it is the prerequisite for things to work out in your lives. So feel that for yourself for a moment, feel your integrity and the sincerity of your love: this is the most precious gift one can bestow on a child.

It's understandable that you feel doubtful, even desperate at times, but at the core there's a deep love that unites you. If things are not going as you planned or expected, then it is not you or her that should be blamed. There is something she wishes to go through and deal with in her life, a special reason why she has this particular problem. It is her intention to be here on Earth in a very pure way. She carries a very pure and knowledgeable energy inside of her, which will touch many people. But a lot of patience is required, on her and your part, to have this energy come down on Earth intact. She has chosen – it's complicated to put into words exactly – to bring a pure and evolved energy to Earth and to be relatively unprotected in this. So her energy is not attuned to the energetic reality of Earth and she needs a translator, someone who helps her make the translation to the reality of Earth. She consciously chose this high and relatively unprotected sensitivity because that way the natural vibration she carries within can remain intact.

One can put it this way (I'm speaking more generally now). If you have a "normal child", in the sense that it easily adapts to the expectations of the outside world, the child will more easily forget themselves, i.e. lose touch with their original soul energy. It will more easily be influenced by the demands and standards of society and even the most sensitive and enlightened parents cannot prevent that. Children with behavioral disturbances such as autism do not adapt so easily. But because of that, the soul energy of the child is more easily preserved; it does not budge so to speak. The people around this child will have to adapt instead of the other way around. This situation is often quite difficult for parents, teachers or doctors. But there's a hidden treasure in the problem. The child's "being different" challenges the environment to find new ways of communicating, reflect upon assumptions that seemed self evident before and to be truly open to the inner reality of the child.

What is asked of you in relationship to your daughter is especially to have trust in this child and to tune into her needs. You do this very well! You have a lot of inner space in your being. Trust that your child has chosen her life path, that she has outlined certain milestones in her life and that she chose you as their parents, so that you together could enable her to shine her light on Earth. You're doing an excellent job.

Additional notes by Pamela: After the session I did a short intuitive reading of this girl for her mother, on the basis of a picture. This showed that her autism was related to a past life experience. This is a literal transcription of the reading:

I see a lot of light blue energy above her head in the form of shining transparent stones which are linked into a standing oval above the crown chakra. There's an energy there of high vibration; it contains a profound understanding of life and the human psyche. I feel she lived on Earth one time and had a strong spiritual or clairsentient experience during which she felt a lot of insight come to her, like an epiphany. As a result, the behaviour and the motives of the people around her became transparent to her, including the silent power plays that were going on in her community. But it was difficult for her to integrate that knowledge into her daily existence. I sense that she got ill, that she got unwell both at the bodily and at the psychological level. She could not express her truth, because her environment would not understand, not grasp it. This made her feel very anxious; she had the feeling she possessed knowledge that could help other people and prevent them from suffering, and yet it was impossible to speak up about it because she would be locked out. My impression is that she could not solve this dilemma during that lifetime and that she broke down due to emotional stress and physical problems which were the result of not being able to integrate that higher consciousness into her physical being. She shut down emotionally and this had an effect upon her throat (self-expression), her heart (connection to others) and the lower three chakras (feeling safe and wanted).

Now (in the present) this higher knowledge (the blue oval) is hanging above her head, exquisite and pure, and it is her intention for this lifetime to integrate it with her physical and emotional reality on Earth. I feel strongly that is the reason why she came to you (her mother). You also carry something of that blue energy (the quality of higher awareness) in your auric field, so there is a natural connection with her. You also have red in your aura near the lower chakras which shows that you are able to stand up for your truth, although it has been hard for you at times. My feeling is that your presence alone has a healing influence on your daughter. That's wonderful. She wants to heal in this lifetime, step by step. You as her parents are part of the solution, not part of the problem.

Both of my sons are highly sensitive, but in very different ways and therefore they fight and argue all the time. This very hard for me to watch. I find myself struggling and arguing with them also, while I am truly someone who needs peace and harmony around her. How do I deal with this?

It is very important for you to stand up for your own truth, to stick to your gut feelings and put our some clear boundaries in relationship to others. Your consciousness easily slips into the highest two chakras (third eye and crown), from which you tune into other people's emotions and understand their reasons for it. But you lose the connection to the lower three chakras, which tell you what you feel, what you need and what you want. You lose touch with your own inner child (the seat of the emotions) and you become ungrounded.

You are very sensitive yourself and your sensitivity contains a lot of empathy and reaching out to others. You have the desire to be connected, to be together with others, but in this you often sell yourself short. It's important for you to take your own emotions of anger and resistance seriously and allow an energy shift to take place within you so that the balance between giving and receiving is restored.

The struggle you find yourself in with your children is there for a reason. It challenges you to become clear about your boundaries and demand respect from them. Often, this is a problem for parents who are very sensitive and who want to understand their children and not hurt them. In the role of parent they often lose their balance because they repress their own emotions and lose track of their own inner child. You should become more assertive and "self-centered" in the relationship with your children.

By becoming more self-aware and assertive, you will be able to set an example for your children and show them what it is like to be both a highly sensitive and a self-confident person. By embodying this energy of balance, you teach them more than words can ever do.

Children pick up your energy, the feeling tones of who you are, especially sensitive children. So allow yourself some space to express yourself and you will see that it'll make you more grounded and give you the real peace and harmony you are looking for.

How do I realize my intention and desire to work with children? I feel inspired to work with children in the manner you described but at the same time I am inhibited by my fears of failure and my doubt that "no one out there is waiting for me". Again and again, I am "interrupted" in my outward flow of self-expression by my insecurity. How do I deal with that?

There's an authentic longing inside of you that stems from your soul. It's important to cherish that longing and treat it in a gentle and caring way. Apart from enthusiasm, this longing also awakens fear inside of you. It brings to the surface an old hurt, which goes back to your childhood and beyond, to previous lifetimes, in which you were rejected for the specific qualities you now want to express once more. The experience of (violent) rejection has left a trauma in your soul. This trauma now makes you resist and waver as another part of you wants to manifest your soul's true energy again. Understanding and accepting this heritage is the first and pivotal step towards healing yourself. By being impatient with yourself and by judging your fears and insecurity, you deny the pain in you that wants to be recognized and brought to consciousness.

Take your time for healing the hurt inner child inside. Your enthusiasm points at the right direction but it can also make you restless, as you are trying to get over your inner wounds too quickly. Remember that essentially, this process you're in is not about your manifestation in the outside world. It is about your healing. The first and foremost goal of any soul incarnating on Earth is self-realization: to love and accept yourself as you are and to experience the intense liberation coming from this. That is the foundation for all truly creative, spiritual energy. Once it is laid, the outward manifestation flow comes easily and effortlessly.

The fact that you want to live and be in the world from your heart, shows you are prepared to go to the core of the fear and darkness that is still with you. The longing to express your very own soul energy on Earth always comes at a time when you are ready for a deep level of self-healing. As you prepare to express your heart's inspiration on Earth, you will, more than ever, let go of your past, your education and of relationships that no longer nourish you. Connecting with your soul creates a lot of movement in your life and it may seem like you are putting one step back before your spiritual energy can gain material form. Changes occur in your life and things may even get chaotic and messy for a while. This is precisely as it should be. Do not doubt yourself when the process of manifesting your soul's desires comes with jerks and jolts along the way. It is these jerks and jolts which make you realize who you truly are and what you have to offer to others. Going through the fear and the insecurity, facing up to them and accepting their presence, makes you all the more loving and compassionate towards others. As you let go of judgment, and truly accept who you are at this moment, you become wise. You understand that it is really about you and not the others. And at that moment, the others will start to come to you. They will see something in you that inspires them. Opportunities to manifest your soul's inspiration will present themselves easily. You are ready and you will know it.

17 - Let joy be your guideline

I am Mary and I represent the female aspect of the Christ being. I would love you to share in the joy and peace that is available for you and belongs to the very essence of who you are. You are not here to suffer, to struggle and merely survive. You are here on Earth to have joy, to be who you are and experience the miracle of it. You are beautiful as you are. We don't need a improved version of you. You are quite well as you are. Can you accept this?

The essence of creation is joy. God did not create you for a grave and solemn purpose. She created you out of joy and a zest for exploration. She wanted to find out about life through you. All of you are the expression of God's love and creative joy, and that's why you are allowed to experience these very energies every moment of the day. I invite you to reconnect to this original flow of energy, God's joy of creation, which pours through each and every one of you.

You tend to make life too heavy and serious. Imagine that you are not here to achieve a goal, but simply to be yourself, including the parts of you that feel dark, doubtful or stuck. Yes, those parts are welcome as well, they are part of this experience, the complete experience of duality in all of its aspects.

Trust that it leads up to something beautiful, something magical, to a new world. You are ever moving and transforming yourselves. There is no fixed purpose, no final destination. You are constantly on the road. Now enjoy being on the road, enjoy the changing currents of life, and such a heavy burden will be lifted from you.

I ask you to go back with me in time, to the moment before you were born on Earth in this body. Do not doubt whether this is possible, just travel along in your imagination. It does not matter if you think you make it all up. Trust yourself and allow yourself to feel how once upon a time, you were free of the body. You were independent of the physical form, you felt unlimited and anything was possible. Life was magical. From this dimension of great freedom, you felt a pull coming from Earth. Your attention was drawn, of all places, to this tiny planet with such grand potentials; potentials of both light and darkness, love and fear. You felt a pull. You wondered about the nature of reality there and you sensed you had something to do with it. You felt there was something there that you wanted to experience.

As a free spirit, you decided to take the plunge and incarnate on Earth. Feel how even now, having gone through so many experiences on Earth, there still is that original sense of magic, wonder and attraction you once had. Feel how special it is that you are here now, that your consciousness has narrowed itself down to fit into an Earthly body, perceiving reality through physical senses like eye, ear and touch. This particular way of perceiving reality is not the natural one; your original perspective is much wider and less limited. Yet you chose this limitation, because something incredibly valuable was to be found in there.

You are here on Earth to express the freedom and magic of the spiritual realms you come from. You are here to bring it into form and matter and make it available for experience to both yourself and others. Yes, you are carriers of light, where light stands for freedom, ease and joy. And you have been on Earth before, with the same desire and impetus to kindle the light of creation here and spread joy and loving awareness. Allow yourself to feel it again. Know who you are. You need not be or do anything special here, you don't have to achieve anything except to remember who you are and allow joy to fill you again. That is your job: to get back to your original state of wonder and joy amidst energies which seem to point in a wholly different direction.

You have been put under pressure. The reality of Earth, the way people think, the beliefs of society can weigh heavily on you and soak you in forgetfulness for a while. Remember, you are divinity in the flesh. Light is pouring through you right now, through your hands, through your eyes, feel it. It has never left you, but all of you have been told at some point of your life that this light cannot flow freely into the open. You believe you have to hide it and keep it inside, for fear of being "different". The constraint to be normal, getting locked into what other people might think of you, that's probably the worst prison on Earth. It's not being in the body that limits you so. The true limitation comes from allowing in the many heavy, fearful beliefs of society and have them diminish your divine radiance.

My wish is to show you a way out of there, and the key is: dare to receive joy again in your life, feel that it is your birthright! It is simply who you are. You are the joy of God made manifest. And to be so, you need not have achieved anything, in the worldly sense of the word. You only need to be one with who you are. You need to feel that you are fine as you are here and now. There is nothing you fall short of, there is nothing lacking. Embrace the totality of who you are now, your fears, emotional blockages, and yet, at the same time, the deep sense of wonder and vitality at the bottom of your being. Life itself flows through you and wishes to impart on you its many miraculous gifts. You have undertaken the journey of incarnation in this body, in this society, in this material dimension. That is enough. By that, you already have shown your great courage and faith. Now trust that you are allowed to receive everything you need in your life. Feel the pure joy of being in this moment. Let yourself relax into it.

Imagine that from now on, there is nothing you "must do" in your life. If you would really grant yourself that freedom, your life would consistently flow smooth and easy. I understand that this runs counter to much that you have been told by your parents, teachers, employers, etcetera. Society imparts on you that you have to work hard and diligently to develop the necessary skills and abilities to cope with reality. It tells you to think small and focus on what is possible rather than on what you dream and hope for. Not only society tells you this, even a lot of spiritual teachings have a rather stern and disciplinary outlook on how to achieve enlightenment.

Imagine that you release the very idea of goals and achievements. Imagine saying to yourself: I am as I am, and I am completely okay as I am. What liberation! If you can allow yourself to be this relaxed, things will start to flow in your life, and you will see that exactly the opposite happens from what society tells you to expect. Things will start to happen for you without having to work hard for it. If you can be at one with yourself and accept things as they are, you will invite a flow of peace which will bring miracles into your life. By accepting yourself as you are, you say "yes" to life, to being here on Earth, and you allow yourself to receive anything you want simply because you are who you are, an indelible part of God, cherished and loved unconditionally.

If you find that peace in your heart, and let go of your tense and high strung expectations, then you allow the magic of life to take care of you. You surrender yourself to her flow and rhythm. I say to you, to start finding fulfillment in your life, to start finding the right job, the right relationship or the right house to live in, start by allowing yourself to experience joy again. The simply joy of being, the joy of being you. Spirituality is all about simplicity and ease. It's about feeling like a child can feel, not thinking of tomorrow, but just enjoying the present and doing whatever it feels like.

I know you believe that this is not possible anymore for an adult. That is such a tragedy. There is such sadness in the fact that you have felt obliged to relinquish the most spontaneous and carefree part of you. Reach out your hand to the child within, that has saved your spontaneity for you. Deep within, it is still there, the child that wants to play and enjoy itself, the child that wants to explore life and trusts that all will be well. This child knows that Earth is a safe place for you to express yourself. Feel it and let it speak to you again. Perhaps it wants to give a message to you right now. If you do not feel anything yet, that's fine too. What matters is that you are willing to reach out to that child, that you say yes to the original flow of spontaneity within, to your soul's inspiration. You are filled to the brim with notions that this is not possible or desirable, that you have to turn outwards rather than inwards to find guidance in your life. But it is not so. Life is to be lived according to other tenets.

True creative power, truly manifesting positive creations in your life, always happens from a state of simplicity and ease. It is precisely when you feel totally relaxed and divinely careless about things, not forcing yourself to do or be anything, that you attract the most positive changes in your life. If you would simply cherish your dreams and desires, and then let go, and have things run their own course, your trust will draw them to you. You will not even wait for them to happen, as you will be much too busy enjoying yourself in the present. Life is exquisitely simple.

We are with you and we understand very well what you are going through. We ask you to trust this message and have faith in the kindness of life and the joy that flows through every living being. Take a look at nature. The animals, trees and flowers are all inherently geared towards the expression of beauty and harmony. They do not doubt themselves. They value themselves in a perfectly natural and peaceful way. Connect to that natural energy of validation and know that you are held within that same web of life. You are safe. God is right here with you, and will never leave your side. Dare to entrust yourself to the magic of life, which is nothing but the divine flow of your own soul, and enJOY!

18 - The dignity of the female energy

This is Mary speaking. I rejoice, and I am here with many: loving guides and angels who want to share their energy with you because we all love you. We are brothers and sisters, united by a common goal: to live on Earth and spread a spark of light, so that peace and joy will be born in the hearts of many.

All of you have undertaken a long journey that leads to this very moment in the 21st century, a moment that is significant in the process of transformation on Earth. People are currently getting involved on a large scale. Their souls have been touched by a desire, a longing, a knowing. Today I want to talk about the rebirth of female energy on Earth. This rebirth is closely connected to the current surge of interest in spirituality.

The past ten centuries have been marked by the suppression of female energy on all levels. Those were (and in some parts of the world, still are) times when women had no basic rights. Additionally, female energy itself – that life-giving, creative and spiritual force – was ignored and looked down upon. Much pain and suffering ensued from the disharmony between male and female energy. You women all carry part of the collective female soul, the bundled energy of female experience on Earth throughout the centuries. Try to feel the pain that lives in that collective soul. There is fear, sorrow, rage, alienation, disempowerment and abandonment. You can feel the very presence of all of this in your own body. Don't be afraid of it. These are exactly the times when this pain wants to be seen and known, so it can be healed by the rising of inner awareness.

Connect with the wound in the female soul. All of you have been raised with certain expectations and tacit assumptions about what it means to be female. Emancipation and the onset of equal rights for women have changed attitudes towards womanhood somewhat – but on the emotional level, in the root and sacral chakras, the energy remains stifled by a past that cannot be forgotten through reason alone. There's an old pain and disempowerment there, one that can topple even strong women. It's that pain that I want to talk about.

The surge of dominant male mental energy

I would like to speak a little about the separation of male and female energy and the way these two forces went on to live a life of their own. Originally, male and female energy were meant to be equal partners in a creative dance. Male and female energy are equally represented in every soul. There are no "male souls" nor "female souls", only souls that choose male or female incarnations. Male and female are not fixed identities; they are aspects of creation. If you incarnate as a man, the male will be temporarily dominant in you. One could say that this soul wants in particular to investigate the male side of creation. However, this will only work well if he continues to recognize his female energy as part of his own being and as an equal creational entity. The man who alienates himself from his female energy, who rejects this energy as something outside of himself and does not recognize it as his own, will become one-sided and distorted. He becomes a man who lacks feeling and empathy, and who has the tendency to steer and control life by reason. The sensitive part of him is more or less closed and he lives with the illusion that reason is superior to feeling. This type of emotionally unavailable man who wants to rule the world with his brain, has been the role model for men throughout the centuries. This has had had a profound cultural impact, especially noticeable in the fields of science, politics and conventional medicine in the West.

This phenomenon has engendered a world view in which humans are regarded as rational, thinking entities who can manipulate the world based on their analysis of it. All of modern science is based on the idea that reality can be known by reason, and that reason is the best tool with which to discover the essence of nature, life and consciousness. Reason is essentially analytical. It explains the whole based on the characteristics of its parts. For a long time (until the dawn of quantum physics), the aim of physics was to describe the essential aspects of life in terms of lifeless particles. The world view of physics is mostly mechanistic. In other words, the world is regarded as an incredibly sophisticated piece of machinery, which theoretically can be known by understanding its parts. Human consciousness too, its ideas, emotions and desires, are understood in purely material terms – as very small particles that interact in ways that are determined by the laws of physics.

This world view has now been challenged by the most contemporary school of physics: Quantum Physics. It suggests that matter, at its core level, cannot be explained without using the notion of awareness or consciousness, in other words that consciousness plays a vital part in the creation of material reality. This new school of physics actually negates the modern, mechanistic world view – but I won't elaborate on this point. The important thing to realize is that the mechanistic view still has a big influence on the way psychology and medicine view people. There is no room for the human soul in that view; the soul has been rejected as old-fashioned superstition. However, if you view humans simply as physical beings that accidentally developed consciousness and emotions, you approach them as if they were machines. This goes against the deepest human intuition that we are living, feeling, individual beings who make conscious choices and influence life with our awareness. A purely mechanistic view of humanity cannot produce healthy, potent psychology or medicine. Regular medicine, of course, has had a lot of success with its analytic and scientific approach to the body. Something precious, however, has been lost as well: a holistic approach to people that first and foremost regards a person as an embodied soul who has certain life goals and desires that influence their body and mind.

The holistic approach looks at the person as a whole, and it understands that the whole cannot be understood only as the sum of its parts. You cannot explain the soul with reason; its language can only be understood by intuition, an inner knowing that comes from feeling and not from thinking. The female is much more appreciated by this approach than by the analytical approach. This doesn't mean the analytical approach is totally wrong. It is in fact tragic that both approaches are seen as mutually exclusive, as ideally they would produce an integrated form of healthy, potent medicine that combines the good of both. A singular approach always falls short. The male, rational approach clearly has its value and purpose, but problems arise when it is put forward as the one and only truth. It then starts leaning towards dominancy and reductionism – it becomes intolerant and arrogant.

In your past, rationality has all but suppressed the female approach. The most tragic result of this is that humanity has lost its intuitive connection with the body and psyche. People, men as well as women, have become alienated from the workings of their body and spirit because they believe that "professionals" (doctors, scientists) have more profound, objective knowledge; they are in the grip of authorities that have "a better understanding of the machine". People have thus lost their grip on life, having lost touch with their birthright to shape their life through their own awareness, as creative beings. This is the core of your existence: you are creative, divine beings who *choose* a body and a life path for the sake of experience and inner growth. If you have a deep inner understanding of this, you will start seeing sickness and mental suffering from an entirely different perspective: not as accidental, mechanistic failures, but as experiences with a profound purpose and meaning. The only thing that can give you access to purpose and meaning is intuition. Rationality cannot do this; only an intimate connection with your inner self can. If people were able to get in touch with their own soul, and medicine would allow it, there would be room for healing of the whole person and not just curing (part of) the body. Mental and rational knowledge would serve intuitive knowledge, and the holistic, female approach to health would not be treated with as much cynicism as is the case now.

Another area where the emphasis has mainly been on reason is technology. Modern technology, which permeates all aspects of modern life, is the fruit of a mechanistic, scientific approach to nature. This approach has been remarkably successful when it comes to managing the forces of nature, the building of machinery and equipment that make life easier, and the development of long distance communication. But again something valuable was lost: the sense of unity with nature, of being part of a living web of interconnected forces. This realization was taken for granted in older civilisations. Nature was regarded as a conscious, living being. The forces of nature (air, fire, earth and water) as well as plants and animals were all considered to be part of a greater consciousness. Later on, this idea was discarded as superstition, coming from a primitive mind. There was indeed superstition in older societies – in the sense that people sometimes projected powers onto natural phenomena that actually belonged to themselves. Also, think about the cruel custom of sacrificing of animals to please the weather gods, or declaring certain animals divine and others impure. We are not saying that the old, holistic experience of nature was in all ways better than the modern, male approach. What has been lost in modern times however is a profound understanding of life's wholeness, the fact that all is interconnected and that there needs to be balance in giving to and receiving from nature.

With modern technology, nature came to be regarded as a thing, a machine. When you abandon the idea that animals, plants and all living things on Earth have their own awareness, and are working towards the completion of their own inner growth, you are but one step away from regarding nature as a tool – one just about good enough to serve human needs. Nature lost her soul in this one-sided mental approach. The dominant male energy at work here was not tempered by an intuitive understanding of the unity between man and nature. Female qualities such as empathy and sensitivity towards nature were suppressed for an extended period of time, and this crippled the delicate balance of giving and taking within the web of life on Earth.

We have talked about the way mind-centered male energy became dominant in your past, and how it displaced the female aspect in psychology, medicine and technology. Now I'd like to speak about the way this has affected women emotionally and psychologically. We are going to address the collective female wound. And we're going to have to discuss sexuality in order to understand the essence of this wound.

Injured female sexuality

The deepest injury to the female energy is in the area of sexuality. Sexuality encompasses much more than just the physical act of having sex with a partner. Sexuality is part of a wider flow of energy that nests in your pelvic area. This flow holds your passion, your life energy, your ability to create and enjoy. Your emotions are part of this flow which springs up from your belly. Your passion, emotion and sexuality enable you to experience life as a human being.

You are essentially spiritual beings who connect yourselves to human bodies to experience and express yourselves on Earth. Your belly, your emotional center is the connecting point between your soul and Earth, between your spirit and your physical body. Your soul speaks to you through your emotional center. Your soul cannot communicate with you clearly when your emotions are confused, in chaos or shut off. There needs to be peace and balance in your emotional center for you to feel your soul's guidance. If you could see the human female as a collective figure, made up of the experiences of individual women throughout the ages, you would notice that her emotional center has been injured deeply by repeated and aggressive sexual attack.

What happens when you sense ongoing contempt and degradation of yourself as a woman, or even are forced to have sex against your will? Your basic sense of safety is violated, your life force diminishes and you lose touch with your passion and creativity. On the energy level, you lose the connection with your three lower chakras (solar plexus, sacral and root chakra). You withdraw to the higher chakras and lose touch with your body, your emotions and consequently with Earth. This type of withdrawal is prevalent in many women. Many of you are spiritually developed, have an open heart from which you share with others, but you find yourself unable to have a true connections with your own emotions. You often do not take them seriously, especially when they urge you to stand up for yourself and be assertive. When you lack the ability to express who you are with dignity and self-esteem, it is hard to manifest what you truly want and envision as the best life for you. You have become uprooted and alienated from your center of passion and creativity. This frustrates and saddens you, and I ask you, my dear sisters, to have compassion with yourselves and the wound you carry, and to start treating yourself with tender care and respect.

To awaken your compassion, I want point out what happens to a woman when she becomes sexually abused. Keep in mind that this has happened to all of you to a certain degree, whether in this or a previous life. What happens when you are sexually abused is that you lose your emotional and physical anchor. Often, your consciousness leaves your body at the time of the event, in an attempt to make the pain bearable, and when your return you are not there fully anymore. You have become a stranger in your own body. You withdraw from your belly, your emotional center to survive emotionally, but the withdrawal itself causes damage to you. By cutting yourself off from your emotions, you lose touch with your basic sense of vitality and well-being. In the worst case, you die inside; your eyes become dull and your actions mechanical and soulless. There's no passion left – you are merely surviving, no longer able to feel enthusiasm, joy and wonder.

One reason giving birth has been so painful is that women are no longer in touch with their three lower chakras. They have withdrawn from this area, or it has become scarred from painful sexual experiences. Pregnancy is an intensely dynamic event that changes the energy balance in the three lower chakras. This can stir up uncontrollable emotions that are hard to deal with, and also severe physical distress. Not all physical discomfort originates from the changes and processes the body undergoes during pregnancy and delivery;

there is also an energetic (psychic) aspect. If women felt more at home in their pelvic area, if they boldly expressed their dreams and desires and enjoyed their sexuality to the fullest, pregnancy and delivery would be less painful. There would be more trust in the body, which would alleviate much of the fear and tension – thus easing the intensity of the pain.

The male wound

The imbalance between male and female energy did not only affect women, but men as well. The dominance of overly-mental male energy has caused men to lose touch with their own feelings. Due to the prevalent idea of what it means to be a man, it is now difficult for men to be openly emotional and to follow their hearts. Female energy has become suppressed in men, and for many sensitive men this has created self-doubt and feelings of incompetence, fear and alienation. In men, suppression of feelings can also lead to obsession with sex – which women perceive as aggressive and unpleasant. What you are seeing when a man takes the archetypical macho pose, is how his original desire for unification with the opposing female principle has turned into to a plain physical hunger for sex. To operate on this hunger will not satisfy the deeper (spiritual and emotional) needs of the man. Even if he has a lot of sex, he'll be perpetually dissatisfied and develop a love-hate relationship with women. He'll be obsessed by them, which shows emotional dependency, and at the same time act tough and untouchable – as befits a "real" man. The only real solution to this predicament is for the man to get in touch with his own female self, and find access to his own emotions, his true inspiration. This is difficult to achieve, however, in an environment that constantly tells you to suppress this aspect of yourself. Both men and women have suffered from the burden of a one-sided, overdeveloped male energy.

In this context, the phenomenon of homosexuality has been a blessing. It has been one of the channels through which men can embody their female energy in a more pronounced way, and blend it with their male side. Homosexuals have played an important progressive and spiritual role in your society. In their own way, with their originality and artistic skill, they have often challenged and gone beyond fixed (social, moral) boundaries. This requires much courage and self-awareness. Homosexuality often deeply challenges prevalent morality, especially in parts of the world where the assignment of sexual roles is tight and rigid. Homosexuality has triggered a lot of contempt, hate and aggression. The deeper the disharmony between male and female energy in a society, the more difficulty it has in dealing with homosexuals in an open-minded and respectful manner. Gay men or women often embody a blend of male and female energy, which from a spiritual perspective is quite a natural state of being for the soul. In societies that struggle with homosexuality, especially with gay men, the ruling energy is often very controlling and there's a deep-rooted aversion to the flowing, feeling, boundless quality of the female energy. This side of the female energy is regarded as unstable, hysterical and irrational – because it can't be controlled by the mind. In women, this aspect of their nature is managed by reducing their role to that of mother, wife and housewife. But when the feeling nature of women manifests itself in gay men, it challenges all traditional conventions is met with even greater resistance. Blind hatred against homosexuals is directly related to fear of emotions and sensitivity and the need to control them. We honor the gay men and women throughout history, brave individuals who moved beyond rigid notions of male and female in the midst of an extremely dualistic world view.

The origin of the male dominion

Why did male energy once take over? How did the cliché of the emotionally underdeveloped, mentally-fixated male elevate itself to *the ideal* for men? What is at the root of the suppression of feelings and the aversion to female energy?

At some point in time, male energy disconnected itself from the female. There was a desire in the male energy to suppress and control the female. This urge had several causes. In ancient times well beyond your written history, female energy once had the upper hand. Before documented "historical times", there was an era where women played the dominant role.

Role reversal is a typical aspect of duality: what once was black becomes white and vice versa. It is certainly not inherent in the female nature to be weaker or less capable of exercising power than the male. Spiritually, women can be very influential with the third eye, and it's definitely a mistake to regard physical prowess as the main factor in determining who will hold power in society. Women can take charge just as well as men, and they have done that in the past. Memories of these times still live on in the collective male mind, memories of pain and indignation that created the desire for retribution.

Interlude by Pamela: example of a society dominated by women

Jeshua once referred to the occurrence of female dominance in the past – see: "Spirituality and sexuality" (published in "The Jeshua Channelings"). I asked Mary if she could explain how and when female dominance took place on Earth. She advised me to visit a past lifetime of my own that took place in a maternalistic society. I did, and I'm adding the account of it to this chapter because it sheds some light on a time when men were dominated by women.

I see myself being born to a mother who receives me with disgust. She is tired during and after her pregnancy and she didn't really want me. The pregnancy was mandatory – she was forced to produce children for the community by a female elite that doesn't bear children. There are three classes in this society: the female elite, the cast of childbearing women, and the cast of men who work as slaves. The childbearing women are as equally enslaved as the men, but they are told they carry out a most honorable task, and they are treated well physically – except for the incessant pressure to get pregnant and produce children.

Growing up, I feel resentment towards my mother. I feel nauseated in her presence. The abuse of her body has severely affected my mother's psychological well-being. More often than not she's listless, unhappy and showing dislike towards me – I am an unwanted child. From early on I know I don't want to be like her. I don't want the future role of mindlessly producing children. I clearly sense the humiliation of it and soon decide to try and escape my fate by climbing the social ladder. There is no father in my life. Fertilization is achieved via artificial insemination of the assigned "child bearer" with sperm that is extracted from a select group of men. There is no sex involved and men have no part in parenting. They are forced to ejaculate without any sensation of passion and pleasure. I see images of a man who's hooked up to some type of machine that stimulates his genitals, causing him to ejaculate whilst experiencing pain in the rest of his body. This is a form of rape. I suddenly understand that repeatedly undergoing such an experience eventually (in later incarnations) leads to perverted behavior (finding pleasure in sexual cruelty).

185

As I grow up in this society, I succeed in advancing to the higher female elite, the women that don't produce children. This social class consists of very calculating so-called priestesses. They hold the governmental and spiritual power. Girls can join the elite if they demonstrate enough discernment, intelligence and mental power during their upbringing and scholastic years. When I join, I find myself in an ambivalent state of mind. I joined the elite to avoid becoming a child producer, but I am not really interested in the power the elite holds. I don't crave for power, I even dislike the abuse taking place. Yet I have to demonstrate unconditional commitment and ambition in order not to betray my ambivalence. My main motivator is actually fear. At some point, my ambivalence intensifies when I meet a man who belongs to the working class – the group of people involved with agriculture and the processing of goods, mostly tasks that demand physical labor. This man has something that attracts me. I fall in love with him, but I'm prohibited from getting involved romantically. Elite women do have sex, but only behind closed doors and without letting feelings of attachment and intimacy get in the way. I do however have feelings for this man, and he does for me. I'm unable to control my emotions and at some point give away the secret of my relationship. I am condemned by the elite and executed.

I'm under the impression that this life took place somewhere during the Atlantean era. When I look at the karmic background of this type of society (why were the ruling priestesses the way they were?), I see images of an even older era. I see how the priestesses were part of a secluded spiritual community in a previous life, a group that had withdrawn from the world. This community was sharply focused on the sublimation of material reality, and had reached a considerable level of asceticism. It seems to me they existed only partially in the three-dimensional world, with the rest of their being steeped in a more ethereal world. At some point during a secular crisis, they were called upon for spiritual guidance. They refused to help. I feel they should have shown compassion and engaged with the world. But they refused, fearing that such an engagement would curtail their spiritual progress. I see then how the spiritual commune comes to a violent end because of the crisis in the nearby community: they are attacked and exiled by foreigners who take control of the entire region. The women of the commune receive rough treatment but are not raped. They have a certain psychic power that scares men – having sex with these women would put a man under their spell. Their biggest shock is the sudden re-immersion in three-dimensional reality. Their consciousness is no longer aligned with their physical body, and they can't deal very well with the emotions that come up with their rough treatment. Consequently, many of them die with a torn emotional body in which they have adopted the vibrations of their (male) intruders, creating a thirst for vengeance towards, and global dominance over, males.

This is only a partial account of an elaborate history. I don't claim to have clarified exactly how and when women came to power on Earth. I do however hope that this fragment shows that it is very possible that women were in charge in certain societies. Women don't seize power by physical force but through psychic persuasion and manipulation. Psychic power can be so strong that men don't even think of questioning and overthrowing the authorities by physical means. In more ancient societies especially, where spiritual and psychic forces were regarded as very real, female energy could easily dominate because of its natural affiliation with those phenomena. With all this in mind it's somewhat easier to understand how in later times the collective male soul could harbor so much resentment and hatred towards women.

End of interlude. Now I let Mary speak again.

The path to self healing

Now is the time for healing. This is the time to come to terms with the rift in balance between male and female energy. Female energy is currently awakening on the heart level. Even though pain and suffering have instilled fear and anger in the emotional center of many women, there is currently a powerful spiritual impulse in the collective female soul.

I would like to offer some pointers to help you in your personal lives, so you can surmount the old pain and frustration, and live with passion and creativity again.

- Make a stand for yourself and be assertive

Ask yourself if you dare to live from your passion, or if you still bend too much to the will and expectations of others. How much space do you allow yourself to pursue your dreams? Do you frequently do what you like? Get in touch with your belly, let your breath gently touch the energy center behind your belly button and connect with the child within. Inside of you lives a child who would love to play and enjoy life unburdened by fear and worry. Can you sense the presence of that child? What does she or he need from you? Can you give it to her or him?

- Beware of self-suppressing thoughts that present themselves as noble and spiritual

Many of you have been told that "it's better to give than to receive" and that it's spiritual to suppress your needs to the advantage of others. Moreover, for centuries women have been raised with the firm directive to serve men and please them with their physical beauty. How does such a message affect the female spirit? It creates a taboo against "doing what you like" and also against "perceiving your body as a source of pleasure" instead of as an object to be judged by others. Despite emancipation, many women still feel bad about being self-aware and independent. They hesitate to embrace their own male energy, to be assertive about their own wishes and desires, to enjoy their bodies as something that pleases *them* instead of others.

If you notice that you deny yourself what your truly want because you think it would be bad or selfish, think again and ask yourself if you're being held back by old moral conventions that don't serve you as a spiritual being. Spirituality is not about rules that suppress your passion. What these times really need is for women to have the courage to firmly engage with their male energy, to integrate it so they become focused and self-centered enough to realize their dreams and desires. Healing comes with strong, independent women who integrate the energy of the heart with a foundation of self-trust in their belly. Well-balanced, tender and strong women attract well-balanced, strong and tender men. What a beautiful example this offers for the new generations of children to come.

- Have compassion with and patience for yourself

To heal the female wound, caused by the history of sexual abuse, it is necessary to proceed with patience, empathy and tenderness. If you notice that it is hard to overcome your fear of self expression or your fear of standing up for yourself, don't judge yourself. Treat yourself with compassion. Your fear may seem irrational at times, but it has real origins – often going back to past lives. The same goes for being overly controlling of your emotions, or feeling resistance towards intimacy. Don't judge or force yourself. Part of your soul is still in shock. Part of you has been traumatized.

Trauma is an unprocessed emotion that has become stuck in the body and psyche. It expresses itself through destructive thoughts or habits. The first step towards healing it is recognizing that the destructive patterns inside you are a reaction to a very deep wound. Seeing it this way, it becomes easier to forgive yourself – and this the key. Acceptance and forgiveness are major aspects in solving old trauma. By loving and accepting yourself *as you are right now*, you are really opening up to change. By judging yourself or *forcing* yourself to let go of destructive patterns, you only give yourself the message that these patterns are bad, but you don't reach out to the wounded, traumatized part of yourself. Understanding and compassion give you the balance, courage and trust that is needed to release the old pain – not all at once, but step by step. Have patience with yourself. Patience is a form of love.

Whole women

Finally, I, Mary, want to speak a bit about the way I have been portrayed as a woman in the Christian tradition. The prevailing image, invented and maintained by the Church, is one of me as a "holy virgin". In most images you see me smiling meekly, in quiet resignation, far removed from the world's turmoil.

There have indeed been times in my life when I attained deep inner peace, but those couldn't have come about without me having intimate knowledge of the contrary. I was a down-to-earth woman full of passion and emotion, just like you. I was in no way perfect or holy. I had a strong sense of justice, but I also was impatient and stubborn. On Earth, I've lived through the entire spectrum of emotions from fear and despair to love and ecstasy. The most difficult 0was my inner conflict when Jeshua was crucified. I was almost entirely taken over by rebellion, grief and anger. Finally, I was able surrender to Jeshua's will; I realized he had chosen his own path and it therefore had a meaning that I couldn't comprehend with my maternal instincts. I let go after a long, intense inner battle. After his passing I repeatedly sensed Jeshua presence, while I was still on Earth, and it became clear to me that he was so much more than my son. Slowly I resigned and at a later age I surrendered to a most wondrous light which came to me and eased my pain. This light lifted me to the awareness that we remain connected to our loved ones beyond the threshold of death.

I ask you to accept me as I was: a woman of flesh and blood, your sister in all regards. Don't make a saint out of me; give me back my humanity and my sexuality. That way I can stand next to you, and the natural link between passion and spirituality is restored. Passion and spirituality are an extension of each other, but in the Christian tradition they have been portrayed as opposites. It was regarded as selfish and impure to live according to your passion, to pursue your natural desire for wholeness and self-realization. Mankind was regarded as inherently sinful, and spirituality was a way to save you from your own human nature.

In the Christian tradition I have been represented as the icon of purity and innocence. There was another woman very close to Jeshua who was depicted as embodying the other extreme: passion, sexuality, *sin*. That woman was Mary Magdalene. While I was reduced to a holy virgin, she became branded as a prostitute. Can you see how Church tradition struggled with female sexuality? It was either Madonna or whore, with nothing in between. No room for inspired passion, building the bridge between human and divine, between belly and heart.

For a long time Maria Magdalena represented the forbidden side of the female energy: independence, spiritual power and female passion. I on the other hand was made harmless by taking away my sexuality and passion. In fact, we were both whole women, just like you are today. We encourage you to be independent and free, to trust your belly and your passion as well as your heart and your spirit. Be a whole woman and take pride in both your humanness and your divine nature. Take good care of yourself. You are beautiful. Feel free to fully express your divine nature through your blessed female body.

19 - Fear as doorway to the unknown

I am Mary, mother of Jeshua. I am here to reach out to you and bring to you the female aspect of the Christ energy. It is direly needed for most of you right now. You are going through a deep process of transformation.

There's a large group of lightworkers on Earth right now and they have partly awakened, partly remembered who they are. In fact one can distinguish between three groups of lightworkers, or three stages in which they may find themselves in this transformation process.

The first group of lightworkers has not awakened yet. They do not yet realize who they are and they feel very lost and lonely because of that. They feel different, yes, they feel like they're not fitting into human society. They feel alone and alienated from mainstream society. These people are suffering. They think they are failing. Often they are highly sensitive. They are dreamers, like all of you: dreaming of another world, even remembering it, from the depth of their soul, but unable to connect the dream with everyday reality. So they withdraw and live in their inner world. Because their light does not radiate outward, they feel unhappy and even suffocated.

Then there's another group of lightworkers, who are starting to remember who they are. Slowly they remember their true strength, the fact that they are really angels, who have incarnated into a human body to bring light on Earth. This light is so much needed right now. As soon as you realize that you are an eternal soul, not bound to the material realm, you gain in strength. You may still feel different, an outsider, but now you feel connected to another world, a world of beauty and harmony. This is your home, the world you truly come from. If you know that, you need not any longer feel alone. Today we wish to remind you of the energy of home.

The ones I am speaking to in this channeling, the people who will hear this channeling, are part of the group of lightworkers who have awakened, who already have connected to their true self, their soul. They know they are here for a reason, they know they're here to make a difference on Earth. We bless you for this intention, this yearning to bring light on Earth and we know how difficult it is to be true to your self in the midst of a reality that seems hostile to the kind of energy you bring in.

There is yet another group of lightworkers, a third group. We may call them the "senior lightworkers". These are the ones who have been in the process of awakening for a long time. They have been working on themselves for years, some even decades, and they have gone through many different stages of inner transformation. They know what it is like to change on the inner level, to become aware of deep-seated emotional burdens and negative beliefs. They have experienced what it is like to release one's old identity and open up to a new one, closer to their true nature. Many of you hearing or reading this message are part of this third group of lightworkers. You feel very old inside. You have gone through a lot, both in this lifetime and in many previous ones. In our eyes, you are revered for your courage and depth of wisdom. You are the treasures of the Earth, even if you feel old and weary. It is you in particular to whom we are speaking.

You have in your life processed a lot on the emotional level. You have allowed fear and other difficult emotions to come to the surface of your consciousness, to be looked into the eye and thereby to be released. You have had spiritual experiences along your path, sensations of bliss in which you were melded into oneness with All-That-Is. Many of you have already started your life's work of being a teacher and healer for others on their spiritual path. You are in your everyday life practicing the light work that you intended to do as a soul.

I am addressing you who are in this third group of lightworkers today, and I am also addressing you who are in the second group. There is not a fixed line between the two groups; there's a gradual development from one to the other. There's no point in pondering too long which group you are a part of; we're not administering grades here. The most important thing is to recognize yourself as one who is committed heart and soul to this process of inner growth. I mean to explain to all of you why this process of awakening can seem so difficult at times.

You see, spiritual growth or evolution does not proceed along a linear way. It's not like there's a stairway that you climb step by step. Growth and evolution occur in cycles. Take for instance the cycle of day and night. During the night you submerge into your subconscious. The relative darkness of the subconscious presents itself as dreams which take you out of the ordinary, out of what is known to you. It thereby enables you to go deep within, and to discover feelings and emotions inside that do not easily show themselves during waking hours. During the daytime, you are gathering experiences as you are participating in Earth reality. The night draws you within and helps you face emotional energies you weren't aware of during the day.

The cycle of day and night enables you to integrate experiences on a deeper level than the mind. There is growth occurring because of this alternation, even if you don't remember your dreams. This growth occurs in ever repeating cycles, and it is the same with spiritual growth. You to whom I speak know what it is to go within, to address old emotional pain and fear and to let go of it. You know what it is like to be submerged in old pain and feel the joy of releasing it, feeling more free and powerful afterwards. You to whom I speak are advanced; you have progressed far, but still, even then, after daytime nighttime comes. New layers of un-consciousness want to be seen, addressed and released. At this time, many of you are in the midst of a "dark night" that summons to the surface a very deep layer of fear that wants to be seen in daylight. It wants to be released in order for you to shine your light upon the world even more brightly and peacefully.

In your life, you are influenced by your own personal cycles of development, depending on your age, gender and soul agreements. You are however also influenced by broader energy currents, which have to do with processes that the Earth, and humanity, as a whole are involved in. There are energy currents at work in this time, which propel old and dark energies to the surface in a pace that may seem relentless if you do not trust the process. Humanity as a whole is not prepared for the release of the old energy that now comes to the surface. The majority of people do not know how to handle deep emotional pain and the destructive energy that may result from it. You are adept at this. Still, it may overwhelm you as well. You may feel submerged into layers of yourself which seem utterly unmanageable and alien to you. You may seem to go crazy. Perhaps you thought you had already dealt with the majority of issues that were on your plate in this life, and now another layer of fear or darkness is banging on your door, one you did not expect. You may feel indignant about it, feel that you have processed enough and are ready to move on to a lighter life. This new pit of darkness may seem too hard to deal with.

I am here today to tell you not to lose heart and to keep faith in your journey. You are now entering a stage of your development in which you can no longer control your growth. The area of consciousness expansion that you are entering is about surrendering and letting go. It's not about doing certain exercises or visualizations, following a certain diet, or pursuing any discipline through which you seek to control life. It is impossible to control the huge wave of energy that now wants to flow through your being.

Your soul wants to lift you up to this flow of energy because it is aware that it is a good flow. However, your human personality is not able to see where it is leading up to. The human mind cannot understand where the flow of the soul is heading towards, so therefore you may feel desperate and out of tune with your intuition, your passion and general sense of direction. If this is how you feel, please know that you're not doing anything wrong. This sense of disorientation and chaos is always there when you are about to make a new start. Truly new beginnings are always preceded by a period of chaos and crisis. The new cannot enter before the old falls apart. You thought you had already let go of so much, and now you have to let go of even more. Please be aware this is a meaningful process even if it doesn't seem so. Try to remain in a space of trust and surrender, because that way you align yourself with the flow of your soul and you make the ride a bit easier for yourself.

You are the teachers. You bring in the new energy on Earth right now, even if you feel you are in the dark, even if you feel down, depressed and don't have a clue where you are going. You are doing the light work that you came for. Light work often means that you travel into the night, into the darkest corners of your soul, not knowing what will happen. You travel through the dark without guidelines or a map to steer by. You are thrown into the darkness and all you can really do is surrender to the experience and trust that you will get through it and that it will have meaning.

As soon as you come out of the darkness and back into daylight again, you will understand the meaning of your journey, not simply with your mind but with your heart. Always, the dark holds a treasure for you. Dark emotions are hidden parts of you that want to reunite with you. The negativity you encounter in yourself is a part of your energy that got stuck, that could not move for a long time. Please understand that as a soul you have had many, many lifetimes, on Earth as well as in other places in the universe. Now that your cycle of lifetimes on Earth is nearing its completion, the most anguished parts of your soul, which got stuck in very different lifetimes, come to you in the present era for release and liberation. Often you do not understand where all the emotional trauma comes from. But in the end it's always about the same thing. It is about fear wanting to be addressed by you. The fear wants to be looked into the eye and it wants to be welcomed. It is a part of you and a valid part indeed. Fear is part of the duality game you are playing in this corner of the universe.

If you could just let it be, if you would not fear your own fear, you would see that it is harmless. That may seem a strange thing to say, because fear can so deeply uproot you. But fear is harmless. It is innocent like a child. Fear is simply a response to the unknown. If a child faces something it doesn't know yet, it often reacts with fear: it has to get used to the new. It has to explore it, get comfortable with it and learn to trust it. Fear is innocent really; it's quite understandable to not feel at home directly with what you do not yet know. There's nothing wrong with fear. However, if you place judgment on it, if you feel uncomfortable with fear and reject it, then it becomes this large dark thing, a demon that terrorizes and paralyses you against your will. Don't make fear your enemy, because then you make it into a dark and alien power. Fear in itself is not dark; it is simply the emotional response of feeling unsettled by something different and new.

Dear friend, you are wise. From your deepest core, where you are Spirit, where you are shining light, eternal and lovely, reach out to the fear that is inside of you. You are much larger and stronger than your fear. You can reach out to it, like you would with a child, and tell it that it is safe with you, that you do not fear it, that you do not fear your own fear. Do not try to get rid of it, because the intention to eliminate fear holds judgment in it. The fearful part of you will get more fearful if you take up battle with it, for then it gets the message that it is no good and that it is unworthy.

Please understand that fear is a necessary element in the universe. Otherwise it would not be possible to explore and experience something new. Fear marks the boundary between what feels safe and familiar to you and what doesn't. Beyond that frontier there is something new which you do not yet understand or have not yet experienced. If you could look at fear in that way, you would release your judgment about it and it would even hold the potential of joy, because fear promises you a new land to discover, a new place for your light to shine on. So trust fear, let it be your light! If there's a situation in your life that gives rise to fear, just notice it. Shine the light of your consciousness on your fear. The fear will not dissolve immediately, but if you do not look upon it as a frightening energy, you will relax more and thereby open yourself to the possibility that there's a hidden treasure inside the fear.

You know, fear will always be there, it is part of creation. Even if you are highly evolved, there is always an element of the unknown that wants to be explored. If this would not be so, the universe would stagnate and lose its vitality and aliveness. It would be like living in a beautiful, lovely country that you truly enjoy and resonate with, however it is not possible to go outside of it, to go beyond its boundaries. You would never be able to explore new land. Would this give you the deepest fulfillment in the long run? Now, I know you know yourselves well enough to realize that you love to explore the new. You are adventurous spirits, all of you. Therefore, please don't condemn your fear, for ultimately it is part of the adventurous, exploring part of you. Fear shows you where there's new land to discover. Once you travel this new land, holding the hand of fear, you will experience beauty and joy that exceed your present comprehension. The secret is: you can never know beforehand what you will discover; otherwise it wouldn't be new to you.

So the delightful experience of venturing into the new, having new and ever deeper experiences of love, beauty and joy, can only occur if you accept the reality of fear, which is nothing else than the reality of the unknown, that which lies beyond the horizon of your current knowledge and experience. Welcome the fear inside, even if it seems irrational and you don't know the cause. Much fear inside you comes from very ancient parts of you, other lifetimes which are far behind in time. Even they hold the promise of a new understanding, something you did not yet discover. Perhaps there's an experience there of being violently rejected which you are afraid of and don't want to feel. However, if you would not fear the experience, if you would allow yourself to feel what it is like to be violently rejected and let the emotion come to the surface, you would feel compassion with yourself and you would understand why certain things are difficult for you now. You would forgive yourself for it and not judge yourself so harshly anymore. The experience of self-forgiveness is an enlightening one. So, if you allow yourself to embrace an experience that seems awful on the outside, if you go through it with trust and no judgment, then this experience might become an enlightening one, even a joyful one. It might enable you to taste the liberation and relaxation that go with self-acceptance. This is how flexible the universe is, how flexible experience is.

If you are experiencing fear in your life, know that right on the other side of it is so much potential for experiencing love, beauty and joy. It is not far away. As I mentioned, spiritual growth is not a linear process, in which you release a little bit of fear in every step. Rather, the fear builds and builds and then reaches a climax, which probably turns your life into crisis, and you feel unable to deal with everyday life anymore. At that point, you are being confronted with your fear head-on; you can no longer suppress it or get around it. It is flowing through you and you are losing control. It seems that at this point, you are defeated. The dam breaks and you cannot keep the water out. This may seem disastrous, but it is not!

The fear wants to break open gates that have closed you down, that have imprisoned you. The fear wants to flow through you, and if you flow with it, it will bring you to another reality, much more liberating than the one you're living in right now. So if you feel that your fear is uncontrollable, if you can make no sense of it, this is not as bad as it seems. You are right on the threshold of the new and you are very close to a breakthrough.

Let it be, let the fear be, don't struggle. Don't think: "what have I done wrong? Has everything I have done on my spiritual path been in vain? Why do I feel completely lost, was I mistaken?" This is mind chatter. This is the mind trying to make sense of something that cannot be grasped by the mind. Your soul knows what it is doing. It wants you to release pain on a deep level and this will happen if you trust and do not try to control it. The more you align with your soul, the less you can have control over life, and you know what? This is so liberating! Letting go brings in the new, brings in the beautiful and refined energy of the unrepressed You. Fear is the gateway to a higher version of you, wanting to incarnate on present day Earth.

I am asking you to have respect for your own inner process, even if it seems to lead you into darkness, even if all logic to it seems to have vanished. Always keep open the possibility that you are not able to understand it from your present state of mind, that you need not understand it, and that the meaning of it will be revealed later. Open up to the larger reality of your soul, be the explorer of consciousness that you truly are and that you want to be!

We bless you for embracing the adventure of being on Earth at this time of change and upheaval. You are courageous; you are in love with life, even if you feel depressed and lonely. If you did not have that love for life, you would not be here, right now.

We are close to you. I represent the mother energy of Christ consciousness. Feel yourself enveloped by it. Perhaps you see it as a soft shining pink, a playful, yet very tender energy, gentle and soft. Allow it into your energy space, it can bring you healing. And by healing I do not mean "taking away your fear", I mean accepting it, accepting it as the doorway to another reality, a more loving and light reality.

Be yourself, simply be yourself. Do not try to change yourself. You are already perfect. You are lovely. We see you, and recognize your struggle. We have much respect and honor for you. Please allow my energy to comfort you. I do not want to change anything inside of you. I just want you to look at yourself in a different way. Even in the midst of your struggle you are an angel. You are beautiful.

Remember: after every night, a new day will come. The sun will shine again. It is inevitable. It is life resuming its natural course. Just like you cannot prevent the night from falling, you cannot prevent the day from coming. So, allow yourself to go through that motion and you will find yourself in a splendid new dawn.

By undertaking this journey within, you are helping many people on Earth, who are trying to find their inner road to freedom. You are paving the way for other lightworkers, who are in the beginning stages of their awakening, and they in turn will help people who are becoming more sensitive, wanting to open up to the reality of their soul.

We thank you for your work, your light work on Earth right now. You are never alone. We are joining you from the other side, please accept our love. It is our greatest joy to remember you of who you are.

20 - The angel and the adventurer

I am Mary, mother of Jeshua. I speak to you with an open heart and I would like to tell you how beautiful you are. You are a channel between heaven and Earth, building bridges between the two realms through your humanness.

At this time there is an opening on Earth towards more light, love and awareness. These qualities are awakening in people's hearts more and more. A global change is occurring. Many people, however, become confused when they open their hearts for the first time. Opening your heart doesn't immediately lead to bliss, love and freedom. More often there is an initial phase of confusion and upset because what you previously took for granted in your life is now leaving you. When your heart chakra opens you develop a high sensitivity which changes everything.

You actually get a glimpse of the unified consciousness of which each of you is a part. You are all kin and on a deeper level you are all one. When your heart opens (which is a natural phenomenon in the evolution of consciousness) you start feeling more than just that which is your own. Your energy merges more easily with the energy of others. Your empathy grows. This is a sign of inner growth and development. You are once more remembering: that we are all one, that we are all connected. This is also the point in your soul's development when your inner angel, the angel you once were, awakens.

At one time, you emerged from the source (God) as a vibrant being of light. You were *you* for the first time. You were an angel, so close to God you could still feel God's hand in yours. You kept holding that hand, even though you knew you would be letting go of it soon; you knew you were leaving on a journey. Because there was another part of you that was looking for experience. I call this part your adventurer. You are an angel at the core of your being, but you also have within you another divine entity: the adventurer. This is the part that thirsts for experience, the part that wants to take on new forms, that desires to incarnate in matter.

Today I will tell you the story of the angel and the adventurer. The angel in you represents your female energy, whilst the adventurer represents the male energy. These are two aspects of creation that play a fundamental role in the whole of the cosmos. Female energy in its highest form is the energy of the source, of Home. You can sense it in your heart, but it is ethereal and subtle so it is easy to overlook. The angelic energy in people's hearts is currently awakening on Earth. After the female energy was repressed, hurt and wounded for a long time, it is now being reborn. The collective feminine energy is going through a process of healing and transformation and this will change the overall awareness of people, both en and women. This change cannot be effected however without the rebirth of the other aspect of creation: the adventurer, the male energy inside people.

The male aspect of your soul is about manifestation, focus and boundaries, thus enabling you to experience what it is like to have an individual self. The adventurer in you separates himself from the whole and sets out to explore new territory, experiencing what it is like to be different rather than one, even to engage in confrontation at times. The male energy is taking you out of paradise, so to speak, meaning the initial state of unified consciousness you were in. The adventurer senses there are creative and fulfilling experiences beyond what is known to you. His desire to travel away from Home is a vital part of God's creation.

Get in touch for a moment with your deep-rooted sense of adventure, the part of you that loves to travel to unknown land and to explore new experiences. Feel the pulse, the urge and the creativity. This part of your soul has pushed you forward, has caused you to let go of God's hand and leave paradise. What does the angel in you think of it? At one time, she consented to go with him. You might say she was tempted by the adventurer's charm. Their tale of seduction was less about sin than about romance; a fairytale you both engaged in.

Imagine you were an angel once; see yourself as a beautiful female figure. Next to you is a man who is inviting you for a journey. You are about to leave Home and engage in the dance with matter, with separation and duality. You found it exciting and scary at the same time. The adventurer said: "Let's go, I'm up for it, I'll stay with you and protect you." You then dared to jump into the abyss, and your voyage started. Together both of you have lived through numerous adventures. Not all joyful ones; you've also known deprivation and profound alienation. The world you live in now, the earthly dimension, has known much pain and suffering.

One cause of the suffering was the separation that took place between the adventurer and the angel within you. They turned against each other at various points in your history and in the more recent stage, the male energy took a destructive turn, wanting to experience itself as the center of all creation. Male energy has explored the limits of aggression, control, subordination and dominance. The abuse of the female energy has caused the angel within to withdraw from the world until it was no more than a shadow of itself. The female energy could not die, because it is an essential part of creation. But it could become severely disempowered, and that's what has happened throughout your times. You all carry this history in your hearts. You *are* this history. You carry the male as well as the female aspect within you.

The transformation of the male energy: from adventurer to knight

The time has now arrived for the angel and the adventurer to come together and reunite. One of the first signs that this is happening is the revival of angel energy on Earth in the form of kindness and empathy. People are more connected now than ever. Their hearts are opening. Sense the soft, angelic energy in your own heart. You are the ones who are now channeling the higher feminine qualities of empathy and connectedness to Earth. This is part of what your soul wanted to do her right now. However, as your heart opens, your worldly personality may experiences this as a burden at times, because it increases your sensitivity. The easier you pick up on and connect with energies around you, the easier your heart and emotions become overwhelmed with the suffering you sense. The negative thoughts and emotions of other people can cause you to get imbalanced and feel very vulnerable. It may make you wonder: "How do I handle this heightened sensitivity, and prevent it from bringing me down?" At the same time, you cannot shut down your heart and it is not does feel right to do so. So you feel open and sensitive and at the same time you struggle with the question how to find your way in a world that is in many parts not yet aligned with the energy of the heart.

The world is awakening however. What is really needed on Earth is not just the return of the feminine energy, but the transformation of the male energy as well. It is only in their joyful interplay, that the feminine energy can truly blossom on Earth. Recall the image of the adventurer. Think about his gusto, courage and focus. It's in his nature to be self-aware – to be aware of what distinguishes you and me, what separates you from me. He is the one helping you become aware of your uniqueness, your individuality. This is a vital aspect of creation! It is only when you have a good sense of your own boundaries, that you can connect deeply with someone else. Blurry boundaries lead to self-loss instead of love. To experience real love, you have to be able to use your male energy as effectively as your female part. Without the male energy, you could not have entered the adventure of incarnation to begin with. To be born as a soul requires male energy. You are separating yourself from the whole when you become an individual. The adventure of creation and the evolution of your soul are dependent on the interplay of male and female energy.

The male energy is valuable and part of your original nature. However, because of your history, the male energy has become associated with aggression and dominance. Many sensitive people, especially highly sensitive women, regard the male energy as inherently aggressive and this blocks them from properly using their own male energy. Many of you have become alienated from the male energy to such an extent, that you are now suffering from an overflow of feminine energy which imbalances you. Your awakening sensitivity would greatly benefit from the male qualities of self-awareness and groundedness. The angel inside you is in need of protection. Not the protection of an aggressor but that of a knight. The true face of the mature adventurer is the face of a knight, who stands beside the angel inside, supporting and guarding her.

The knight's mission is to enable the angelic energy to manifest itself safely and freely into the world. The knight enables the flower of the heart energy to blossom by *the sword of discernment*. The knight makes you aware of the balance between giving and receiving. He lets you know when you are taking in too many outside energies and risk losing your center, your balance. Through physical and emotional sensations he signals you when you commit yourself to others in ways that deprives you of your energy. Your inner knight is continuously giving you signals. When you learn to trust him again, you will see that heightened sensitivity doesn't necessarily mean weakness and exhaustion. The knight within you creates a buffer between you and the world. Not a buffer of resistance and aggression, but one of awareness.

I invite you to feel the interplay of angel and knight inside of you. Focus on your heart. In the middle of your chest lies the center of your heart chakra. Imagine a pretty lotus flower floating on water there. The water is very quiet and you see the flower slowly opening itself up. Ethereal energies in all manner of soft shades swarm around the flower and remind you of who you are: a lovely angel holding God's hand. You are directly connected to the source of all life. Feel this angelic energy flow through your body, through your belly, tailbone and legs. Feel its subtle qualities, its refined beauty, and welcome it inside you. This angelic part of you contains the qualities of intuition and compassion; it is the feminine energy in its highest form. Allow it to flow through your entire being. Remember your origin.

Now feel the male energy inside yourself as well. Let the adventurer take the shape of a knight who radiates awareness and determination. Take a closer look at this knight and feel how he wants to serve the angel within you. The knight is in a state of admiration and tenderness for her. He is in love with her. Now see if you can allow both of them to interact. Perhaps they want look each other in the eye or touch hands. Watch what happens. Ask the knight what he needs to be able to help the angel. Ask the angel what she needs from the knight.

When you fall prey to the imbalance caused by too great a sensitivity, you sometimes end up cursing life on Earth and thinking: "Why am I here, I don't belong here, I don't feel at home." What began as a delicate and precious opening of the heart, ends in a sense of depletion and alienation. This you can prevent by holding hands with the knight inside you. When you make peace with the male energy, with your inner knight, you hold the key to a renewed engagement with the world. Your knight is able to cope with circumstances here. He is the adventurous part of you, ready to explore the new. He *wants* to be here, and as he is maturing, he will help the angel shine her light in a balanced and safe way. He is the key to keep yourself grounded and centered, especially for highly sensitive people.

High sensitivity and the pitfall of giving too much

High sensitivity means that you feel and observe a lot about what is going on around you. You are aware of the floating energies, thoughts, moods around you even if you cannot put words to it. You feel them as if they were your own. Sensitivity in itself would not be a problem if the feelings and energies of others flow right through you. You would be aware of them and yet be transparent to them at the same time. High sensitivity becomes a problem when you *hold on* to the energies you perceive. Then they become a burden to you. This often happens unconsciously. You are not aware that you are carrying other people's moods and thoughts around in your energy field.

The problem, strictly speaking, is not your sensitivity, but the – often unconscious – tendency to take in other people's energies and regard them as your own. You often do not distinguish between their energy and yours. The problem is that you are not aware of what is happening as you take in other people's energy. You need the male quality of discernment to distance yourself from energy that is not your own. This is difficult for many of you. Often, what happens is that you swallow negative energy of people around you and you start reaching out to them. Often, you dive right into it, wanting to alleviate the other person's pain, wanting to save them. At this point, you are becoming imbalanced. You are giving your energy away, and you don't realize that what you are doing may not be beneficial to either of you. By empathising and sympathising too much, you lower your own energetic vibration: rather than resolving and elevating these negative energies, you start vibrating to their pulse.

There is a big difference between *sensing* energy and *holding on* to energy. *Holding on* is what causes trouble for you. Why does this happen so easily? Why do you absorb someone else's negative moods so easily, and why is it so difficult to stay centered and grounded around the suffering you perceive. It is part of the global awakening of the heart center in this time that people care more for each other and start feeling their underlying oneness. This is a beautiful and natural occurring. However, becoming depleted due to your high sensitivity has another reason, which goes back to your childhood. Most of you were born as sensitive children who were ahead of your parents in the sense that your hearts were already more open than theirs when you were born. You could easily feel the emotional pain of others, but you were not taught how to handle this. One way for you to try to deal with the pain you sensed in others was *by becoming their knight*. Instead of becoming your own knight, you became theirs. You devoted yourself to them, taking on their burdens, often unaware of what you were doing. By suffering along with your dad, your mom, or your family, you seemed to lighten part of the load. This was often the only way for you to connect emotionally with your environment. In order to make a connection and resolve the chaos, you had to lower your energetic vibration.

This is when, in many of you, it became a habit to give too much of yourself to others. As a grown up, you naturally sense other people's pain and sorrow, and you offer yourself as their problem solver. This has often become your only way of connecting deeply with people. Silently, you hope to receive their love and recognition in return. During your childhood this way of relating to others became your emotional survival mechanism; the alternative was isolation and despair. As an adult, however, it creates imbalanced relationships that make you unhappy in the end. By making your energy available in such a way, you repress your own wishes and desires. Sensitivity becomes the equivalent of self-deprivation and exhaustion. This is how the angel energy so purely present in the child becomes a burden as you grow up. Some of you now wish you could turn off your heightened sensitivity and empathy, because it robs you of your life energy.

Sensitivity is not however the problem; it is the habit of giving too much that is blocking you. There is a way of using your sensitivity so that it serves you rather than disempowers you. You are used to employing this gift for others; now you have to learn to employ it for yourself. You have to take ownership of your inner knight and connect him with your inner angel. Your knight is meant to protect her and create firm boundaries around you if necessary. Look at beliefs that are blocking your from focusing on *your* needs and desires. These may be beliefs such as "I have to be there for others; I can't let them down; it's not spiritual to put myself first." Or: "I have to be nice and accommodating to be loved and accepted". Beliefs such as these are to be re-evaluated. Is it really un-spiritual to remain balanced and calm around negativity and suffering? Will other people reject you if you dare to stand up for yourself and tell them what you need and desire? Really, it is not your high sensitivity that is the problem, but the outdated, false beliefs that you clung to as a child in order to survive emotionally.

You can practice this for yourself in the following way. Think of a person who means a lot to you. We are going to look at the energy exchange between the two of you. Imagine standing in front of him or her with a red rose in your hands. The rose is pretty and in full bloom. It represents your vitality, your life force and passion. Hold this rose in front of your solar plexus, near your stomach. Now imagine you give the other your rose. You share your passion, your energy, your being with them. See if they accept your gift and look at how they treat it. What happens with the rose as the other person receives it?

If the exchange is uplifting and energizing, you will notice that the other person receives the rose with excitement and gratitude. Notice how their reaction also uplifts you. See what they are giving to you in return. Imagine you are receiving a flower from them. How does that make you feel? Is it an equal exchange? If you feel that your rose becomes withered in the exchange, it's important to examine if you still want to give it to that person. Notice clearly if there is fear inside you. Are you afraid to lose the other's appreciation if you stop giving? Can you decide to withdraw the rose and stick to your own path? Deciding to stop giving too much is an act of wisdom. Being highly sensitive and living from the heart is not about giving without end. Rather, it is to be open and receptive with the sword of discernment in your hand - angel and knight both fulfilling their roles.

21 - From hypersensitivity to high sensitivity

By Gerrit Gielen

This article by Gerrit is based on his personal experience with high sensitivity and on his extensive work with highly sensitive people as a spiritual counsellor and regression therapist.

Many people are hypersensitive. They cannot stand the noise, aggression and hasty pace of modern society. Often they suffer from psychosomatic disorders and insomnia. What other folks take for granted, for example going to a family party, is quite a chore for them. Simply doing what other people consider normal often turns out a disaster for them.

As a child they are often misunderstood and underappreciated. Because it's hard for them to stand up for themselves and because they easily dream away, school time is tough. Building a career and becoming successful according to society's standards often doesn't work for them. They more or less muddle along at the fringes of society. Participating in mainstream activities is experienced as exhausting and draining. Because of all this, their self image isn't very positive; they often feel insecure and inferior. Their thoughts are gloomy and may repeat themselves endlessly.

Of course, this image is somewhat of a caricature. Yet many people will (partly) recognize themselves in it. Let us now focus on some of the positive traits of hypersensitive people. They appreciate peace and quiet and long to live in harmony with their fellow humans. They are sensitive to beauty, especially the beauty of nature. They are very empathic and open to the spiritual. They have a rich imagination. To their own surprise, people who are in trouble are naturally drawn to them and come to them for guidance.

What is the matter with these people? The answer is that they are not (just) hypersensitive, they are highly sensitive. In fact, they are angels in disguise.

What is high sensitivity?

Every living being emits a certain vibration or aura: flowers, the sun, people, animals, plants, and also human society at large. You are highly sensitive when your vibration, your aura is more refined and delicate than the vibration of human society.

Imagine a radiant, beautiful angel descending from heaven to be born in a human body in a modern metropolis. The angel has a hard time coping with the noise, the chaos and the ugliness of the world around. Where is the serenity and beauty of nature, where are the flowers? Where is the deep inner knowing, the sense of unity with the cosmos? The angel feels shattered and alienated. The world around does not nurture or acknowledge him (or her*). The angel starts to think that there's something wrong with him and he becomes sad and depressed. As he does not feel at home here, he withdraws and vaguely longs for another reality. The people around him consider him to be a dreamer who does not want to face the facts of life. The angel's light diminishes. Whereas he was a high sensitive at first, he has now become a hypersensitive.

You may wonder why this angel incarnated on Earth.

Many angels are incarnate on Earth and every angel has their own motive to be here. There is however one general motive: to help Earth. Through the presence of all of these angels, human society as a whole gains in light and sensitivity. The angelic presence raises the vibration of the world. This happens especially when the angels remember who they are and when their self-confidence is restored. That's when their light will truly shine.

Now imagine that *you* are such an angel.

What can you do to become radiant again, to transform your hypersensitivity into high sensitivity?

Step 1 – Realize that you are an angel

Realize that you are an angel and don't be afraid to show it. Believe in your own light, your creative abilities and overcome your fear to show yourself. This is the first step.

How do you do this? It's important to connect to the spiritual. See the world from a spiritual perspective, remember the timeless realm of love and beauty that you originate from and to which you belong. You have always been in touch with this subtle, ethereal reality. Now take another leap and really believe it to be there. The moment you connect with it, you also get in touch with your own inner core and start to realize who you really are. You remember that your consciousness is eternal and that it is a magnificent source of light and creativity.

The moment you feel a part of this other realm, which is your true home, the judgment that human society places on you becomes much less of a burden to you. You realize that your stay here is only temporary and that this hectic, chaotic society will disappear one day and make place for a more peaceful, harmonious and happy society. What this current society thinks of you and expects from you is not so important anymore. More important is what you are here to do, how you are going to manifest your light in this world.

By sensing your true origin, you kindle your own light. Light is creative and transformative. You will notice that your environment will start to respond to you differently. Life will flow more easily and people will take you more seriously. You have taken a fundamental first step in the transition from hypersensitivity to high sensitivity.

Step 2 – Become aware of your male energy

You are able to truly give your light to others only if you are also able to *not* give it. If you cannot say "no" to people, your "yes" has no meaning. Learning to set boundaries and to stand up for yourself is crucial. If you don't do this, your energy flows into a bottomless pit and you will permanently feel weak and drained.

To prevent this from happening, you need to get in touch with your male energy. Many people who are inclined towards the spiritual, have a negative image of the male energy. It is associated with violence, oppression and aggression and considered to be not spiritual. As a result of this negative attitude towards the male energy, many spiritually inclined and hypersensitive people feel disempowered and unable to stand up for themselves.

The solution is to understand that there's nothing wrong with the male energy per se; it is the *imbalance* between the male and the female which causes the problem. By regarding the male energy to be inferior, many people weaken their own strength. This happens particularly in sensitive women. Especially when you go through a process of spiritual growth, it is of prime importance to connect with your male energy.

As soon as you take step 1 and become more aware of who you really are, you will distinguish yourself energetically from your environment. Your light will be noticed. This will attract to you what I call energy leeches. These are people or other entities, for instance the organization you work in, who will feed themselves with your energy. They deprive you of energy without giving something back to you. If you're not able to protect yourself in such an environment, you get stuck.

At this point, you need to use your male strength. Embrace the male part of you, your inner man, and trust him. Let him take the shape of a sword in your hand which severs the bonds between you and everything that deprives you of energy.

A common pitfall in using the sword of your male energy proficiently is the notion of equality. "We are all equal and therefore I should not distinguish myself from others, and I should share what I have with them." The idea of equality is right to some extent. At the level of the soul we are equal. At the level of manifestation however we are not. Some people are more able to let their inner light shine through than others. By not acknowledging this, we give energy leeches free range. Especially people who radiate much light and who have much to give, should protect themselves. Be aware of who or what you give your energy to. Not everyone is ready to receive what you have to offer. Do not let your most precious gift be dragged down by people or organizations who do not match your vibration. Use your male energy for this purpose.

Step 3 – Realize that mother Earth is your friend

Many hypersensitive people feel resistance towards living on Earth. This resistance is partly due to the fact that they do not feel at home in modern western society. The energy of society does not match their own and they feel alienated by it. They want to leave; they subconsciously remember their spiritual heritage and long to be "home" again. They want to go back to the peace and harmony of the heavenly realms, which contrast so sharply with the noise, fear, aggression and anonymity of present day human society.

Apart from this reason for feeling resistance towards living on Earth, sensitive people also have intuitions about what happened in their past lives on Earth. Often they carry memories within of war, persecution and other forms of aggression. They remember trying to be and do good on Earth and being violently rejected for it.

To overcome your resistance to being here, it's important to distinguish between the energy of human society and the energy of Earth itself. To do so, find a beautiful spot in nature. Go there on a weekday when it's quiet. Feel the energy there, the serenity and peace. Open your heart to this place in nature and feel all the energies present there. Apart from you there are nature spirits such as fairies and leprechauns, who work closely together with Earth. Now feel Earth itself. This is the Earth you came for, the Earth who reaches out to you and who wishes to support you. Open your heart to her energy and love.

By entering into this connection with Earth, you are able to truly take your place and shine your light in this world. You are able to change the world and make it more beautiful. There's a place for you on Earth where you feel at home. This place will become a beacon of light that transforms the world around you.

Hypersensitive people hide for the world. Highly sensitive people radiate their light freely into it.

Step 4 – Use your female energy to become even more sensitive

Your female energy can make the difference between fearing someone and loving someone. It enables you to look behind the mask that someone's putting on and see their vulnerability. In our hearts we are all good. God is in everyone's heart. You can use the female energy within to become even more sensitive, to use your empathy to really understand what it's like to be in the other person's shoes. Understanding the other from within can help you put into perspective their hurtful remarks or offensive behavior. It may help you let go of it.

This becomes possible when the male energy inside is strong enough to protect your female side. When we are hurt by what another person says to us, we are often not hurt by the words themselves, but by our own oversensitive interpretation of those words. Often people are not out to get us, it's more that they blurt out something which isn't aimed at you personally. Your male energy can help you to not take things personally. Your female energy helps you feel what is really going on in the other person. By using the female gift of sensitivity, we now see a lot of lights in this dark world around us. Becoming even more sensitive, we take a step towards the heart of our fellow humans, which is often warmer and brighter than we thought. By noticing the light in the heart of the other, this light will burn stronger.

Becoming even more sensitive works in two directions: not only do you get a deeper sense of who the other person is, they also get to know you better. They feel something sensitive, warm and beautiful in you that they had not noticed before; by acknowledging the other person, they acknowledge you. This is how you start to feel at home on Earth.

To be an angel is to be balanced

Every human being gives and receives. To stay spiritually and physically healthy, we need to be in equilibrium with our environment. The flow of giving and the flow of receiving need to be balanced. The moment we radiate more of our light, make the transition from hypersensitivity to high sensitivity and become the angel that we are, the flow of giving increases. We exude a creative and beautiful light and share it with our environment, often without knowing it. The energy we put out into the world wants to come back to us in the form of (physical) abundance.

This causes problems in many sensitives. Hypersensitive people often do not believe that life can be beautiful, rich and abundant for hem. They feel it would not be right, that they are not worth it and so they block the flow of receiving that wants to come to them. Religious traditions which teach you that it's better to give than to receive, or that it is sinful to enjoy yourself, support this line of thought. Fear and doubt keep out the natural abundance that wants to come your way.

Be attentive of this. Check for yourself if you are really open to what the universe would like to give to you, to all the love that is there for you. As long as you do not say "yes" to what the universe wants to send your way, you have not truly said "yes" to yourself. Say a loud and loving yes to yourself, to all of you. Accepting the flow of receiving in your life will then become natural for you.

Messages from Earth

22 - Your inner connection with Earth

I am the voice of Earth. I salute you in joy. I am pleased about the connection we are making. You are my child and at the same time, you are my parent. I am your mother, and you are my keeper and caretaker. You have been born from my womb. I enabled your soul to take material form in a physical body. You come forth from my hand of clay and in my hand you are still cherished. It is my continuing desire to guard and nurture you with love and encouragement.

Feel my presence in and throughout your body. We are not separate. I communicate with you through your body. Let me help you relax in this very moment. Let go of any tension in your head, your neck and shoulders. A warm shower of gentle Earth energy now releases you of all the thinking and worrying that you humans are so used to. I am here to tell you that you are fine just the way you are. My energy feels warm and familiar, with a spark of humour. Let me flow though your heart, your belly, your legs and your feet. Let me touch the ground through you. Recognize your kinship with me. We are one.

The great secret of life on Earth is that all that lives is one at the core. The rocks, the plants, the animals and the humans are connected by a web of consciousness that encompasses all beings. All of nature is silently aware of this. It is only the humans who seem to have forgotten. Surrounded by a multitude of life forms, all conscious at some level, they feel lonely and lost in the universe. This is tragic – though not without meaning or purpose. Humanity has embarked upon an adventure, and forgetting was part of the journey. Sweet human child, you have not made a mistake in the ordinary sense of the word. You have plunged into a great adventure, once, when you departed Home.

Home is not a place. It is a primal sense of safety, a natural Beingness without questioning yourself or worrying where you are going and what it is all for.

Home is a state of consciousness, a place in your spirit where you feel safe and free. A place of peace and quiet. Home is not up there in heaven, nor does it reside in past or future. Home is in your heart. You left Home the moment you forgot you are one with everything around you. When you started to believe you were separate from everyone else, that you were independent and autonomous, you lost the self-evident sense of connectedness that all beings of nature unconsciously possess. Then you started to experience fear and loneliness.

The experience of forgetfulness and getting lost marks both your great strength and your great vulnerability. The very possibility of disconnecting yourself from the all-pervading oneness and deeming yourself independent from the web of life, shows that you have a strongly focused consciousness, which is a creative force. Your consciousness was so strong and dynamic that it wanted to transcend the boundaries of what was self-evident. To discover and experience the self-evident as such, you first have to disconnect from it. You probably know the saying: "you don't know what you got until it's gone". You had to forget the truth, before you could truly and consciously know it. You had to leave Home to recreate it within your own hearts. Your consciousness had to turn itself inside out in order to understand what and who you are. This turning inside out created the illusion of separation and fear. It leads to a wrong image of reality, but it also shows your great creative power.

I do not have that kind of creative power. I do not create like you. I will give you an example to illustrate this. When a human holds a flower in their hand and really admires it, something happens to the flower. If you had etheric eyes, you would see a flow of light going to the flower, absorbed by all of her cells. The flower will gain in life force and beam even more. Humans can give life force to plants and flowers by their appreciation and admiration. The flower receives this energy and treats it like food. This spiritual food will reinforce the flower's self-awareness, and thereby make it even more lovely and strong. In this manner, humans can inspire nature and help it gain in self-awareness. My, or nature's, power is not to create but to receive. I receive and pass on. I receive energies from the cosmos, from the sun and the planets, from the realm of humanity, and I transform and let these energies take form in an earthly way. I am a big transformer of energies. I give and receive but I do not create like you humans are able to. I am like the flower who gathers your light and beams it back to you.

I and all my realms of nature admire your creative power. Through your creative consciousness, I am able to grow in awareness. As you lose track of the self-evident, I can remember you of it and thereby become more conscious of myself. Because at this stage of your journey you feel homeless and lonely, you are starting to long for unity and connectedness again. This longing leads to growth in consciousness among humans. The realms of nature benefit from this. They grow with you. They are becoming more consciously aware of themselves. As you become more conscious of the unity and connectedness between all that lives, you become the keepers and teachers of the nature realms on Earth. As I told you, I am your parent but I am also your child. I want to learn from you, share in your experience, so that I myself acquire experience and raise my awareness.

Do not be ashamed of being a human. Being a human is something grand. Humans are the great forgettors (smile) but also the creators of new paths in consciousness. You are masters at opening up unexplored territory. You are pioneers. Humans have received the gift of free will. They are able to disconnect from the whole and steer their own course. They can create new realities based on their desires, dreams and intentions. This freedom has been granted to man because in the heart of the cosmos there is faith in humanity. There is much fear, anger and stubbornness in humans. In the past thousands of years humanity has explored the extremes of pain, destruction and suffering. Yet deep within the cosmos there is still faith in humanity, faith in you. Being human can lead you to become entangled in persistent illusions of fear and greed for power. Yet there's also a great promise in the heart of humanity. The moment humans remember the oneness and connectedness of all being, they themselves become divine, loving beings who elevate life all around them and inspire it to grow in self-consciousness and self-realisation. Human beings have a type of consciousness that can give a powerful evolutionary impulse to all living beings on Earth.

I am waiting for you. I, Earth, and the realms of rock, plant and animal, of air, fire, water and earth, are waiting for you. We wait for your awakening. If you awaken, your collective consciousness will lift us to a new level of consciousness. We do not wait passively. We are reaching out to you. We can help you remember who you are – remind you that you are safely held by powers who transcend the human ego and have your best interest in mind. We long to embrace you.

219

Tune into nature and feel that you are allowed to fall back into the unconditional safety of Being itself. You need not fret and stress so much to get your life together. Let life itself take care of it. There's a rhythm and wisdom inherent in nature which is communicated to you through your body and your feelings. You are used to thinking much and basing your actions on your thinking. But the flow of feeling inside you often points to another direction. Feeling comes from within and thinking often comes from the outside. Often there's a conflict between what you feel deeply within and what you think you ought to do or be in the outside world. I invite you to trust your feelings more and let the voice of the heart speak openly.

Concretely you can do this by giving more attention to the signals your body is sending you. The body is an extraordinarily rich instrument. It is not a mere shell, a material frame you cloak your soul in. Your soul manifests itself in and through the body. Through the body your souls speaks to you much more directly than through your thoughts. Make it a habit to frequently ask your body how it is feeling. Is there tension or pain somewhere? Direct your attention to those areas. Ask for the emotion behind the bodily sensation. Don't make it too hard on yourself. Do not *think*: what emotion could be possibly hiding here? *Feel* what is there. If you don't feel anything, let it go for a while. The answer will come to you. Wait patiently. The attention you directed toward those tense and painful spots has already been beneficial. If you do this every day, you get used to going within continually and aligning yourself with what goes on inside of you, instead of letting your energy unconsciously be absorbed by the hectic outside world. By going within frequently, you connect stronger and stronger with your unique, individual flow of energy. Your intuition becomes clearer and you are able to stay more attuned to what fits you and what not.

As a soul you have chosen to incarnate in an earthly body. Through that incarnation, by becoming flesh and blood, you wanted to know yourself more profoundly. The more you are connected with the Earth and your body, the more fully you are incarnated. The more fully you are incarnated, the more you are able to realise your soul's longings in the realm of Earth. Is it possible then to be only partly incarnated? Yes, it is. If it is difficult for you to feel your body and therefore you also have trouble connecting to your emotions, you are only partly incarnated. Part of your consciousness has not fully been anchored in your body and does not feel at home here. This causes feelings of unrest, irritability and insecurity. There are spiritual traditions on Earth which encourage you to transcend the body and which place the realm of heaven in opposition to the realm of Earth. But heaven and Earth are not adversaries, just like soul and body aren't opposites. They are meant to complement and mutually enrich each other. The heaven you are looking for, the Home you long for, is present in all the cells of your body. The light that you call God flows through all of Earthly creation. Your spiritual goal is much more about truly valuing the realm of Earth than it is to transcend it. I welcome you and invite you to use my healing powers for your self-realisation.

I also like to tell you what you can do for me. Many of you would like to know this, because you are concerned about the condition I am in. If you ask me, Earth, what you can do for me, my answer is: accept me, appreciate me, enjoy me. This is the calling that sounds from my heart to you reading this: bless me with your loving attention. I ask you for a blessing. You are gods in the making, do not underestimate the power of what you radiate with your consciousness. The moment you connect with a plant, an animal, a rock, you touch and influence their consciousness. You can treat an animal carelessly for instance, as a means to satisfy your needs, or as a unique being who wants to be cherished as such. The way in which you approach the animal has a direct impact on its self-awareness, the way it feels about itself. If you bless it with your loving attention, with your spiritual knowing that you are part of one great Consciousness, you awaken something in the animal. It will experience a gain in life force, health and self-awareness and it will develop a bond with you which will affect both of you positively. The same goes for all living creatures in nature. When you hold a flock of birds in the sky with a loving gaze, admire a colourful sunset, or feel thankful for a fine, nutritious meal, you bless the Earth with your love. This is what I ask of you.

Now you may wonder whether it can really be so simple and if you are really helping Earth in this way. It may seem that by appreciating and blessing Earth you do nothing particular against the pollution of the air or the water, the climate changes and other negative developments you take note of in the media. However, I say to you: I am a living consciousness. I am affected by your inner attitude towards me. I am a sensitive being, not a thing. Your blessings reach deep into my heart and I am able to better regenerate myself if you make the inner connection with me. From this connection I can communicate with you and also tell you what you may do for me in particular. The most important step however is to make the connection. This is not something self-evident in your culture.

221

Connecting with me is also connecting with your body. Your body is part of Earth. I speak to you through your body. Many of you detest your body. You don't approve of the way it looks, you resent the physical complaints it may give you or you simply feel caught in or restricted by your body. Because of this attitude, no message can come to you from your body. You first need to recognize and appreciate your body as the refined and unique instrument it is. Your body is your closest friend. It reacts to everything you think, feel and sense. It is the mirror of your soul and it wants to help you manifest your soul on Earth. If you are able to feel this and let go of the external judgments of your body, the inner connection can be made. Once it's there, you will probably change some things on the outer level too. Perhaps you will eat, breathe or exercise differently, and create more quiet time for yourself. You will in any case treat your body with more respect and probably want to go out in nature more often. When these outer changes in behaviour are born from an inner connection with the body, the changes will be lasting and give you joy and satisfaction. It's no use forcing yourself to change your behaviour with regard to your health or with regard to the environment. When you approach the problems of the body or the problems of Earth from such an external point of view, you are all too often inside your head and you are approaching it like a battle.

As an example, think of what happens when you are on a diet to lose weight. If you do this from an external approach, from the head, you start from the idea that your body is not good as it is. It is fat, ugly or unhealthy and that has got to change. There is contempt for the body as it is. Sticking to the diet will depend on your will power, your ability to subject your body and your emotions to your will. Diets usually fail this way. They are not born from an inner sense of respect for the body as it is, for you as you are. A change of eating habits can only succeed if you work together with the body, if you can first accept it like it is and if you can be forgiving and loving about your emotions regarding eating. If you bless the body with your appreciation and respect, even if it does not comply with the many external demands it is supposed to meet, it will start to tell you what it needs to be healthy. A unique flow of communication will arise between you and your body, a love relationship which helps you realise your deepest potential.

It is the same way in your dealings with me. I ask you first and foremost to see and recognize me for who I am. Revel in my beauty, take in my abundance. I am a mirror to you, just like your body. Enjoy what I have to offer. Have faith in my power and ability to self-heal. You need not save me. I am perfectly able to save myself. I know who I am and I trust the cosmic powers that accompany me. My spiritual essence is indestructible and I do dot fear annihilation by human hand. You do not support me by being angry and worried about the damage done to nature on Earth. You help me by taking up your natural role in relation to me. In that role you are both child and parent, both small and vulnerable and great and majestic. Allow yourself to be a child again who entrusts itself to the great powers of life that carry, cherish and sustain you. Dare to embrace your vulnerability and surrender to powers that transcend you. Yet be self-conscious also and accept your responsibility as a creator and inspirer of life. You are gods in the making, but you can only truly embody your divinity if you know yourself to be one and connected with the great web of life which supports your very existence. Humility and surrender on the one hand, self-esteem and self-consciousness on the other hand, are the qualities that reinstate the original role play of giving and receiving between man and Earth. I invite you to dance with me. Dancing together, heaven and Earth will merge and miracles will abound.

23 - Grounding yourself through joy and creativity

I am the voice of Earth. I salute you all in joy. It warms my heart to experience your presence and openness towards me. I long to connect with you. We are meant to develop together and jointly walk the road to a different, new world.

I would like to take you back to the very origin of our mutual connection and cooperation. I am a living creature. I am a conscious being who has received you here on the planet in very ancient times. I was receptive to your arrival here on Earth and wanted to learn and grow through your presence. You are not from the Earth, you come from the stars. You carry a light within that is new and inspiring to Earth and all the realms of nature here. Let me explain.

As a planet I absorb light from the outside. The light of the sun warms me and helps me bring forth life on the planet. I am inspired by the great force of the sun and I need it to create and sustain physical life on my skin. The sun is a star. You are representatives of the sun. You carry star light within your soul and bring this light to Earth as you are born here.

What was the meaning of this light descending on Earth? What was the intention behind your coming? You are here to bring the light of consciousness to me and all of the realms of nature. You are here to awaken us to inner life. Whereas the physical sun helps me to create and sustain physical life on Earth, your star light helps me to evolve at an inner level, to grow in consciousness.

To offer a simple illustration of this principle, think of what happens when you hold a flower in your hand and look at it in awe and admiration. You see the exquisite beauty of the flower; you sense its purity, marvel at the colours and enjoy the scent. The flower itself is not aware of its beauty; the flower is simply being itself. But because of your admiration, your presence, your consciousness enveloping the flower, something awakens inside it. She will start to experience itself as something beautiful and valuable. She enjoys your attention and a spark of soul light is awakened in her.

You will see that plants and flowers you give conscious attention to, simply by enjoying them and caring for them, will grow more abundantly, have more life force and develop stronger roots into the Earth. You are creators. By your thoughts, intentions and self-consciousness you are able to add life force and creative power to living nature on Earth. This is exactly what nature longs to receive from you. All the realms of nature seek to grow in self-awareness, to reach out to the stars, make the connection and absorb star light within.

Think of the animals you keep in and around your house, your pets. So many of you have a special bond with them. Whenever you enter into an intimate relationship with an animal, you receive their unconditional love and loyalty. The animal however also receives something back from you. The animal is touched by your human presence, and the particular type of consciousness that belongs to humans. Your presence lights a spark of consciousness in their being and it helps them evolve in their evolution towards greater self-consciousness.

Everything in the universe is growing and evolving towards self-consciousness. Self-consciousness brings one closer to awareness of one's own divinity, one's indestructible light and creative power. Everything in the universe gradually grows towards a state of consciousness in which it realizes: I am part of God. I am Creator myself. To celebrate your divine creatorship and handle it with responsibility is the purpose of creation.

You are creators, and you as souls have come to Earth to learn to deal with your creative powers in a conscious and responsible way. As creators, you are meant to contribute to my evolution, and to inspire the realms of nature which in turn provide you with many services and blessings on the material and ethereal levels. When you look at the current condition of the planet, it is hard to perceive there was once an original intention for a mutual cooperation between you and the planet.

Things have not worked out as planned and many would say things have gone wrong. In this moment however, I ask you to remember your original excitement to embark upon our mutual adventure. Your loving intention is still alive within your heart, even if you notice all around that humanity has used her creative powers unwisely and has damaged Earth because of it. Humanity has veered off its course, taken a detour, one might say.

Originally, you came down to Earth from a great source of light, like angel-children. You were innocent and pure, but as your journey progressed, you were led astray. Humanity came to a point at which it refused to cooperate with the forces of nature, and instead placed itself in opposition to nature. Humanity then lost its connection and roots into the greater whole. Out of fear, people sought to gain power over others and over nature, in order to secure a place for themselves on Earth. One could say a fall from Paradise took place. Where you had originally intended to serve life on Earth, to nurture and inspire it with your creative powers, you now experienced the opposite. In the present, you see what happens when nature is not recognised anymore as a living partner in creation.

Humanity's lack of respect for nature and the planet deeply saddens many of you reading this. There is sadness in me too about all that has happened. The realms of nature, both animal, plant and rock, have absorbed part of the darkness and negativity spread by humanity. They have experienced in their own way a sense of abandonment, a crack in the all-pervading sense of oneness that once was.

Yet, in the very heart of me, there is lasting love and compassion for all of you, and I ask you to also feel compassion for yourself and the whole of humanity. You are involved in a grand learning process. In any such process it is inevitable that mistakes are made. It is part of growing and learning that you embark on detours and dead-ends.

In this age, the collective consciousness of humanity is changing. There are more and more people nowadays, who carry in their heart a remembrance of the original bond between man and nature. They have a silent awareness of the true and blessed relationship that humans are meant to enter into with me, their home planet. Feel again, how deeply you are connected with my being.

I love you so. You are my angels of light, and still my faith in you has not withered. I ask you to acknowledge me and allow my energy to pour through you again. I am a living partner walking right beside you on your path of incarnation on Earth. By connecting yourself more intimately with me, by *grounding* yourself more, you bring your star light deep into the material realm. You let it shine and radiate and that will bring the changes on Earth so direly needed right now. By connecting to me from the heart, your true self will come out. Every human being has a unique contribution to make to this grand adventure. Your unique gift inspires me, adds life force to nature and inspires other people as well.

What is grounding about?

I would like to say some more on the meaning of grounding. What does it mean to be connected to Earth, to be grounded? Being grounded means: being present in your body, being able to feel your body from the inside out, feeling the flow of life in every part, from your head to your toes to your fingertips. Check for yourself if you can experience this flow. Can you simply feel your fingertips at this moment? Your toes? Can you feel the life inside of it?

Being grounded means that you anchor your star light, your soul light, deep into matter. The part of the material world closest to you is your body. The cells and molecules of your body are open to receive your light, your soul. You are the sun for your own body. Your consciousness makes your body alive and endows it with healing power, life force and vitality. The anchoring of your soul into your body gives you the strength to fulfil your truest desires in life. Be aware of your creative power. The more you anchor it into your body, the more you truly incarnate on Earth and create the changes in your life that you long for.

When you are grounded, you feel clear and quiet. You are open to your soul's inspiration and at the same time you are connected to all that happens around you in everyday life. Making the bridge between cosmos and Earth, feeling that connection, is what it means to be grounded.

Many of you carry your soul light in the upper half of your body, around your heart and head. You find it difficult to let it truly descend into the lower part of your body, your belly, legs and feet. One reason why this is hard for you is fear of your own greatness. You have fear of being the radiant angel and star that you are and to make a difference in the world. This fear is old and its roots extend further than only this lifetime. In the past, you have incarnated on Earth many times and you have often felt unwelcome. You are all in the process of healing this old pain.

I will suggest two ways of grounding yourself and feeling that you are indeed welcome on Earth, in your greatness, your creative power and your divinity.

Grounding yourself through joy

The first way is through enjoyment. You are really not used to enjoying. Enjoying what? Everything you can experience on Earth. Your body offers many possibilities for enjoyment, but many of these have been deemed sinful or inferior in your culture. Enjoying the movements of the body, the sunshine on your skin, eating and drinking, the warm touch of another. Being able to enjoy this has to do with being able to truly *receive*. Why is this difficult for you?

Many of you feel there is something wrong with you, that you are somehow not right the way you are. You feel you have to achieve and work hard in order to receive acknowledgement and appraisal. This is a silly idea, seen from the perspective of nature. Have you ever seen a wild animal work hard to gain recognition? Well no, the animal simply *is* and takes its right to be for granted, not as something it must deserve. The animal is able to enjoy without reserve the sun, the food, a water bath, the seasons and natural rhythms of life.

You are all invited to *receive* and to experience yourself as a divine being who is allowed to receive simply because of who you are. You are invited to enjoy the simple things life in a body has to offer you. Receiving seems to be easy, but it is not. It requires a deep level of self love, a deep recognition and appreciation of who you are. Dare to reach out to that level of self love. Choose one moment every day, in which you ask yourself what you can do for yourself now that truly pleasures and fulfils you. What do you really feel like having or doing? Then do it. Do it for you, because you honour yourself and because you are here on Earth to enjoy yourself.

When you truly enjoy, whatever it is, without guilt or shame, you are grounded. You are completely present in the now moment and all is well. There are no thoughts of the past or the future. Enjoying is being in the now, fully grounded.

Grounding yourself through creativity

There is a second way of becoming more firmly connected to Earth, more grounded. It is the way of creativity. This is what you are made for. Every human has a natural longing to express themselves, to manifest themselves in the world. This has nothing to do with achieving fame or success in society. Rather, it has to do with finding a way of expressing yourself that gives you real satisfaction. It may be the case that raising a family deeply fulfils you, or that leading a company inspires you. Perhaps caring for animals in some way is your heart's desire, or it may be a type of artistic expression that feels natural to you. Every soul longs to express itself in some manner. The moment you answer to that longing, you feel fulfilled. The moment you allow the natural creativity inside to unfold, you feel "yes, this is me, this is how my energy wants to flow".

In that moment, your soul connects to the heart of Earth, the heart of this reality. It is important to find out what you truly long for in your life and to make room for the creative flow inside you. This is where your divine essence touches Earth and finds material form.

Now, I would like to impress on you that you should really stand up for yourselves a bit more in this respect. Many of you suppress your impulses to do what your heart desires. So often you think of "how you should behave", what is expected of you, your duties and responsibilities. In that way you will not find the key to the unfolding of your creative power. Your creative power speaks to you from your belly, from your gut. It is not concerned with all the limiting rules and obligations that you have internalized. Break free from this! Feel the fountain of fire and passion springing from your belly, and let it flow freely. Sparkles of light will find their way from your belly, to your heart, from the inside to the outside, and you will express yourself in your own original way on Earth. You will see that your creativity will touch other people and that it will make them joyful and inspired. Following your passion and desire has a much more positive effect on the world than virtuously doing what you've been told and forcing yourself to comply with limiting rules and structures.

This is a time of change. It is a time to be brave and take risks, to hear the voice of your heart and act according to it in all areas of your life. By truly surrendering yourself to your heart's guidance, you dig your roots deep into Earth, and you start to feel that life here is truly worth living.

Full circle

The first way of grounding yourself was to enjoy and receive. This is an ingoing flow. The second way is about an outgoing flow: creating and giving. By creating from the heart, you give yourself to the world. Receiving and giving, enjoying and creating, together make a full circle. It is a healing circle.

The more you dare to enjoy and find yourself worthy to receive, the more you connect with your natural inspiration, the energy you are meant to share with this world. And as this flow of inspiration becomes stronger and finds a creative form in the world, the more you enjoy the love and joy that will befall you on your path. The flows of giving and receiving, creating and enjoying, mutually reinforce each other.

I, Earth, benefit from this healing circle of receiving and giving. In this flowing, dynamic circle, I am working with you. It is my desire to nurture and stimulate your divine creative power, this unique sparkle in you. Human beings who have developed the capacity to enjoy and create, will naturally enter into a different connection with Earth. They will be aware of their greatness, their divine nature, and for that very reason understand also that they are held and carried by a force of Life that connects all beings together. Experiencing your own greatness goes hand in hand with a sense of smallness, the realisation of your being embedded in the great web of life that sustains you. Humans who honour and respect themselves, naturally cooperate with their living environment, other humans, animals, plants, all of nature. Knowing your greatness goes together with recognising your place in the larger whole, and deriving joy from the part you play in it.

A journey to the New Earth

In closing, I would like to ask you to travel with me to the future, to a new Earth. Imagine that the evolution we are now in together has progressed a few steps further. I am myself evolving towards a more expanded self-awareness. This new awareness has been awakened inside me, urged by both the good and the bad times on Earth. I am becoming more self-conscious and creative in my being. There's a longing in my heart for a reality in which humanity and Earth reinstate their original bond of love and companionship. A new Earth on which we joyfully cooperate and I am again inspired by your love and thoughtful attention, while I provide you with all that you need, living in a physical body and attuned to the rhythm of nature.

Imagine this new Earth that you all so long for, present in the now moment. In our hearts it is already alive, as a seed. Let us nurture this seed with consciousness and have it sprout in our imagination. See yourself living on this new Earth. What is the first thing you notice? Humans are living in harmony with nature here. Technology is used to support nature rather than manipulate it. See whether you can find yourself a house on this new Earth. There is a place and a community there in which you feel like you belong. Let your imagination guide you, and feel no restrictions. Where do you live on this new Earth? Can you find a natural surrounding in which you feel comfortable? Feel the climate, feel the ease and simplicity of life there. Life is pure and simple there, as it is meant to be.

Now take a look at what kind of work you do. Work means anything that inspires you and gives you a sense of fulfilment. What are you doing? You probably live in a small community of kindred spirits and you do exactly what your soul inspires you to do. What form does your creativity take?

When you see or feel this, know that your soul is speaking to you in the present. What you are seeing is something that you long to do right now, and something you *can* do right now, if only you trust and dare to be who you are. This is the work of your heart.

Now in this imagination of the new Earth, feel also what it is you truly enjoy. Let your inner eye provide you with a situation in which you truly enjoy yourself and receive something from what Earth has to offer you. Let an image of what that is spontaneously well up in your mind. What is it that truly makes you feel: all is well and I am content.

Feel the flow of giving and receiving in this place, this new reality. And hold on to it when we go back to the present.

Earth is in a transition stage and the more people remember what their inspiration is, what they are here to give and to receive, the sooner the new Earth will be here.

24 - From heart to belly: bringing your soul's light down to Earth

I am Earth speaking to you. I am your mother and carry you in my lap, your whole life long. You are cherished by me, even if you are not aware of it and are too busy and caught up in your day-to-day affairs. I hold you and invite you to connect with me, as I wish to stir your memory and remind you of something sweet, old and forgotten. It is about the natural safety of being on Earth.

To remember the natural safety of being, you can look at nature all around you. Watch the seasons, how they come and go all on their own, see the plants and animals go about their daily life, listen to the rustle of the wind or the murmuring of water. In this way, you are briefly reminded that the most important things in life happen automatically, as a result of nature running its course. Nature is all around you and it is in you as well, for you also have a nature and it is part of nature as a whole.

Especially in the West, you have become so oriented to living from the head that you have forgotten you are a natural being, like the plants and animals. Look at the animals, how naturally they surrender to life. They almost can't do otherwise. They do know emotions such as fear and resistance, but they cannot oppose themselves to life as much as humans can. Human beings can by their excessive thinking create a cage for their own nature which will cause problems after a while. Life cannot be organised and controlled by human thinking. The primal forces of nature are vaster than that. Sooner or later you'll find out. There will be a moment in which you have to surrender to nature.

Often you reach such a moment through crisis, when you get stuck in a situation that asks of you to release control, because you have no grip anymore on things inside or around you. Releasing control hurts and it can be a struggle. Yet it will bring you home. You think you are lost and drowning in chaos, but you are actually coming closer to the natural safety of Being itself. Life holds and loves you. Crises often seem to be cruel and unjust, but in truth they always carry inside nature's, or if you want God's, invitation that says: "come home, come back to me". There's a guiding hand within the crisis, which seeks to support you and show you the way.

All of you who read this are on the inner journey to wholeness and completion of the self. You are seeking to bring your soul alive in a human body of flesh and blood. On this path you go through different stages. The soul gets embodied - or descends into - the body in different stages. When you've only started the inner path, you will probably have become acquainted with it through your head. For instance, you may have become attracted to certain books or people, who throw a different light on ideas and values you always took for granted. You may be shaken by their new thoughts, and yet strangely attracted to it. It will fascinate you to read and hear more about it. You will let go of some of the more rigid structures of your thinking and open up to something new. Reading and speaking to other minded people can be helpful incentives in this process. This is how the journey within begins for many. You devour spiritual books like they're cookies. Deep within you, something wants to awaken and change, and this translates itself first as the need for a new way of thinking.

After some time you start to long for more. You start to think: well, I understand what they're talking about in those books, but how do I apply all of this to my own life? How does this knowledge come alive and how do I truly translate it into my feelings and actions on Earth? This question may haunt you and drive you to despair, but you cannot force life. Yet at a certain moment something will happen in your life which will help you make the breakthrough from head to heart. Often it is a crisis of some sort. Changes may occur in the area of work, relationships, health or loss of a loved one. Whatever it is, at a certain moment feelings will arise inside you which are so intense that they cannot be ignored. You have to allow them in and let the transformation take place. That is when your soul incarnates deeper into your heart.

First your soul had descended into your head, inspiring you to take in new ideas through books, talks etcetera. Then the soul knocks at your door at a deeper level, the level of feeling. You will get acquainted with layers of emotions you never knew existed before. Crises spur these on; they will make old emotions from childhood come to the surface, perhaps even memories from before this lifetime. You will explore these layers of emotions and this is how the center of your heart opens up. Your soul incarnates even deeper, filling the heart chakra with its energy.

The transformation that takes place at that stage may give rise to several complications. You start to look at the world with different eyes and your relationships with other people change as well. Deep within, the awareness of oneness awakens. The awareness of oneness means that you realize that all of us, man, animal, plant, nature, are held together by a divine force, and that we are bound to each other, each a mirror to the other. This awareness can be overpowering and for many of you the breakthrough from head to heart causes a great sensitivity inside. This high sensitivity may create imbalances. Boundaries with others get blurred, you may take in a lot of other people's emotional stuff not knowing how to release it and your moods can go from very high to very low. The breakthrough from head to heart, however, though powerful and essential, is not the last stage in the incarnation of the soul. The soul wants to descend even deeper, into the belly.

When the soul has descended to the level of your heart, you have partly awakened. You are aware of your feelings, you dare to look at your emotions, you are prepared to go within and face your inner wounds. But you also feel weakened by your high sensitivity and the unstableness that arises because of that. Because your heart is so full of feelings, you lose your grounding at times, and this can be difficult. This happens to many of you. When the heart center is opened radically, your sensitivity may become too much for you and you may want to withdraw from the world. You will not express yourself creatively anymore, because it is all too much and too overpowering. This can make you feel anxious and down.

The answer to this problem is not in going back into your head. The answer is in your belly. You are ready for the next step in the incarnation process of the soul: the transition from heart to belly. The soul wants to flow even deeper into your body. In the middle of your belly there's a space or point of silence. Go there with your consciousness now as I speak. In that space there is no language, no thinking, no concepts. You may hear the rustling of leaves in the wind or the sound of the beating of waves. Those sounds can help you become aware of the silence that is within this center.

At this level, your spiritual knowing and feeling become instinctual, or as one calls it, second nature. There is no need to think or even feel it over. A deep knowingness is present from which you act and life pours through you easily. Your soul has then become your nature, it has descended to the level of instinctual awareness. This gives you the balance you need! You can remain centered and calm amidst a demanding and turbulent environment. Your feeling center (your heart) wants to connect with your belly, in order for it to be truly grounded and for you to feel safe on Earth.

Let us now visit that place in your belly. Trust that it is there. Tell your soul it is welcome there. Allow your soul to flow from your head, inspiring your thinking, to your heart, radiating love and kindness, to your belly, giving you trust, self esteem, a profound inner knowing that you are who you are and that you are fine as you are. Feel your belly opening up to you. Sense how the golden light of your soul flows down to your root chakra and connects with me, Earth. Go deep within. Be the center of silence and know that from there, your high sensitivity will be balanced with peace and calmness. In this balanced state, you will know how to put boundaries around your feelings. You will know when to open up and when to keep your distance, staying close to yourself. You determine when to say "yes" and when to say "no", when to connect and when to let go. The key is in your belly.

To help you connect with this center, I suggest you imagine an animal that represents the inner power residing in your belly. Take the first animal that comes to mind. Remember, animals are very spontaneous creatures, they live from their instincts, their natural reflexes. This animal reflects your instinctual inner knowingness. It is already there. It is waiting for you. You do not need to create it, you only need to see and recognize it. Invite this animal to come near you, say hello and look it into the eye. Now ask it whether it has a message for you, helping you to descend deeper into your belly.

Let the animal speak. The animal embodies the wisdom of the instinctual and you can receive that wisdom, because you have a head and a heart. You can feel and articulate this wisdom. That is the beauty of the cooperation between head, heart and belly. Not one of them is better or higher than the other. Rather, it is their balanced cooperation which makes you whole and complete. Your head can give you much pleasure. Thinking can be useful and fun. It gives you the opportunity to communicate with others, as it provides a common language. The heart offers the possibility to experience joy and the whole range of emotions human life comprises. It is a beautiful gift. The belly gives you your foundation, your I-ness, if that's a proper word. It allows you to really be *you*, firm and rooted, drawing your own boundaries and using your discernment. From this foundation, the interaction with your heart and your head becomes a joyful play. If these three layers are aligned with each other, you feel whole, and life is worth living on Earth. It can be full of inspiration, love and happiness. You can surrender yourself to what moves and inspires you, while at the same time not losing your basis, your inner point of silence. You can remain close to yourself, and at the same time freely give and receive what life offers.

I salute you all. My love and compassion are close to you always. I am playing this game together with you and I am part of it. You are beautiful and rich as human beings. Have faith in the beauty and power of the instruments available to you, the instruments of thinking, feeling and being.

25 - Journey through the elements

I am the voice of Earth. I speak to you from beneath the ground under your feet. I carry you constantly and I am present in your body. The body you dwell in enables you to experience life here. I represent Home just as much as heaven does. I am a primal force wanting to provide you with a sense of safety in which you can relax and be free. Being home means essentially to feel free to be who you are. Being yourself is something simple and yet incredibly abundant. You all long to be yourself. You all long to be free from worry, fear and sorrow. Make the connection with me. I wish to nurture you, receive and carry you. We are one. I am present inside you through your body and the body continually sends messages to you about your life's path.

Let us go on a journey with the body, travelling through the basic elements of nature: water, fire, air and earth. These elements represent life energies which together weave a web of creation. Follow me, and see this as a game. Keep it light and playful.

Imagine you are in nature. Your bare feet rest upon the earth. You stand on the shore of a lake. You are nude, without clothes. There is no one there, just you, and you feel free. You are not ashamed because you are naked; it feels natural and comfortable. You feel the ground beneath your feet. Then you put some steps forward and feel the water wash over your feet. The water is warm and soothing. It calms you. You feel no resistance. It is delicious. You go deeper and deeper into the pool and you sense the healing power of the water. It is from a pure source. It helps you let go of what you do not need anymore. Now float on your back in this pool and feel the element water all around you.

Feel it wash also through your body, through your blood, which contains the element of water. Water is in and around you. Let it cleanse you. You hear the reassuring sound of the water and now feel within your body if there's something in particular you would like to let go of. Do not ponder whether it is possible to let go of it. Just feel the longing to be free from it. It may be a situation in your life that is difficult or an emotion that bugs you. Name it and surrender it to the water. You do not need to know how it will happen. Just say to yourself: "I release this. The water may rinse it from me and cleanse me." The water brings flow and change. Surrender yourself to this flow. You gently float back to the shore.

While you are floating on your back, you see the sun shine above you, a ball of fire in the sky. You get out of the water and lie down on the shore. The sun dries your skin. The sun beams are warm and nurturing. As you feel your body basking in the sunlight, you now feel the energy of the sun and connect to it. Feel its essence flow through you in a gentle and soft way.

There's a place in your body connected to the power of the sun. It is your solar plexus, the area of your third chakra, located near your stomach. Feel a warm, relaxed flow in that center and ask yourself what is it I would like to create in my life. What is it that inspires me?

You do not need to find the words for it, just let the feeling be there. There's an inner desire to manifest your unique quality, your love on Earth. Let the sunlight make you aware of that inspiration. It is your inner fire, warm and full of life. Let the energy of the sun also pour through your throat. Your throat is the energy center of self expression, showing yourself in the outside world with trust and self-worth.

Quietly you sit at the side of the lake and feel how the elements of water and fire assist you on your inner journey. You then notice a soft breeze on your cheeks. It is air, the element of space and openness and at the same time safety and playfulness. You can play safely within the grand cosmos that surrounds you. Feel the air come into your body through the breath. Breath in, feel the air in your belly and breath out. Air brings room to play and move. Air is the most cosmic among the elements and brings inspiration to you from your soul. Feel light, light as the air, air that does not take any solid form. Float and fly. Dare to be free. You are not truly bound to your body, or to any form. The element of air reminds you of this. You are free as a bird.

Now feel again how you are sitting on the ground at the shore of the lake and connect to the element of earth. Sense the firmness of the ground beneath you. Notice the fertility of Earth which shows in the many plants, trees and flowers surrounding you. Feel the maternal power in me. I am a female energy. I flow through all of your body and you can clearly sense me in the tail bone, the first chakra at the base of your spine. Sense how a cord connects your tail bone chakra to the heart of Earth. Note the flexibility of this chord. It is not a chord that binds or imprisons you. It is a chord that enables you to be here and express your deepest inspiration joyfully.

Know that the four elements are available to you. They flow inside and all around you. You are home here. You belong to us. You are creators and you are meant to be master of the elements. They want to serve you.

Today we have spoken about the difference between the dimension of nature and the human world. Many of you feel stuck in the realm of human society. The hurry and agitation often present there dictate an unnatural rhythm that unsettles you. Do not be frightened of this. You are strong enough to handle this. Do however dig your roots deep into the realm of nature. Play with the elements, for there lies your home. It is the energy of natural living that your souls want to contribute to society in this era. The spiritual transformation now occurring in humanity is about a return to Earth, to a way of living in which your life flow is aligned with nature inside and outside of you.

In human society, much emphasis has been placed on thinking and controlling life. Many of you try to bring structure to your life from pre-set notions, which come from the head rather than the heart. If you do so, you walk past the great powers, both earthly and cosmic, that shape your life. You plan and control life from your heads, and when life runs counter to your expectations, you interpret this as adversity and ill fate. The art of natural living is to let go of thinking and controlling so much. There has been an excess of this in your society. This time invites you to align yourself with the natural rhythm and flow of Earth.

I am your home, allow me to nurture you. Let the elements in your body speak. Ask what you need and it will be given to you. I hear your heartbeat and want to help you find you way. Now hear my heartbeat too. You bring inspiration and cosmic light to me. I absorb you and am grateful for your presence. Restore your unity with me.

26 - Angels on Earth

I am the voice of Earth. I have known you forever. Your every footstep is felt and acknowledged by me. At the deepest level we are one. There is one consciousness that envelops us both. This consciousness is majestic and unnameable. It is the spirit of God. It is mysterious and at the same time deeply familiar. Within the hand of this creative Consciousness the game of our togetherness enfolds. Together we play a game; we are partners in a relationship that has evolved over time. This relationship is now ready for transformation. We are entering a new era. But first I will tell you more about the beginning of this process of our cooperation together. It is different from what you may have expected.

At our first coming together, you were not yet human. You did not possess a physical body. You were not incarnated upon Earth. You were an angel. And you were not just any angel! You belonged to a family of angels who intended to pave the way for a new adventure in the cosmos. What was that adventure about? I will put this in very simple terms. In the cosmos, there is a law that like attracts like. For instance, after you die on Earth, you are automatically drawn to an area in the spirit world that mirrors your state of consciousness. Your surroundings are a direct reflection of how you feel inside. There is *unity between inner and outer*. In the spirit world, there are realms of light and realms of relative darkness. These realms are separated. This is not the case on Earth, or so it would appear. On Earth many different types of consciousness are present together and interact with one another. There is great diversity, and therefore Earth is like a huge melting pot of different realms of consciousness.

Even here, it is the case that you create your own reality by your inner state of consciousness. However, this is something you gradually come to understand in the course of a deep spiritual quest. At first, you are greatly distracted on Earth by an external world that does not seem to be created by your own mind at all. On the contrary, you seem to be the product of that reality rather than its creator. In the spirit world, the unity between inner and outer is simply a given, concrete and palpable. On Earth, it takes a highly evolved consciousness to realise that oneness, and to take responsibility for oneself as creator.

On Earth a special experiment takes place. When you are here in physical form, a veil is put over you so that you do not recognise your own divine creative power. It remains there until you awaken and see that you *are* God at the core of your being. Then the veil drops and you also recognize the deep underlying oneness that pervades all living creatures on Earth. The process of awakening on Earth is intense, and the very existence of Earth gives a powerful evolutionary impulse to the entire spirit world. In the spirit world especially, there can be a lack of dynamics and of change. Indeed stagnation has taken place because all realms are so neatly separated. Change, growth, evolution occur when you meet and confront *otherness*. When I speak of meeting up with otherness, I do not mean having a polite chat with it, but rather a truly plunging into it. You learn and grow from diverse forms of consciousness not by studying them "from above", but by *becoming* them. This is exactly what happens when you plunge into incarnation on Earth. You take a dive into the deep, and by incarnating you connect to diverse realms of consciousness. This is how you forge a bridge between realms of being which would not have connected otherwise.

Being human means to be a bridge between widely varying realms of consciousness. In the forging of that bridge lies the hope for an expansion of consciousness in all the realms of the spirit world. Even the highest evolved realm in the spirit world gains an impulse of growth and renewal from the great experiment on Earth. Humans are able to explore the extremes of light and dark, and eventually recognize the oneness behind all forms and appearances. When human beings attain this consciousness of oneness within, they become conscious creators on Earth, and their presence will have a transformative and healing effect on all living creatures they come in contact with.

Creating unity consciousness is the goal of your adventure on Earth. I started this tale by mentioning that when we first began this process of cooperation, you were not humans but angels. Your consciousness had not yet attached itself to any material form, and you felt strongly connected with the other angels around you, your brothers and sisters. There was such a strong bond among you that you experienced yourself like the cells of one organism. You

246

would work for a common good in a selfless, obvious way, being of the same mind and heart. At a certain moment, you heard a calling from Earth. You were invited to embark on a journey with this planet. Why you? To make a long story short: you were the bold ones among the angels. You were fearless, passionate and yes, somewhat stubborn and self-willed. The claim has been that you were banished from paradise because of your desire for knowledge and your wilfulness. And yes, you were indeed curious and a bit unruly too. But that was precisely as it was supposed to be! Did you think God made a mistake in creating you? Well no, God knew precisely what she/he was doing and by the way, God does not deem anything wrong or sinful easily. God is perfectly capable of living with your "sins". You are the ones suffering most from it.

Although it is understandable that as a human being you may regret your own acts, it is not wise to be endlessly weighed down by them. In this respect you have suffered a lot from your religions which have put such a strong emphasis on guilt and punishment. God is more gentle and compassionate that you would ever hold possible. You are forgiven even before you trespass. God whole-heartedly grants you the space to make mistakes. She/he rather prefers that you look upon your own mistakes with equanimity than that you beat yourselves up about it. All those "mistakes" are steps on the journey within, the journey on which you fully get to know yourself. This journey need not be straight, it is meant to be erratic. Without twists and turns, there is no experience, and without experience, no awakening. You first have to get lost to be able to come Home consciously. You were the ones taking the experience of "lostness" fully upon you, with the passion and the self-wilfulness that God him/herself planted in your hearts. However, I am straying a bit from my subject!

Once you heard the call from Earth, you entered my dimension. You found a planet rich in vegetation, with green forests, endless oceans and a burgeoning animal kingdom. You were moved by the beauty and richness of life upon me. You felt invited to participate in this life, to inspire and nurture it with the angel energy that was at your disposal. I was happy with your arrival. You were my shepherds; you helped to take care of life and even implanted seeds of change and innovation into the existing life forms. How did you do this? You were so close to the Source of creative power, that you had magical abilities, as one would call it today. You allowed yourself to imagine new, exciting life forms and these imaginings grew into spiritual seeds which attached themselves to already existing life forms. You impregnated life with new ideas. That is how biological evolution came to be. All life forms are born from Spirit. Physical, material forms are the manifestation of spiritual forces. The spirit is much stronger than you assume. You have been raised in a materialist frame of mind, which tells you that the physical – as described by the science of physics – is the foundation of reality. In fact the opposite is true. The spirit is not a product of soulless matter. All matter is pervaded by a creative consciousness that sustains it.

Let yourself go with your imagination for a moment. Remember who you were in those ancient times. It is possible! Your soul is open and unlimited. It knows no space or time. Imagine that you float above the oceans and forests in a very refined and ethereal body. You feel enchanted about the beauty you see, about the adventure that is about to take place here. See yourself as an angelic being guided by joy and passion. You feel as free as a child who can do anything it wants. Now imagine you gather up your powers to express your sense of joy and respect for life in a magnificent flower. Allow an image to come forth of a flower which particularly allures you. See its colours and feel them from within. Hear the flower's laughter welling up from its heart like little bells ringing – it is like music to your soul. Now pass on this image to me, Earth. Imagine how it falls into my womb and how it is nurtured there by physical and ethereal powers which help this spiritual seed gain material form. This is what you did in those ancient times. You let yourself be carried away by the flow of your inspiration and impregnated me with it. And I was receptive. I, the awareness present in this material realm, wanted to be impregnated and to absorb your thought forms.

Our partnership and cooperation stem from that time. It is the reason why you can be so moved by the beauty of nature and the innocence of non-human life forms. You are not only touched by their physical beauty, you are also reminded of the old connection there is between you and life on Earth and the joyful game you once played. You made your contribution to the creation of many life forms on Earth. As an angel you were the spiritual parent of life on Earth. This is how deep and far your creative power reaches.

During the time I am speaking of, there were also dark powers present in the universe, who got fascinated with the flowering of consciousness on Earth. Dark powers are nothing but energies who are not yet aware of their divine nature and therefore believe they need something outside themselves to be whole and complete. These dark powers wanted to feed on the life on Earth that radiated such vitality and life force. As a reaction to the intrusion of these dark powers, you wanted to protect life on Earth. Your emotions were much like those of a parent who wants to shield their child from danger. To meet and confront the intruders, you had to have denser bodies and live in a denser vibration, less thin and subtle than the realm of the angels. Essentially, the intrusion by the darkness lit a spark of passion and a fighting spirit in you, and this in turn drew you deeper into matter. The next step in your journey was for you to let go of being an angel, and you took the path of incarnation.

With this step, you in a sense lost your innocence. Just before this step, there was a moment of hesitation in which you realised that by becoming more material, you were going to let go of something very precious. You would lose your angel wings, which symbolise freedom from time and space, freedom from birth and death, freedom from fear and illusion. Yet there was something that deeply attracted you toward the adventure of incarnation. You were a passionate and bold angel, as I said. And that was as it should be. Apparently, your journey took a negative turn when you let go of being an angel and engaged yourself in a battle with the dark forces. You got mixed up in several conflicts and wars for a long, long time. On the other hand, this plunge into the deep made it possible to spread your angel energies to the farthest corners of the universe. Your angel energy is an unalienable part of you which, even if it is temporarily veiled, can never be taken away from you.

Your first mortal bodies were not made of physical matter as you know it on Earth. They were much less dense and compact. One would not be able to see them with human eyes. Your consciousness was less focused than it is now. You still went in and out of your physical forms easily and you experienced reality in a way that is similar to how you now experience reality in the dream state. You were less aware of yourself as a separate entity, your "I-ness" as opposed to the outside world. Presently, you are very much attached to your physical form. Many of you think they *are* that form and that they will perish with the physical body. In your earliest incarnations this was not yet the case, and in many ways you were much freer to go and do what you pleased. Nonetheless, you did feel confused. Although you were guided by the intention to struggle for light and to protect life, you now also had to deal with dark emotions such as fear, desolation and doubt. As soon as you start to battle someone or something, you cannot but partly absorb your adversary's vibration. If that would not happen, there would be no common ground to start the battle from, and you would simply let go of the other completely.

As an angel, you really only had high and elevated feelings. There was joy, enthusiasm and a strong sense of connectedness. When you went down the road of incarnation, an emotional body formed around your soul. This energetic body contains emotional responses that arise when you do *not* perceive reality from the standpoint of oneness and connection. The feelings of the angels have their seat in the heart. The emotions you experience when incarnated are related to the lower three energy centers (chakras) which in your body are located around the stomach, the belly and the tail bone. These three chakras form the ladder to incarnation: through them you trade the experience of oneness for the experience of duality. It is also through them that you go up the ladder and rise from duality to oneness. Your emotional body presents the greatest obstacle to inner peace and liberation, because it contains fear, sadness and anger. Yet the way up, to freedom and enlightenment, *goes through the emotional body* and not alongside or around it. We will speak of this later.

As your emotional body grew heavier and denser, and you lost track of your origin, the possibility arose to incarnate as a human. You had become widely-travelled souls in the meantime; you had become experienced in both the light and dark aspects of life. The energies of duality had taken hold of you, which means that, for a long time, you have believed in the illusions it creates. If you live in duality, you believe deep within that you are alone, fearful and powerless, and that you need something outside of you to protect, feed and acknowledge you. From this notion, you start to exert power over others and you hide your vulnerability. Or you may become too vulnerable and give your power away to another power who wants to feed on your life energy. Whether you are offender or victim in this game, the fundamental error you make is that you think you cannot experience wholeness within yourself. There is a hole you want to fill, either by being boss or by being slave. This game is very painful, as many of you have experienced. In that distant past, there was a moment in which you strongly realized this. This was a moment of change. You had experienced both extremes of the game and knew there was no real solution in either of them. You knew something had to change, but you did not know how. You had become far removed from the original freedom and joy of the angel inside you. Yet your emotional body held a memory, a longing for home. You knew there was something you wanted to go back to, some Home, a state of being that felt like heavenly ecstasy to you. Your emotional body now embarked on a new path. Having explored the extremes of duality, it now started to turn within. This change of consciousness created the impulse to incarnate upon Earth as a human.

The human being at that point already existed on Earth as a biological life form. When you entered that life form however, you added something to it, which made the human being less animal and more self-aware. Human biology is related to the animal kingdom, but the human being was forged by powers which do not solely spring from natural evolution on Earth. What separates man from animal is the ability to be self-aware. Through this ability the human being is able to transform their emotional body and spread the energy of the heart consciously on Earth. Whereas the non-human realms of nature radiate the joy and connectedness of the angels unconsciously, it is humanity's mission to transform it into a conscious energy.

By incarnating into the human being as it then existed on Earth, you added something to its development, and this addition has been controversial. On the one side, self-consciousness holds a great promise; on the other hand it can lead you astray. By becoming human on Earth you hoped to reconnect with all life on Earth and be the gentle creator and keeper you once were. Being human is a rich and complicated reality. Many aspects of reality come together in the human being: you are partly animal, plant and mineral, partly a cosmic being with a long galactic history. Human beings are dark and light, the lost ones and the saviours, the cause of suffering and destruction, and at the same time messengers of hope, love and creative power. In the human being many powers converge with the purpose of reconnecting and cooperating. The consciousness of man holds the possibility to connect widely diverging realms of being and reinstate the notion of underlying unity. Because of the possibility of realizing this beautiful ideal, humanity is granted the opportunity to make grave mistakes. The goal can still be attained. Hope is not lost yet.

In this age, hope rises as never before. Great changes occur in the collective consciousness of man. I just referred to a moment in the past in which you realised that your salvation could not come from the game of stealing or giving away energy, but that the solution lies in finding wholeness within. This insight now germinates in the consciousness of humanity. It is only a seed, not yet a plant. But a change is at hand and something is awakening in the heart of mankind. The heart is the connecting force between the many realms of consciousness represented in man: the earthly, the galactic and the cosmic. The call for peace and fellowship now resounds through all of these realms and this collective call creates a wave of energy that engulfs me, Earth.

If you feel touched by my words, and recognise yourself in it, you are one who has heeded this calling of the heart. You are someone who wants to contribute to the transformation of consciousness on Earth. I welcome you and wish to assist you. I am telling you this long story, to make you aware of who you really are: an angel at the core of your being. Your growing self-awareness helps me. If you remember who you are, we can again have a partnership.

I see your longing, I feel your home-sickness. I see you reaching out for the joyful and carefree state that once was so familiar to you on the one hand, and now still so far and distant on the other hand. It is time now to return to who you are. It is time to climb that ladder and embrace your emotional body with your heart. Surround your pain, your sense of heaviness, your sadness with the angel consciousness of mildness and compassion that is natural to you. You can heal yourself.

You are now becoming an angel who is able to hold her light in the densest realm of reality. You are becoming a conscious creator, who has learned to manifest themselves in realms both light and dark, without losing themselves in it. You are carrying a seed of consciousness that is transformative for your environment. You are becoming a spiritual teacher. A spiritual teacher is not someone coming down from the highest realms to explain to the ignorant what life is all about. A true teacher has gone though darkness himself and reaches out their hand to you not from above but from a deeply sensed inner unity.

The adventure you once started as a creative angel is nearing its end. Especially in this final chapter of your journey, you are invited to reconnect with me, the life form on which your experiment took place. Allow yourself to travel in your imagination, become the dreamer and visionary you once were. Own the greatness of what wants to manifest itself through you on Earth. Become again the angel who graciously entrusts itself to the magic of life. Let yourself be guided by what gives you joy and inspiration. The angel inside you wants nothing more than to become fully human. By feeling one with the angel within, you bring a piece of heaven on Earth.

Message from Mary Magdalene

27 - Return of the wild woman

All three of us are present here today: Jeshua, Mary and Mary-Magdalene. We are honored to be here with you. We see you as our brothers and sisters. We are one at heart and for me, Jeshua, it is especially liberating to be here alongside my female friends. Because I am often seen as the one representative of the Christ energy. That is not the whole truth, however. There were women at my side in my life who were essential to my mission. In those times, it was not acceptable for women to do what I did, to be a public teacher. But my mother and Mary-Magdalene were both spiritual warriors. They helped me plant the seeds of the Christ-consciousness.

Today we speak of the male and female energies. My female soul mates and I speak in one voice. In your history, the female energy has become wounded in a profound way. This has had important consequences for both women and men on Earth. It is not just women who have suffered from the male dominion, men also have been wounded.

We will first discuss the female wound. We ask you to imagine a female person. She represents the whole of the feminine energy. Now the female energy has been degraded and treated with violence. The effect this had on women is that they withdrew from the lower part of the body where their power resides. Especially when there has been sexual violence, the emotional trauma causes women to retract their consciousness from the lower part of their body. It becomes hard for them to be self-aware and grounded. Envisage a woman in front of your inner eye. It represents the collective energy of women. In this image you can see that there is a kind of hole in the area of her belly. She has withdrawn her consciousness from this area and she feels insecure because she lacks foundation. Inside her belly you can hear screams of anguish and pain. And we would like to invite you all, both men and women, to radiate light out to this woman, to her belly. In this way you are also giving it to yourself.

Now Mary-Magdalene wants to speak.

I am Mary-Magdalene. I love you deeply. I am always with you. I have risen above the female wound and I now wish to touch this area of pain very gently to help women heal. I would like to see them being born again with joy and firmness, so that the power of the female can return in a peaceful way. I do not wish to fight or struggle. I come in peace and I have a special plea to women. You have all been wounded in history, but in this time you are regaining your strength. This is your age, this is your time. I wish to remind you that men need help now as well. You as women are familiar with the wound in your belly, the pain and trauma of being degraded. But what happened to men?

Because of the dominating male energies in the past and the energies of power and oppression, men were forced to close down their hearts. They had to be strong and harsh, this was the ideal picture of being male. But in that way men became alienated from there feeling side. Many men got locked up in their heads; it became difficult for them to express their emotions and their feelings. The inability to connect with your feeling side, your feminine side, is also a wound. You do not live life fully if you cannot access your feelings. In fact, you are disconnected from your soul. In many men, there is a sense of loneliness and alienation which can be perceived as a hole in their hearts.

So you see: both men and women have been wounded in the past. Women's wound is located in the belly, men's wound is like a hole in their heart. I wish to say to women today that as you regain your power, as you recognize your true strength: reach out to men. They need your help; they have become estranged, alienated from home. Have the kindness in your heart to be compassionate with them. The New Earth can only be born if the two of you make peace. If men and women understand each other's wounds, they can build a bridge between them.

I ask women to join me in sending light to the hole in your belly. From that light, a cord develops and goes right into the Earth. Feel your connection to mother Earth as a woman. Your feminine energy is so powerful and essential to life. Remember your true strength. As you feel your self-consciousness grow, reach out to men and send light to the hole in their heart.

You are on the verge of a new time in history. Your are meant to join together as men and women. You are invited to have joy and laughter again as human beings. In many of you I see tired warriors; you have struggled and struggled and some of you a very tired and disappointed. The answer to your pain lies in a very simple life. By that I mean: feeling truly connected to Earth again and enjoying the simple pleasures of being human. To experience the love between man and woman, to have friendship with likeminded people and to live in peace with your surroundings and with nature is the promise of the new Earth.

In my life on Earth I experienced the female wound deeply. I was a dear friend of Jeshua. I could feel his strength and wisdom but also his pains and doubts. There was an intimate understanding between the two of us. I experienced deep grief and sorrow when he had to leave Earth, when he was killed. Often, when he would speak to us, I could feel his messages not just in my head but throughout my whole body. I did not like to argue about his ideas, about his messages, like his male disciples did. In that respect, I was a little different from them. They sometimes mocked me and I felt lonely at times. I was regarded as a "wild woman", I was unconventional. Presently, I am really joyful to see that wild women are welcome again in the world! Much has changed since the times of Jeshua. I tell you: wild women will be the leaders of the new world! I invite you all to stand up in your true power. In the past, when women were "wild", meaning independent, unconventional and passionate, they were often labeled as hysterical. In the Middle Ages, they were called witches. But really, those women – I was one of them - were moved by love. Now it is time again for women to show their true power, not in any aggressive way but in a way that reconciles the male and female energies.

An Interview with Pamela Kribbe

By Colin Whitby

First published on <u>www.themagicofbeing.com</u>

This month we have been very fortunate to catch up with Pamela Kribbe who has published what was for me the most inspiring channeling I have read this year. Her work is available for free on her web site, or your can purchase a copy of her book The Jeshua Channelings to read at your leisure (my preferred method). I do hope you enjoy the interview.

How did your spiritual awakening start, and how were you to lead towards self expression and a more heart focused approach to life?

My awakening started when my heart was broken because of a love affair. At 26, I was pursuing an academic career and I was writing a PhD thesis on modern philosophy of science. I was enmeshed in a very rational approach of life and was married to a scientist. Then I met someone who was a philosopher also and who I had amazing conversations with about metaphysics and spirituality. I had always been interested in spirituality and the esoteric, but I had been suppressing this for quite a while. I fell deeply in love with this man and I thought he was the love of my life. However, things turned out differently.

While I got divorced, he decided to go back to his girlfriend. I felt shattered by this experience and suddenly, my fascination for academic philosophy completely disappeared. I was so devastated emotionally and so thirsty for real knowledge - the kind that speaks to your heart - that I was completely finished with intellectualism. I completed my thesis in 1997, but I left the university and started to read a lot of spiritual and esoteric literature. In 2000, I met a woman who was a spiritual teacher and psychic reader, and meeting her was the beginning of a deep inner transformation. She helped me become aware of old emotion pain, pain that stemmed from my early childhood as well as multiple past lives which I started to remember. With her help I relived these painful emotions and was able to rise above them. I felt liberated and free for the first time in my life. It was like I had died and been reborn as a new person, but at the same it felt like I could finally be myself.

Immediately after I went through this period of catharsis and liberation, I met Gerrit (my husband) in 2001. I stumbled upon his website on spirituality and reincarnation on the Internet and we started a lively correspondence. Connecting to him felt miraculous. There was a kinship between us which was unexplainable and yet so familiar. Unlike the devastating love affair in the past, our coming together was not surrounded by drama, but by a deeply joyful, quiet knowing that we belonged together. Gerrit had always been deeply interested in the esoteric and it was only natural for us to start working together as spiritual therapists. After our daughter was born in 2002, we built up our own practice and I could do what my heart most longed to do: to work as an energy reader and teacher and to explore philosophical questions about life in a meaningful, practical way.

How did you come to learn about channeling and when were you first drawn to it?

I got acquainted with channeling around 1995, by reading the work of Jane Roberts, channeler for Seth. At that time I was spending a semester at the University of Harvard, in the U.S., doing research for my thesis. I had become thoroughly disenchanted with academic philosophy, as I mentioned before. I discovered the Seth books in a little bookstore nearby the university and soon got fascinated by this "forbidden fruit" (forbidden by academic standards). I felt that these writings were both philosophically profound and very loving and inspiring. Reading these books deeply affected me. I now feel it was the universe's - or my soul's - way of waking me up and showing me a new direction in life. In the years after that, I read a lot of channeled books by other authors as well. But Seth made the most impact because it was all new to me at that time. Now, I hardly read anything anymore.

When did you come to "notice" that Jeshua was with you and how would you describe his energy?

One evening in 2002, I was doing a personal session with my husband Gerrit, when I noticed a presence near me which I had not felt before. I was used to speaking with spiritual guides, who I often felt around me and who would uplift me with their loving suggestions and cheerfulness. These were personal guides. But when I felt Jeshua's presence, it was different. It felt like a solemn and deeply aware energy, very grounded and focused, not like anything I met before. It frightened me a bit at first. I asked the energy "Who are you?" and then I saw the name "Jeshua ben Joseph" spelled out in front of my inner eye very clearly. I instantly felt it was true. My mind started to raise skeptical objections at once. But just before that, in a flash, my soul had recognized Jeshua as a very familiar presence. My mind argued it was extremely unlikely and presumptuous that he would be next to me in my sitting room. But my heart reassured me that it was quite normal for Jeshua to be so close to us.

Jeshua is not really an authority far and high above us. He means to be our friend, someone you can trust and be open to, as he never judges you. As I have come to know Jeshua, he is never judging me, although he is very direct and upfront. He asks of me to be really honest with myself, to look my fears in the eye, and not cover them up by self-serving theories or justifications.

So he is stern in a way, but it's a very loving way. It makes you realize what love is about. Love does not necessarily feel nice and comforting. Often it asks of you to get out of your comfort zone, to be courageous and vulnerable.

For me, expressing myself publicly as a channel for Jeshua, raised a lot of fear and insecurity in me, which have been very hard to overcome. My instinct (or survival mechanism) has long been to withdraw from the world, which I considered to be a very scary place. Jeshua is teaching me to feel safe in the world, to remain centered and self-aware while connecting to people instead of fearful and fragmented. I'm still learning how to do this, but I think I made some progress. I have received so much because of that: through the Jeshua channelings, I have connected to my soul family across the word. People from all over the world have written me to tell me how touched they are by Jeshua's messages. I feel more at home on Earth. And what's most important: despite the fears, I sense the deep fulfillment of doing what my soul really longs to do on Earth right now.

Your messages are very down to earth yet explain complex concepts so clearly. How do you receive the messages from Jeshua, do you "translate" them in some way?

Indeed, the messages are quite clear and down to earth, despite the fact that they are highly metaphysical. I think this is due to a number of factors. First, as I know Jeshua, he is quite direct and clear in stating his messages. He doesn't beat around the bush and he seeks to address our heart, not our intellect. This goes against my own nature a bit. I was trained as an academic philosopher and I used to write articles that were unreadable to "normal folk", because they were so intellectually complex and abstract. Jeshua is definitely not in that business.

On the other hand, my philosophical training has also helped me develop the ability to break down complex concepts into simple words. In that way, it has proved to be very valuable in my work as a channeler. I think my own education as a philosopher also accounts for the way the Jeshua messages are stated. Thirdly, I sometimes feel that it's simply a human expectation that spiritual teachers or "ascended masters" (don't care much for that phrase!) express themselves very stately and formally. It fits our image of a wise and revered teacher. Jeshua however seeks to be close to our hearts, and not create any distance.

By the way, I think that channeling always involves a kind of translation. Every channel has some influence on what comes through because of their upbringing, their culture, their specific interests and talents. Something I became thoroughly aware of while studying philosophy of science is that it is naive to assume that we can ever perceive reality purely and untainted by subjective elements. The ideal of objective perception, perception that blocks out the perceiver altogether, has become deeply problematic, ever more so with the rise of quantum mechanics. Likewise, channelings are always filtered by the personality and cultural background of the channel. The best thing to deal with that is to be aware of this and, when you listen to channels, use your discernment and pick whatever resonates with you.

How would you describe your relationship with Jeshua during the channeling process?

When I sit down to channel, I go into a light trance. This means that I focus my attention within, let my body relax and become as quiet and silent as possible. I then feel Jeshua entering my energy field and often, I feel a little jolt down my spine as we connect. It takes a minute or so for our energies to meld and then I hear "Go ahead" within. I start speaking and I am aware of what I am saying, yet there's a flow of energy pouring through me which "gives me" the words so to speak. I feel enveloped by this very loving and compassionate flow and I feel lifted above my ordinary, daily consciousness. Often I sense great peace and I am aware that there is so much more meaning to life than we ordinarily feel and think. I also feel that the vast energy of love and compassion coming through me from "the other side" is hard to put into words. The words often seem limiting to me as I channel.

My relationship to Jeshua during the channeling process is one of an active receiver I would say. On the one hand, I am as open as possible to whatever wants to come through. On the other hand I am active and alert, and I need to focus on getting the message across in human concepts and language. My mind needs to participate to make the translation, and I need to let that happen without interfering from the level of my personal will or belief systems.

This is a delicate process and I do not claim to be perfect at it. I am sure that in translating Jeshua's energy into human speech, I am filtering the message somehow. The problem is that it's very difficult for a human to know what filters are still in them. The most persistent filters are blind spots, presumptions you take for granted because you are not aware of them as such. I think the more we grow and open up to the true reality of love, we let go of our filters. This is a gradual process in my experience. Instead of mourning the fact that our perception is filtered, I think it's much more joyful to look forward to dropping ever more filters on our way. Channeling is a human affair, but that's okay. We are here to experience what it's like to be human, and to revel in the awakenings we experience as humans.

I found the lightworkers series (part of **The Jeshua channelings***) so helpful in putting into context my own experiences; did the material impact your own life and spiritual development?*

Yes, it did. It was the first series of channelings I received from Jeshua. He said to me the messages in it were meant specifically for lightworkers. He said that they would be the first ones on Earth to embrace a new, heart-based consciousness. The material is meant to support them in their awakening, so that they can go out and be the teachers for the ones who follow.

For myself, this series made me understand better who I am and what it means to be a lightworker. I read many stories in books and on the Internet about lightworkers, and I felt deep resonance with it, but I never quite understood one thing. Lightworkers were said to have a mission to bring light and consciousness to Earth, they were said to be natural teachers and healers and to have sacrificed much to be here and do their work.

Lightworkers were very much "the good guys". In fact, they almost seemed to be a kind of martyrs: always giving of themselves and carrying the world on their shoulders. It all sounded a bit too holy for me. I myself felt huge resistance to being on Earth, carrying a lot of old sadness and anger within. I wanted to know where that came from and what my purpose in life really was.

Jeshua's story in the Lightworker Series (part of the book *The Jeshua Channelings*) reveals that we in fact played very dark parts also in earlier lifetimes, some of them in Atlantis and some in times before we incarnated on Earth. In that ancient era, we explored ego-based consciousness to the fullest. Getting to know and understand the dark parts of our/my history satisfied my sense of justice, my sense of balance. I also feel it gave me a healthy sense of humility.

What helped me also is that Jeshua stresses in the Lightworker series that we are not here to save the world. We are here primarily to heal ourselves, to face our dark side, to understand and treat our own emotional hurts with love and compassion. When we do so, we become "enlightened" - we enter heart-based consciousness. We radiate a peaceful, loving energy to others, but this is not something we do (as in a job), it naturally happens because we are who we are. So, the notion of light work as "working hard to heal the world" is misplaced according to Jeshua as I receive him. Light work is about you and not about the world, and it is a state of being rather than a doing. Realizing this has helped me let go of the urge to "save others", which I think is a deeply ingrained habit of lightworkers. It has helped me to be more centered and focused within.

Jeshua takes great care to separate himself (his Earth life as Jeshua) from Jesus as portrayed in the Bible, what would you say is the key difference between their portrayals?

I think the greatest difference is with his portrayal by Church tradition. In the Bible, there are authentic stories about what Jeshua did and said, of course related and interpreted by humans with their own cultural and psychological